EVERYDAY JUSTICE

Everyday Justice clearly demonstrates the value of revitalizing the category of justice in ethnographic work by revealing how both justice and injustice are woven into everyday life in manifold and widely differing ways. The contributors account for this complexity across multiple particular social relations, places, and times, such that concepts and experiences of justice are made analytically visible without essentializing the construal of justice both as an idea and in practice. In the best scholarly tradition, *Everyday Justice* provides theoretical readings of justice and injustice, justice and law, and relational justice, each designed to cut through the specificity of myriad social, political, and legal conjunctures in a clarifying way. One outcome is to suggest future research possibilities to readers by highlighting theoretically distinctive yet ethnographically specific questions about justice. *Everyday Justice* will be essential reading for anyone interested in justice in theory and practice.

SANDRA BRUNNEGGER is an Official Fellow and College Lecturer at St Edmund's College, University of Cambridge.

CAMBRIDGE STUDIES IN LAW AND SOCIETY

Founded in 1997, Cambridge Studies in Law and Society is a hub for leading scholarship in socio-legal studies. Located at the intersection of law, the humanities, and the social sciences, it publishes empirically innovative and theoretically sophisticated work on law's manifestations in everyday life: from discourses to practices, and from institutions to cultures. The series editors have longstanding expertise in the interdisciplinary study of law, and welcome contributions that place legal phenomena in national, comparative, or international perspective. Series authors come from a range of disciplines, including anthropology, history, law, literature, political science, and sociology.

Series Editors

Mark Fathi Massoud, *University of California, Santa Cruz*

Jens Meierhenrich, *London School of Economics and Political Science*

Rachel E. Stern, *University of California, Berkeley*

A list of books in the series can be found at the back of this book.

EVERYDAY JUSTICE
Law, Ethnography, Injustice

Edited by

Sandra Brunnegger
University of Cambridge

CAMBRIDGE
UNIVERSITY PRESS

CAMBRIDGE
UNIVERSITY PRESS

University Printing House, Cambridge CB2 8BS, United Kingdom

One Liberty Plaza, 20th Floor, New York, NY 10006, USA

477 Williamstown Road, Port Melbourne, VIC 3207, Australia

314–321, 3rd Floor, Plot 3, Splendor Forum, Jasola District Centre, New Delhi – 110025, India

79 Anson Road, #06–04/06, Singapore 079906

Cambridge University Press is part of the University of Cambridge.

It furthers the University's mission by disseminating knowledge in the pursuit of
education, learning, and research at the highest international levels of excellence.

www.cambridge.org
Information on this title: www.cambridge.org/9781108487214
DOI: 10.1017/9781108763530

© Cambridge University Press 2019

First published 2019

Printed in the United Kingdom by TJ International Ltd, Padstow Cornwall

A catalogue record for this publication is available from the British Library.

Library of Congress Cataloging-in-Publication Data
Names: Brunnegger, Sandra, editor, author.
Title: Everyday justice : law, ethnography, injustice / edited by Sandra Brunnegger,
    University of Cambridge.
Description: 1. | New York : Cambridge University Press, 2019. | Series: Cambridge studies in
    law and society | Includes bibliographical references and index.
Identifiers: LCCN 2019038253 (print) | LCCN 2019038254 (ebook)
    | ISBN 9781108487214 (hardback) | ISBN 9781108763530 (epub)
Subjects: LCSH: Justice.
Classification: LCC K240 .E85 2019 (print) | LCC K240 (ebook) | DDC 340/.114–dc23
LC record available at https://lccn.loc.gov/2019038253
LC ebook record available at https://lccn.loc.gov/2019038254

ISBN 978-1-108-48721-4 Hardback

CONTENTS

CONTRIBUTORS

Santiago Abel Amietta is a Lecturer in Criminology at the School of Social, Political and Global Studies, Keele University. He holds a PhD from the University of Manchester, an MA from the Oñati International Institute for the Sociology of Law, and an LLB from the National University of Córdoba, Argentina. His research interests span the legal professions, lay participation in criminal justice, migration and integration, and state recognition of indigenous nations, with a continued regional focus on Latin America.

Sandra Brunnegger is an Official Fellow and College Lecturer at St Edmund's College, University of Cambridge. Her research interests are social movements, transitional justice, human rights, and environmental conflict. Relevant publications on justice include *A Sense of Justice: Legal Knowledge and Lived Experience in Latin America* (co-edited with Karen Ann Faulk) (Stanford University Press, 2016) and a forthcoming symposium (as a guest editor) in PoLAR: Political and Legal Anthropology Review.

Carol J. Greenhouse is Arthur W. Marks '19 Professor of Anthropology at Princeton University. Her primary research interests are in the ethnography of law, especially in relation to the federal United States. Her most recent books include *The Paradox of Relevance: Ethnography and Citizenship in the United States* and, as editor (with co-editor Christina Davis), *Landscapes of Law: Practicing Sovereignty in Transnational Terrain.*

Eve Houghton is a social anthropologist based in the United Kingdom. Her work engages with manifestations of law and justice in physical and digital places. Her research exploring the village courts as presented in this volume was conducted as part of an Economic and Social Research Council project exploring Grassroots Law in Papua New Guinea.

Laavanya Kathiravelu is Assistant Professor at the Division of Sociology, Nanyang Technological University (NTU), Singapore. Her research and teaching interests lie in the intersections between migration and citizenship, urban studies, and race and ethnicity. Her first book is *Migrant Dubai: Low Wage Workers and the Construction of a Global City* (Palgrave Macmillan, 2016).

Agathe Mora is a Lecturer in Social Anthropology at the University of Sussex and an Editor at Allegra Lab. She conducts research on international governance and post-conflict reconstruction in Kosovo and Europe.

Ronald Niezen is the Katharine A. Pearson Chair in Civil Society and Public Policy in the Faculty of Law and Department of Anthropology at McGill University. His books include *The Origins of Indigenism: Human Rights and the Politics of Difference* (University of California Press, 2003), *Truth and Indignation: Canada's Truth and Reconciliation Commission on Indian Residential Schools* (University of Toronto Press, 2017), and a co-edited volume (with Maria Sapignoli), *Palaces of Hope: The Anthropology of Global Organizations* (Cambridge University Press, 2017). His current book project, *HumanRights: The Technologies and Politics of Rights Claims in Practice*, will soon appear with Stanford University Press.

Kathleen M. Sullivan is an Associate Professor in the Anthropology Department, California State University Los Angeles. Her research examines the intertwined roles of legal and economic social relations, public forums, knowledge-sharing practices, technocratic governance, and bureaucracies in the development, conservation, and governance of marine and coastal environments. She has published in *PoLAR Political and Legal Anthropology Review*, *Studies in Law, Politics and Society*, and *Latin American and Caribbean Ethnic Studies*.

Sari Wastell is an independent researcher and international consultant. After taking her PhD at the University of Cambridge in social anthropology (specializing in legal anthropology), she lectured in London for fourteen years. She is the author of the forthcoming *The Mouth That Tells No Lies: Law, Custom and Political Ontology in Swaziland* and one of the editors of *Thinking through Things*.

ACKNOWLEDGMENTS

This volume is the fruit of a conference I organized at the Centre for Research in the Arts, Social Sciences and Humanities (CRASSH) at the University of Cambridge, with the financial support of the Department of Social Anthropology at Cambridge and an APART fellowship from the Austrian Academy of Sciences, both of whom I wish to thank for their generosity. My thanks also go to the People Programme (Marie Curie Actions) of the European Union's Seventh Framework Programme (FP7/2007–2013) under REA grant agreement n° 629510, whose funding afforded me the intellectual space to think through the matter of justice.

This book would not have been possible without the generosity of all the individual authors. I am grateful for their critical contributions. I also thank the many people who shaped the volume and offered encouragement and advice. In particular, I would like to thank John Borneman, Jean Jackson, Sally Merry, Beth Mertz, Lawrence Rosen, Rachel Sieder, and Jothie Rajah. Finally, I thank the Anthropology Department at the University of Chicago and the American Bar Foundation, in Chicago, which gave me both physical and intellectual space in which to sketch out this introduction and map the contours of *Everyday Justice*.

ACKNOWLEDGMENTS

CHAPTER ONE

THEORIZING EVERYDAY JUSTICE

Sandra Brunnegger

> *Justice is unwilling to be captured in a formula. Nevertheless,*
> *it somehow remains a word of magic evocation.*
> —Cahn 1949: 13

Everyday Justice aims to expand our understanding of justice and the multifarious and interpenetrating ways in which the category 'justice' operates – justice, that is, as a category of both analysis and of practice.[1] In bringing together a range of ethnographic accounts – from street graffiti in Montreal to a village court in Papua New Guinea – this volume eschews any essentializing construals of ideas or practices of justice. It does not envisage justice solely as a descriptive category; indeed, it does not seek to fix it in any single category.

Although no single narrative or reference exhausts what is meant by 'justice', it remains central as a non-derivative term. Law is a dominant frame of reference for justice – in that justice is shaped by its relation to law. But justice also stands in close relationship with morality, ethics, cultural norms, religious principles, and kinship in ways that are constitutive of justice. Scholars, of course, treat all these relations in different ways.

Justice may be treated analytically as a moral virtue (Rawls 1971), or as political capability and freedom (Sen 1999), or as recognition and redistribution (Fraser and Honneth 2003), or as a matter of right actions (Kim 2015). Justice may lie outside the law or legal edicts. Or it may be embodied in material or non-material terms. Political philosophy – possibly the dominant scholarly tradition within which justice has been conceptualized – treats it mostly as an analytical category.[2]

As a category of social, political, or legal practice, justice may be invoked in the context of both institutionalized (e.g. juridical) and non-institutionalized (e.g. as a mobilizing ideal) discourses, and in the multiple ways in which non-institutionalized discourses of justice are invoked in institutionalized settings. In these terms, justice may represent both a starting point and an (imagined) end point. Justice, then, is a motive and purpose in and of itself; but, as Carol Greenhouse puts it in the Afterword to this volume, an 'outcome may be just, but justice is not an outcome'. This formulation envisages justice as a process; whatever is recognized as just will contrast with, or occur in a state of tension with its social, political, legal, and moral implications, against which it will be judged. Disciplinary interests dispose anthropologists to attend to justice as a category of practice as a starting point. This allows them to ask different sets of questions, such as: how is justice understood, sought, and rejected by people; and how does it contrast or endure in a state of tension within particular social, political, and legal settings? The category of 'justice' may then subsequently, for instance, be excavated and elaborated analytically as intractably relational and contextual (Rosen 2000), or as an ideological value-concept (Nader and Sursock 1986).

Each category – analysis and practice – has its possibilities and limits. A broader question regarding categorical framework is: to what extent is focusing on categories – whether of analysis or practice – helpful at all? On the one hand, it may be productive to look carefully at the separation or distinction between justice as a category of practice and of analysis, in the sense that it may open up new spaces for discussion. This may help illuminate the manifold, and even conflicting, ways in which the category of 'justice' is put to work or used. At the same time, we should neither consign justice too hastily to systematic categorical binaries (practice *or* analysis) nor easily conflate these categories (Ferguson 2007: 383; Brubaker 2012). Understandings of justice are further complicated because of the ways in which social actors reflectively and discursively invoke these categories (Ferguson 2007). Categories of analysis and practice are not mutually exclusive. Rather, it is possible to acquire critical purchase by treating this apparent duality reflexively (Ferguson 2007: 383).

This kind of ethnographic enquiry (and thus reflexive approaches to justice) can throw new light on these categories of practice and analysis, making it possible to see more clearly the complexity of these categorical frameworks and, at the same time, tease out their pervasiveness. The broader aim of this volume is to point to slippages, entanglements, and frictions between justice as it is theoretically abstracted and as it is enacted, actualized, reworked, and represented (see Clarke and Goodale 2010). Justice needs to be seen as a textured *object* of analysis; it needs, in other words, to be interrogated, excavated, or exposed, rather than to be used simply as a ready-made *instrument* of analysis or measure to be eventually worn out (Brubacker 2012: 6). This volume takes stock of the interpenetrating and transformative ways in which justice works, as both a category of analysis and a category of practice. In this way, it addresses contemporary conceptual muddles about justice.

Anthropology and related disciplines have in the recent past shown surprisingly little analytical interest in the concept of justice, while also displaying a sense of urgency in the search for fresh empirical and ethnographic analyses related to justice (see Brunnegger and Faulk 2016; Salamanca Villamizar and Astudillo Pizarro 2016; Merry 2017; Sieder 2017). This is neither to provincialize a long history of work in the anthropology or sociology of law, nor to discount much current work in, for instance, the multidisciplinary scholarship on transitional justice.[3] Our contention seeks, rather, to draw attention to how anthropology has tended to eschew attempts to explore justice in the recent past (i.e. more widely) as a *central* category. Anthropology's failure, or maybe even its refusal, to theorize justice, or to give it adequate foundational theoretical consideration, may in fact derive from the vagueness or polyvalence of justice itself as a concept (see Rosen 1989; Goodale 2017). Teubner testifies to the recent inattention of scholarship to embodied or grounded forms and kinds of justice, which has contributed to a distinct lack of theorizing: 'There is no socio-legal theory of justice' (Teubner 2009: 2).

This volume strives to come to grips with contemporary confusions about justice. Ethnography is important in facilitating fresh analytical re-conceptualizations of justice, in alignment with an emerging body of scholarship that attends to the concept of justice through ethnographic lenses. In this way, the authors in this volume join a handful of recent scholars who are seeking to rescue justice both as an analytical category and as object of enquiry for anthropology and beyond. We aim to shape and advance an underdeveloped theoretical field: the anthropology of justice (e.g. Rosen 1989; Borneman 1999; Clarke and Goodale 2010; Sapignoli 2018). More than this, we strive for a multicentric outlook, and do not privilege any particular epistemological or ontological tradition or starting point. By doing this, we hope to forge fresh *anthropologies* of justice. This also recognizes that diverse global/ regional anthropologies are shaped by their many different traditions of justice as categories of analysis.[4] The suggestion coming from this volume, and other recent scholarship, is clear: multiple, often competing, and even incommensurable meanings of justice operate at different scales and in distinctive forms and interfaces, and different regimes of justice – both parallel and overlapping – exist within the same cultural context. Notions of justice whose meanings are contingent on context and the specific ways in which justice is practised and imagined can fester as an 'implicit idea' (Rosen 1989: 38) or be an artefact or result of political contestation (Clarke 2009). Or notions can emerge from negotiations within a 'market for justice' (Besky 2014: 17), further highlighting justice's malleable character.

Everyday Justice engages with justice with a view to generate fresh theorizations.

First, from the outset, this book grapples with the category of justice broadly and reflexively to elicit such fresh understandings. On the one hand, it pays attention to how and why different people invoke, enact, or depict different ideas *of*, and *about*, justice (Brunnegger and Faulk 2016: 5). On the other hand, it asks: what does justice, as an idea or a practice, do? What is at stake and what are the possible ramifications? The authors in this volume recognize that in some cultural contexts, justice may not be expressed, identified, or characterized as such, and that justice as an idea or idiom may be taken by some as simply a political or legal trope or an ideological – and mainly – Western concern. In this regard, justice is not a neutral, still less a natural, category – although, of course, people may claim it as such. If we aspire towards an ontological understanding, we may encounter different kinds of justice that may be incommensurable (see Chapters 3 and 5). This volume thus serves as a resource for further critiques of narrower views of justice. Its goal is to ensure that justice as a category remains an object of analysis (keeping in view 'object multiple'[5]), rather than designating the category as an analytical instrument of inchoate or unexamined definition (Brubacker 2012). In other words, scholarship needs to consider reflexively how ethnographic categories are shaped and held in place by a theoretical object – in this case, justice – and how far one can or should be responsive to 'local' and lived conceptualizations. *Everyday Justice* removes at least some of the muddle.

Second, the chapters generate new theoretical readings by locating the question of justice within particular textures of everyday life, within particular social relations and places, and at particular times. The contributions evoke the elusive nature of justice as a feature of ordinary life, suggesting that it may be usefully perceived through the 'everyday'. This notion admits complexity and contingency (e.g. to changes in practices) and heterogeneous understandings, both in the same place and across different locations. The contributors to this volume, whose ethnographic studies in different settings occur across the globe, take up the everyday in many of its various registers, with different enactments and manifestations as their points of departure as they seek to elucidate justice. The authors' examples show that the everyday is marked by possibilities, limits, and ruptures, and that justice remains the context for people's aspirations, and manifestations, as well as unexpected appropriations by various actors. These studies cover diverse contexts, from a mass claims transitional justice mechanism in post-war Kosovo (Chapter 4) to the selection of lay participants in trial procedures in Argentina (Chapter 7). These ethnographies excavate fresh material to illuminate the category of justice in 'thick', or textured, terms and thus in its social, political, economic, and cultural specificities and realities. This affirms the importance of grounding justice in ethnography on its own terms to understand it more productively. The book's guiding intuition is consonant with Goodale and Clarke's (2010: 18) sense of 'the constitution of everyday justice' as an integral feature of how actors experience and imagine their world. More broadly, *Everyday Justice* shows the potential value of bringing back the theme of justice to ethnography.

Third, and finally, in yoking the everyday to the category of justice, this volume hopes to provoke fresh theorizations and prompt further reflection. It offers a theoretical account of the everyday in the context of readings of justice and injustice, justice and law, and relational justice – domains that emerge as the conceptual grounds of the individual chapters. *Everyday Justice* reveals dynamic and asymmetrical entanglements, and opens up the sometimes paradoxical nature of interactions between justice and injustice and between justice and law. *Everyday Justice* also addresses justice as a mode of relations. Above all, *Everyday Justice* marks out a fresh research agenda concerned with unpacking in new ways how everyday conceptions of justice circulate

SANDRA BRUNNEGGER

and change, and how they are imagined, legitimized, and negotiated within particular spatial settings and temporal regimes. *Everyday Justice* shows that justice needs to be explored in spatially and temporally specific conjunctures because it is expressed – and often condensed – in both time and space.

This introduction elaborates these perspectives in more detail. It first deals with the dialectical nature of spaces and temporalities and (everyday) justice. It then turns to three axes of analysis: relational justice, justice and law (including moving away from seeing justice solely in relation to legal realms), and justice and injustice. As we will see, these domains usually overlap, transform, and impinge on each other; and they are often shaped by multiple disjunctive or conflicting imaginings, modalities, or logics of space, and temporality.

'JUSTICESCAPES': TEMPORALITY AND SPATIALITY OF (EVERYDAY) JUSTICE

The everyday is the fundamental context of social space. Greenhouse (1996: 1) makes the critical point that time is a culturally specific concept, not a universal one; her emphasis is on 'the ways people talk about and use representations of time in social life, ideas that developed independently of whatever "real time" might be'. In this sense, she warns that anthropologists need to take care not to get caught in the trap of re-inscribing a hegemonic *linear* conception of time. In understanding space and time, and relating temporality to and with spatiality, this volume takes as central the idea that these categories are assembled, fabricated, reproduced, manipulated, and/or negotiated by social actors (e.g. Munn 1990; Boyarin 1994; Weszkalyns 2010). It also holds that temporal and spatial logics rest in people's situations; in their deliberate, non-deliberate, or tacit acts; and in shifting and altering ways that may conflict. Hence, temporality and spatiality are seen as entangled 'qualities' – or conditions, virtues, or conjectural modes – 'of social relations' (Weszkalyns 2010: 16). Both spatial and temporal relations are experienced within the everyday of actors' lives, making people particular kinds of subjects in their everyday actualities.

Justice necessarily has coordinates or vectors in time and space; it is not cut off from temporal and spatial frames but located in space and time. Justice is at once polytemporal and polyspatial in character, which necessitates that it be reckoned with in all of its spatiotemporal dimensions, horizons, and matrices. 'Time', as Bakhtin (1981: 84) said

6

in reference to time–space relations (in his seminal theory of the chronotope), 'thickens, takes on flesh', and 'likewise space becomes charged and responsive to the movements of time, plot and history'. Justice, with its multifarious nature, is constantly in motion and flows through time and space, and across multiscalar registers of meanings within social, political, and legal discourses, which are then experienced and understood in multiple social realities. The complexity and multiplicity of the dialectical nature of spaces, temporalities, and justice can be framed, this volume suggests, by the metaphor of 'justicescapes'.[6] The coinage is intended to point to the dynamic nature of ideas; to their particular and entrenched social, political, and legal character; and to the ever-present possibility and potential of rendering present and future in alternative ways.

Temporalities of Everyday Justice
In both time and space, justice can be framed within the domain of the everyday. Justice can be excavated, for instance, as an everyday site in which the future is brought into being. In these terms, justice funds an administration or management of time and space by tacitly or deliberately contributing to social and political imaginaries. Time is an integral component of everyday encounters, interfaces, representations, and practices; temporal affairs both transform and are transformed by everyday lived experiences; and varying concepts of time and temporality engender corollaries, significances, and effects in everyday life. The chapters of this book locate the matter of justice within particular social relations, places, and times to demonstrate how justice is woven into the fabric and texture of the everyday at different scales and in manifold ways.

In the vast scholarship that takes stock of the everyday – in different theoretical traditions and with extensive theoretical refinements – the everyday is elusively defined and intensely argued, and thus remains cunningly unclear.[7] The work that takes the everyday as its object constructs it in different ways. *Everyday Justice* is concerned, in the first instance, with the social spheres in which a vocabulary of everyday justice emerges, and in which the agency of the everyday becomes apparent. It recovers the everyday meanings of justice by looking at the everyday as a site that discloses the different meanings attached to justice. It also attends to different cultural literacies in the production and reception of justice by showing that the 'everyday' is fuelled by possibilities while also being marked by ruptures. Our conception of the everyday also opens up an ontological position: the everyday is dynamic, contingent, and multiple.

'Whose everyday? Whose place?' are the questions posed by Kathleen Sullivan in Chapter 6, on the case of the Drakes Estero estuary and Drakes Bay Oyster Company, in Northern California. It hints at an epistemological, even ontological, starting point for any study of the entanglement of justice in its temporal dimension with regimes of spatialization (see Valverde 2015). These questions – Whose everyday? Whose place? – are also pertinent in highlighting how there will always be competing notions of justice and injustice. This case study features different stakeholders and constituents (i.e. oyster company campaigners, First Peoples, and environmentalists) with a range of views on the future of the estuary, its nature, and its potential as a place, which determine their stances in a legal process concerning the local oyster production business. (The company has now been dissolved by court decision.) For Sullivan, competing notions of justice and injustice in the conflict are moored in contending 'notions of a coupled "everyday"' and a sense of place as 'each constellation ... mobilizes an illusion of a coherent, common-sense everyday place as its own starting point and end point'. Different constituents invoke place in terms of their own temporal–historical schemes, from the First Peoples claim of sovereignty over the land on which the oyster farm was located, to the oyster company itself that situated itself within a lengthy history of human occupation. This occupation includes a long history of indigenous settlement, which purportedly rebuts ideas that the location should be designated as a wilderness. The complexity of the disputes over place 'explode[s] the everyday as [a] situated sense-making essence of social order' (Marcus 1993: 244). Sullivan suggests that with Drakes Estero estuary, it became impossible to conceive of a single 'everyday' equal in import for each participant or stakeholder. Law, she argues further, cannot appeal to such an essentialized everyday as a source in shaping a social order. Sullivan draws on George Marcus's (1993) critique of the dogma of the everyday as that which is pitched against the law and is categorically distinct from formal procedures, rules, codes, systems, and so on (see also Valverde 2003: 95). As Marcus (1993: 237, 244n9) said:

> In both social theory and legal discourse, the everyday occupies the space of the moral, the pragmatic, the accessible, and the commonsensical and is the last bastion of simple coherence and order. ... In such studies, the order in everyday life takes on a certain virtue and politics

that finds hope in the quotidian against fears … of a 'totally administered and commodified world'. … [E]veryday life [is] where the most
abstractly conceived issues can seemingly be resolved in concreteness
and the virtues of simple, unreflected upon existence.

Santiago Amietta, in Chapter 7, writing on the lay participants in
Argentina's criminal trials, also draws on Marcus's and Valverde's
insights.[8] Amietta problematizes the boundaries between everyday
justice and its institutional counterparts as justice operates in legal
spaces. A discourse of the everyday arises from a 'negative constitution'
(Valverde 2003), or construction, of how ordinary citizens serve as
jurors and have a measure of juridical power vested in them within
the law's own working. These people, conceived as legal subjects or
arbiters par excellence, are entirely separated from their ordinary lives
while at the courthouse. Amietta, however, neither poses an opposition
amongst the everyday and institutions' legal spaces, times, or persons,
nor resorts to the binary of formal–informal 'as epitomic of ontologically discrete realms'. Instead, he suggests a juxtaposition of the formal
and the informal within judicial proceedings as a 'heuristic device',
turning these very boundaries into part of what is studied
ethnographically.

Amietta's main conceptual claim is that boundaries between the
everyday and formally legal may be appropriately conceived as
'power-laden attempts at governing the very formal–informal, legal–
extra-legal divide in discrete contexts'. His ethnographic vignettes
show that jurors – positioned by authorized legal discourse as bearers
of the everyday – do not always behave as expected and as their casting
as 'ordinary persons' might suppose. Uncertain of the nuances of legal
processes, jurors make considerable efforts to observe formalities during
proceedings. When they make a mistake, however, it is sometimes not
acknowledged as authenticating or 'ordinary' but called out as trans-
gressive of legal processes. Amietta argues that this dynamic has related
effects: it re-inscribes an othering, even as it serves jurors' self-
identification with the everyday and facilitates the portrayal of legal
professionals as 'guardians of the law'.

These accounts underline – and make it worth re-emphasizing – the
salience of bringing an ethnographic gaze to the enactments of justice
in generating penetrating accounts of the everyday life of justice.
Ethnography has always studied the contingent practices of everyday
life as expressed in interactions, articulations, and transformations; this
includes enabling to reveal multiple 'time/space-specific structuration

of relations' or encounters amongst actors, institutional agencies, and 'wider socio-spatial structures' (Paasi and Zimmerbauer 2011: 167). Temporality can be a window into a society's political dynamics, differentials, and forces. Exploring the articulations of distinctive – sometimes conflicting – temporalities may reveal the political economy of certain 'time representations' (Greenhouse 1996). Sari Wastell, in Chapter 5, draws on Greenhouse's (1996) 'time politics' in describing the post-conflict period in Bosnia and Herzegovina (BiH) as a 'transition without end', a formulation intended to contrast with a conventional understanding of peace-building as 'linear and progressive'. International institutions have spoken of BiH as being involved in a transition, or linear movement – from 'affective', 'primordial', and 'ethnic' allegiances', said to dominate during a 'time of conflict', to an 'order of the Rule of Law, market capitalism, and democracy'. According to Wastell, the war continues indefinitely in BiH by other means. Many of the operations that should have brought peace led instead to a 'temporal stalemate' or 'void'. As she shows, in implementing transitional justice arrangements, the international community has been unexpectedly complicit with the infighting of ethno-nationalist politicians and their plans and intentions; that is, with the shoring-up of local politicians' power bases and their unjust enrichment. A 'time politics' emerges in which there are, at minimum, three versions of the conflict's history, which allows ethno-nationalist politicians and the international community to 'legitimize the enduring transition on the grounds of an intransient tripartite ethnic divide ... What is shared is a politics of nostalgia that feeds the temporal void of the present.' Ethnic distinctions have been established in nearly every sphere of post-conflict life in BiH. In fashioning and sustaining an 'enduring transition', politicians and community representatives organize memory and trauma so as to exclude any rupture of the 'boundaries of ethnic affect'. Justice, as invoked by ordinary persons, 'gets lost in translation' from their everyday lives to institutions that might fairly represent them. Transitional arrangements fail in terms of socioeconomic justice – for example, in the badly regulated disposal of factories in which leftover wealth is carved up amongst ethnic placeholders. As Wastell tells us, the actions of the international community in BiH continue to turn 'on an ahistorical dyad of the time of affect versus the time of order. ... In so doing, it helps to complete the work of the conflict and plays into the hands of ethno-nationalist politicians who benefit tremendously from a transition without end.' Justice remains to be done, because it has been repeatedly deferred in the interest of certain specific sections of society. As one of Wastell's informants powerfully says, for ordinary people, justice resides in the 'waiting room'. This ever-deferred, not-yet quality raises the topic of political philosophy, which is, as noted, possibly the dominant scholarly tradition in the analysis of justice.

Im/possibilities

A philosophical concept of justice could gain theoretical purchase by, for instance, preventing a sense of 'justice' from being exhaustively determined by its context. The difficulty is that this would (seem to) seek to establish a mode of justice performing outside time and space, or, as Teubner (2009: 3) points out, to underwrite 'legal philosophical claims for a temporally and spatially universal justice'. Further, such philosophical theorization is often 'nomothetic', 'universalizing', and transcendental, regardless of scale or context; as such, it stands squarely against the 'idiographic', 'particularistic', and entrenched temporal and spatial domains through which the everyday explodes (Roohi 2015: 2).

At the same time, we should remember that philosophical reflections on the im/possibility of justice, within more than one philosophical tradition and line of thought, discriminate between temporally differentiated positions. In metaphysical thinking, justice is often understood in a linear mode (i.e. in terms of past–present–future temporal relations). For the political philosopher Rawls (1989: 246), justice must 'fall under the art of the possible' – in this sense, he is a constructivist – while the concept elsewhere operates for him atemporally. Derrida subjects justice to a temporal distinction in his critique of certain forms of metaphysical undercurrents, exploring the temporality of the future, in particular through the examination of a certain temporal mode, namely, *l'avenir* (the 'to come') which he discriminates from what one calls the future. As Derrida (1990: 969) wrote:

> Justice... may have an *avenir*, a "to- come," which I rigorously distinguish from the future that can always reproduce the present. Justice remains, is yet, to come, *à venir*, it has an, it is *à-venir*, the very dimension of events irreducibly to come. ... "Perhaps," one must always say perhaps for justice.

Derrida oscillates between two positions. He is dedicated to the possibility of justice while clearly engaged with the impossibility of justice's demands: justice remains impossible in that it is always to come. This both grants the impossibility of justice's demands and entails a

11

'constructivist commitment to the possibility of justice' (Bankovsky 2012: 4). According to Bankovsky (11), for Derrida 'the defence of impossibility is of little value without assuming the possibility of constructing new and better forms of justice'. Justice, then, comes to represent a temporarily deferred promise and an ever-deferred not yet. This double stance indicates Derrida's 'possible–impossible aporias' (e.g. his idea that there is no continuity between the sense in which justice may be possible and a sense in which it is not). It is an interplay of paradox: the im/possibility of justice is a paradox of the always radically provisional.

This kind of thinking and our commitment to ethnographic concerns in this volume exhibit a certain congruence in thinking through justice as an ethnographic and theoretical object. Thinking of justice as indeterminate in some ways, or as radically provisional, is productive insofar as it may unlock our thinking in both theory and practice. For one thing, fracturing the concept of justice allows it to be seen as both possible and impossible in different moments, matrices, and dimensions (Clarke and Goodale 2010). In this way, the concept retains an open-endedness, partialness, and unboundedness. One may also then entertain theoretical possibilities of justice that are yet to be realized, or even understand that 'justice is ... unknowable as a practical matter' (Greenhouse, Afterword to this volume). But, for Greenhouse, this unknowability goes even further as she explains in her Afterword. The source of the deception 'is not that justice is unknowable as a practical matter, but that it cannot be known primarily by interrogating what states or law do' because 'some part of the apparent elusiveness of justice is actually the elusiveness of the state'.

Further, a temporal reading of the future–present quality of claims for justice, or an idea of justice as belonging to a future–present, should be understood as an invitation to re-think how justice is understood or acted on in people's everyday contexts, and how an orientation towards the future can open up the present bounds of everyday life. However, conceding this is nevertheless consistent with remaining agnostic towards Derrida's suggestion that the future of justice is precisely what may not arrive, including when justice is envisaged as a process. Furthermore, our conception of justice as inhering in different senses of time engenders an ontological stance and entails a non-linear temporal conception. Opening up to the future does more than simply 'explode' the everyday (Marcus 1993); it makes the future continuously present and continuously plural and multiple within the texture of ongoing, everyday life, even as this future remains speculative, provisional, and embedded in different social realities. This kind of thinking can deliver a fertile opportunity for a fresh understanding of the complexities of lived experience.

Political philosophers treat justice as an analytical category differently than ethnographers. Some political philosophers, like Derrida, can take thought back to the point where there is no explanation.[9] Further, Derrida is not analytically concerned with how a just decision may be made – which can be the subject matter of ethnography. An ethnographer may want to understand justice beyond a philosophical ideal and to shun particular metaphysical associations or undercurrents attaching to it before it has become the object of ethnography. It could be that in capturing justice in formulae of indeterminacy, ethnographic accounts can, nevertheless, reveal and fill these formulae with the lived experience of actors. And actors, in their search for justice, may conceive of it as filled with hope. Justice in this sense sponsors new social imaginaries and even utopian visions (Brunnegger 2016). So, unless we bring to bear an ethnographic gaze on justice in the everyday, observing interactions at specific temporal and spatial scales, and in micropolitics, we risk eliding the social and political dimensions at work. Cassatella (2015: 108) has said of Derrida's stance towards justice as being forever deferred and not yet, that 'the benefits of the future are indefinitely deferred while its guiding principle, the telos, is placed beyond the reach of critical scrutiny or even removed from the possibility of failure'.

Rather than entering into the wider discussion of the relationship between philosophy and ethnography, this book seeks to turn to the potential rewards of returning the theme of justice to ethnography. It thus strives to avoid a fixed outlook regarding the significance of philosophical thinking or the exposures to such thinking (Das et al. 2014: 4). It, however, acknowledges the critical take on the relationship between philosophy and ethnography as forcefully expressed by Borneman and Hammoudi (2009: 16), which questions the 'slavish subservience of the anthropologist to particular philosophical schools'. Biehl's (2013: 575) caution, notwithstanding his own engagement with Deleuze, is also not to 'reduc[e] ethnography to proto-philosophy'. Biehl (587) finds academic philosophy too susceptible to opaque prose and insular discussions, so that, as a result, it risks depriving people's 'lives, knowledge and struggles of their vitality – analytical, political, and ethical'. Biehl's niggle is also aimed at ethnographers who consider (unfortunately) that ethnography is eventually only cherished insofar as it crafts some sort of advancement to 'theory' (Moody-Adams 2014). Biehl (2013: 575) claims:

> [Their relationship is] productively ... one of creative tensions and cross-pollination. This sense of ethnography in the way *of* (instead of *to*) theory – like art – aims at keeping interrelatedness, precariousness, uncertainty, and curiosity in focus. In resisting synthetic ends and making openings rather than absolute truths, ethnographic practice allows for an emancipatory reflexivity and for a more empowering critique of the rationalities, interventions, and moral issues of our times.

A related point is made by Fortun (2012: 458), who suggests it is not desirable to seek 'to validate ethnography through philosophy'. Ethnography can, in this sense, yield something other than philosophy; possibly, it is ethnography that accomplishes 'the work *for* theory' (458). The relationship can be conceived as involving an alternation between different kinds of thinking existing in a state of fruitful interaction and possible tension.

This insight allows justice to be analysed in terms of how it may work as an analytic category in the context of anthropological enquiry. Returning for a moment to the heuristic of justice as a 'category of analysis' and a 'category of practice' noted at the beginning of this introduction, anthropologists tend to favour a category of practice framework. It is then that the category of justice may be excavated analytically. Thus, ethnography, for instance, may conceive of justice as a temporal *enacting* rather than as a matter of 'timeless givens' (Orford 2012: 624). On this conception, justice is always value-laden and subject to multiple temporal and spatial logics.

Moreover, as noted earlier, we should also think about the possibility of gaining critical purchase by treating the categories of analysis and of practice reflexively. Reflexive ethnographic enquiry (and such approaches to justice) can shed new light on these categories, showing that these perspectives depend on each other, and reinforce, undermine, and enfold each other in complex ways.

James and Toren (2013: 1–2) remind us that, often, the anthropologist reflexively unravels apparent contradictions – not to mention divergences, flaws, and ambiguities – between ideas and practices. These divergences are unravelled in terms that would make them intractably and analytically paradoxical; that is, apparently contradictory. But paradoxes need not necessarily be actual contradictions; they can also be generative and illuminate the analytic functionality of certain sets of ideas or practices, as well as the limitations of our current analyses. James and Toren (2) tell us:

Understanding that social processes are bound to inform the constitution of ideas (and thus their very continuity and transformation over
time) entails the realization that [justice, in our case. –Ed.] ... as an
analytical category has little purchase on the world unless the use of the
term itself is made the object of investigation.

To draw further on James and Toren, justice lends itself in turn to
becoming an object (or an 'object multiple', if we are concerned with
an ontological understanding) of ethnographic enquiry. Ethnography
enables us to look reflexively at how the idea of justice is used within
social practices. For example, diverse histories mean the same objects
or concepts are likely to be understood differently, both generally and
concretely, across contexts (3). In other words, justice becomes legible
in its spatiotemporality and sociality. The ethnographies in these
chapters circumscribe the contours in each case, allowing an understanding of how a specific idea informs agents' lived – and thus
changing – perceptions of themselves and their social and political
surroundings (2).

This volume's premise, then, is that, in these terms, justice is simply
too important to be removed from ethnographic analysis and left
merely as a concept couched in empty formulae, which can then be
instantiated in a normatively invariant way across contexts (see Sarat
and Kearns 1998). This conviction motivates scholars' attempts to give
analytical contours to the idea of justice as 'implicit' (Rosen 1989), or
as resting on a 'sense of justice' (Brunnegger and Faulk 2016) in such a
way that can illuminate questions of justice in theory and practice of
what justice means and can be.

This volume suggests that justice's polyvocality and polysemous
meanings emerge through its plasticity: its content is momentarily
fashioned, its meaning is always evolving over time, and it is multiply
elaborated. It remains an elusive, or maybe even an incomplete, concept; it is never trapped in any one moment or formulation, and it
resists summary formulation (Cahn 1949: 13; Rosen 2000: 153). In
short, the chapters in this volume orchestrate a plurality of everyday
temporal experiences, contexts, and understandings of justice. Since we
are reclaiming justice as a central category, we also are insisting on a
concept of justice as a saturated and flexible phenomenon of everyday
temporal reasoning at different scales, and within social, political, and
historical contexts. 'Justicescapes' is a useful framework as it points to
justice as an idea or practice constantly in motion: it attaches to, and

traverses, an array of spatiotemporalities, scales, semantics, and discursive contexts.

Locating Everyday Justice

The idea of 'justice' may appeal to a normative state of being *just*, however understood. Of course, the contexts and circumstances – the spaces and places – of some projected future in which this state will transpire will be irreducibly particular; that is, tangibly achieved, enacted, reproduced, and experienced. Any possible tactics of (temporal and spatial) administration will be specific. This book insinuates itself into the interstices between summoned futures and present actualities. By reading the graffiti of the everyday on Montreal streets (Niezen, Chapter 2), spending time at different public places in Singapore (Kathiravelu, Chapter 3), being at the Kosovo Property Agency office (Mora, Chapter 4), visiting places in Bosnia and Herzegovina (Wastell, Chapter 5), attending to oyster farms in California (Sullivan, Chapter 6), observing in a state court in Argentina (Amietta, Chapter 7), or sitting in on a village court in Papua New Guinea (Houghton, Chapter 8), the authors reveal the plurality of meanings that accrue to the concept of justice in everyday life. In traversing these settings, we strive to enact an agenda of 'putting place into space theoretically' (Agnew 2011: 324). Both place and space are articulated, constituted, gendered, and negotiated through everyday social practices and interactions. This understanding permits us to unearth many layers of political, economic, and social processes as they are shaped by forces acting within a continually shifting sociopolitical landscape.

Terms like territorial justice (Harvey 1973), spatial justice (Soja 2010), and socio-spatial justice (Mitchell 2003) have acquired currency outside geography in connecting spatial distributions to concepts of fairness, while 'treat[ing] justice as socially (re)produced' (Bromberg et al. 2007: 2). All the authors in this volume either explicitly reflect on or take as a given the embeddedness of in/justice in the spaces and places in which they are produced, enacted, contested, and neglected, or where justice has failed.

Eve Houghton, in Chapter 8, traces how a village court in Papua New Guinea is convened and how a case is made through tracing the life span of summonses that carry relational ties. A case starts with the making of a summons and ends with it being 'ripped up'. Houghton describes how a bandstand in the village is transformed into a courtroom on a weekly basis through a particular placing of chairs and tables.

The temporary creation of a spatial/material/cultural arena for law – a court space made through the repurposing of furniture such as chairs and tables into props – is a reminder that the localization of justice can reveal itself not just as a materialization of thought but also as an association of perceptions in the theatre of justice. The court remains a flexible place, temporarily fixed, and called on when needed. A summons thus serves to materialize the law in confining and specifying an injustice. For Houghton, the court – and injustice – materializes only provisionally in time and space; the fluidity and material and non-material qualities of in/justice are exposed in the performative making, and unmaking, of the village court.

Through the lens of relationality, in Chapter 3, Laavanya Kathiravelu finds that for South Asian migrants in Singapore, their everyday perception of justice is nested within the socio-spatial changes in Singapore's Little India and in the everyday metropolitan spaces. Kathiravelu conjoins plural notions of justice with plural notions of urban rights (Harvey 2003). These migrants are calling for 'justice with an equal right to the city' – access to city spaces without constraint, regardless of citizenship standing – and the possibility of participating in 'the formal consumption economy, or phenotype'. This kind of justice and access to it are needed 'to build community and social networks and to perform cultural identity'. Public space in Little India is controlled, for instance, through a ban on the open consumption of alcohol, which allegedly leads to rioting. South Asian migrants, already seen in Singapore as 'dangerous, hyper-masculine, and threatening sexual predators', are thus discriminated against further.

Ronald Niezen finds that an understanding of space is extended by both graffiti written on particular walls and internet groups that support this work. He shows in Chapter 2 that graffiti is connected with online activism through a closer-than-expected juncture of the material and the digital, informing yet another kind of relationality. These networks of graffiti artists and online activists are specific to a person's socio-spatial imagination; and these imaginaries mirror ideas or fictions of 'located connection, not new virtual spaces' (Green et al. 2005: 817; Agnew 2011: 328). These networks not only dispense with place in favour of cyberspace but also imbricate it with the physical, of which graffiti is the manifest sign. Niezen's ethnographic vignettes explore how boundaries are ignored: graffiti on walls in Vienna, where graffiti is legally permitted, is compared with graffiti on walls that are considered illegal spaces. Different spaces are also visible to different degrees in terms of eligibility; for example, English written on walls in Vienna may communicate to an audience of urban sophisticates, or to a self-styled subculture, while refusing the terms of other engagements.

RELATIONS AND JUSTICE

The dialectical nature of spaces and temporalities implies relationality. Justice is embedded in social relations. In everyday life, justice cannot avoid being (inter)subjective and relational. The intimacy of everyday life can be observed in its fluidity, constant change, and circulation of interpersonal relations; and the shifting of social, political, and legal contexts. It is this particularized justice, traversing diverse temporal and spatial frames that interest the authors in this volume, who share the perspective that notions of justice are constitutive of social, political, and legal relations – and vice versa (see Clarke and Goodale 2010). To put this another way, justice can be said to emerge from the dynamic relations among people and between people and institutions and any of their 'relational discontinuities' (i.e. between people's and institutional – or normative – understandings; Wilson 2000).[10] At the same time, justice as a practice also possesses the capacity, through its own processes, to forge unexpected relations and connections. Nevertheless, assent to certain understandings of justice may also lead to a surrender of any or some of the relationship networks that circumscribe sociality in communities (Rousseau 2008: 26; Chapter 8 in this volume). One implication is that any form of justice acceptable to any actor must be produced in social, legal, and political terms.

Anthropology as a discipline has always related to the fabric of society by studying the weaving together of relations that form its tissue. Rosen (2000: 170), in his ethnographic study of Islamic law courts of Morocco, shows, for instance, that Islamic justice 'needs to be considered' (or should be thought of) as a form of justice that is a 'relational, a contextual concept'. He adds that its actors, in speaking of justice, refer to 'context and relationship' rather than to 'rights and entitlements', unlike in the Western legal tradition (173). Comparable observations have been made in Papua New Guinea (see Robbins 2010; Demian 2016).

Eve Houghton's work on the village court in Papua New Guinea takes stock of the relationality that penetrates so many facets of life, including legal disputes. She argues that rather than exploring an individual case, an analysis of the constitutive relationships of Papuan life requires an attention to how injustices are mediated in multiple legal arenas. In her vignette, she tells of a person sent away from the village court for lack of a summons. This document was not needed to satisfy government-established court procedures, but nevertheless counted as a requirement 'to make the case' for the local magistrate of the village court. The summons became a signifier for the entangled relationships involved in the case; in materializing these relationships, it got caught up with encoding injustice in context. Papuan village dispute forums thus emerge as instruments adept at recognizing particular 'threatened' relationships and furnishing disputants with means for 'repair'. In this sense, the village court not only presumes social relations but also works to (re)produce and (re)shape them.

For Houghton, what these summonses make possible is the detachment of a single relationship from the nexus of those entangled in any dispute. A summons serves momentarily to suspend one thread of a dispute from the numerous other expectations caught up in it, which may also stand in need of redress. Therefore, by detaching the law as a governing body of reference in disputes and instead examining relationships and how actors interrelate with one another, Houghton studies what conceptions of injustice are actually 'doing' when articulated in a Papuan village court.

These ethnographic observations depend on concepts of justice as a category of relational practice because any form of justice inheres in social relations. To return to Niezen's chapter on graffiti, he shows one affective-relational aspect of justice, namely, the anonymous subjects – the audiences as well as authors of graffiti – who are connected by relationships through this medium when making and receiving claims about public justice. Niezen is mostly interested in the legal and political claims and understands graffiti as their articulation. The graffiti artists are 'solitary' yet angle for solidarity with those who agree with their claims. For Niezen, the public tends to be simultaneously emotionally responsive and 'jaded' (or sceptical). The public may be receptive to 'the spectacular, the unusual, and the emotionally affecting aspects of justice' while also being guilty of the simplification of complex issues, all qualities that make them susceptible to spray-painting.

Laavanya Kathiravelu, in Chapter 3, explores the unequal relations amongst low-wage migrants, welfare workers, and state agencies within their co-created discourses of social justice in Singapore through Glick-Schiller's notion of relationality. She adopts an analytical stance that recognizes how power permeates every scale of encounter, including the everyday, while also conceding the possibility of a plural conceptualization of justice. Her point is to outline a conceptualization that emerges from marginalized migrants' own understanding. In focusing on Tamil low-wage migrants' experiences of injustice and their understanding of what is just, she finds, both semantically and linguistically, that justice is a term that cannot be translated without a loss of 'conceptual richness'. Kathiravelu explains how the word for justice in Tamil, *neethi*, denotes a mode of law that is principally enforceable by the state. Yet the term for 'fairness', *neirmai*, which means what is right or appropriate, is more often used to articulate nonlegal understandings of justice located in everyday life.

LAW AND JUSTICE

Scholars have examined tensions and relations between law and justice in many Western contexts and traditions (e.g. in jurisprudence and legal theories; Kearns and Sarat 1998: 1). Kearns and Sarat (1) show how Western scholarship has historically accepted an inescapable, linear, and stable connection between justice and law, which has 'the virtue of making the boundaries of justice more or less clear' (3). As they explain, this Western tradition understands justice to be defined and circumscribed by the law, as set out, amongst others, by the seventeenth-century philosopher Thomas Hobbes. Hobbes accepted that even unjust laws must be taken as just, contrary to most natural-law thinkers, who allowed more of a distinction between de jure and de facto law and who accepted in principle the idea of an 'experience' of justice. More recently, a conceptual separation between justice and law has crystallized in 'postmodern theorizing about ethics'. It has done so without upsetting the formalized suppositions that justice needs to reside centrally within the law and that the (primarily main) concern of the law is with justice (3). Balkin (2009: 64) explains this insight in language accommodating postmodern concerns: 'Law is never perfectly just – indeed, it is often not very just at all. And yet it is an indispensable condition for justice.' The relation has since been further complicated, as Jennings (2006: 19) summarizes, by an understanding that 'justice necessarily exceeds, questions or even destabilizes law even though justice also is the provocation of law and its (provisional) legitimation'.

Several chapters in this volume explore forms of the classic relationships between justice and law. Law allocates the pursuit of justice in a judicial context to certain agents and delimits its social and institutional space; for example, one functional activity of state law is the pursuit of 'justice', even though the performance of law clearly does not automatically lead to a just outcome.

The conceptual specifications of justice and law, as different terms, emphasize the need to address questions concerning their spatial and temporal relations. As this volume shows, alternative and contending ideas of the place of justice, combined with constitutive legal settings and moments, determine what people understand as 'justice'. For example, Sullivan suggests in Chapter 6, in describing the conflict over the Drakes Estero estuary, that physical places often anchor claims of justice or injustice and, thus, how a specific place is delineated and made either accessible or off-limits. In these terms, court and judicial systems may satisfy visions or conceptions of justice or they may fall short. For Sullivan, while the court may sort through contestation as to what is 'the local' and how it is constituted, 'there is little or no impetus to seek a means for practicing a more equitable, respectful shared civics' when private property dominates both as a matter of right and as the only meaningful attribute of the everyday. The law, according to this understanding, *is* the mode of property rights. For Sullivan, the law in this context cannot claim neutrality as a content-less form of dispute resolution because it already encodes a certain understanding of justice.

The authors in this volume demonstrate that the terms 'justice' and 'law' should not be conflated or seen as stable or unidimensional. Specifically, the contributions fit loosely to any suggestion that justice is enclosed within the everyday procedures of the law, evidenced, for example, in the analytic grappling with the question of how justice in the everyday exceeds these enclosures, freely acknowledging the restrictive terms and relations in which justice is usually framed by law.

One clear connection between justice and law is the political (see Clarke and Goodale 2010). Young (1990: 34) is emphatic: 'Justice coincides with the concept of the political.' The question of how the political plays out must be answered ethnographically, as otherwise the power dynamics of politics are restricted to too narrow a sphere. Sari Wastell, in Chapter 5, offers a reminder of how the political is entrenched in legal activities, specifically innovations within the framework of transitional justice in BiH. She studies how the political arrangements put in place after the Dayton Accord have been manipulated by the political elites of various nationalist factions.

Legal approaches to justice both underline and embody certain values – one being impartiality, as Agathe Mora outlines in her treatment of transitional Kosovo in Chapter 4. For Kearns and Sarat (1998: 6), regardless of some 'ambiguities', justice ostensibly exemplifies impartiality in its principal nexus with the law. Concepts embedded in Western legal culture, such as procedural fairness and impartiality, powerfully denote a certain standard of morality and truth – even as these concepts are susceptible to being angled towards and made subservient to the agendas of controlling agents (Balkin 2009: 67). Mora does not describe the political 'capture' of impartiality; rather, she is concerned with the social 'making' of impartiality in everyday lawyering, which, in her case, is mostly achieved through the work of the national lawyers of the Kosovo Property Agency (KPA). For Mora, the very messiness of the 'local' context and the range of notions of justice at work there paradoxically secure a contextual achievement of impartiality. This impartiality is both emergent and contested, and not with any particular authority. Institutional mechanisms were set up in Kosovo to uphold the impartiality of national lawyers' work, but this impartiality has been reduced to techno-procedural concerns and does little by itself to diminish possible biases alone. With 'technocratic mechanisms' and a 'global' ideal of 'justice as human rights' being insufficient to ensure impartiality, the division of work at the KPA can only seek to render technical actions that, for Mora, will always have a political character. But 'impartiality' is not just stymied on this basis alone. Mora shows how the 'nationalistic bias' of Kosovo Albanian lawyers safeguards due diligence and upholds a tenet of regard for the rule of law. A detachment persists between the personal sense of injustice felt by Kosovo Albanian lawyers and the impartiality that the KPA requires of its staff, meaning that these lawyers remain conscious of the politically sensitive nature of their work. Nonetheless, they see themselves, and are perceived as, impartial. Impartiality, then, is not solely a matter of detachment but involves a conscious, lived-out sense of intrinsic contradictions between the 'global' and the 'local'. Mora's ethnography illustrates not only how these different, possibly incommensurable, senses of justice coexist, but also how conflicting senses of justice are contingent on one another to generate a social setting disposing agents 'to a subjective enactment of impartiality'.

Another concept embedded in Western legal culture is procedural fairness. Santiago Amietta explores in Chapter 7 how Argentinian court officials have interpreted the need to find an impartial means of selecting jurors – using lottery draws or randomizer software, taking specific measures to find younger people, or selecting amongst citizens with landline phones. The legal bureaucrats' authority in choosing jurors allows them to judge their performances according to their own criteria of participation. Amietta does not suggest officials intend to curtail participation by how they handpick jurors. His interest is rather in determining 'how, where, and why everyday informalities' can be instituted within a process usually understood as a series of de-personalized bureaucratic procedures. For Amietta, 'the incorporation of jurors does not simply bring the extra-legal spontaneity and [candour] of the everyday into the otherwise legal rules-bound courthouse. It finds them, instead, involved with and affecting the enmeshment of formal and informal practices'.

This volume also shows how a de/localization of justice may prise apart justice and law to allow a critical examination of their relationship. For example, Niezen describes a process in which an idea of justice is localized in the form of graffiti as a spatially specific practice, while internet communication entangles and mobilizes another spatiotemporal expression of 'public outreach'. He argues that there is a continuity between the singular pleas for justice of individuals or small groups and the strategic repeated messaging of organized campaigns, produced through both cheap forms of technology and mass graffiti – for example, in the stickers, stencils, flags, banners, and posters seen on the streets of different cities. Online communities organize their members to hold the state to the proper limits of its power by motivating graffiti; it cannot be a detached 'act of communication'. Houghton, in her chapter on Papua New Guinea, suggests that detaching the law as a governing frame of reference in disputes allows her to consider what conceptions of injustice are truly doing or enacting when expressed in a dispute forum. The law here may be a spatially designated holder for extra-legal relations. If this is so, it prompts the questions: who is using the courts? And why?

Justice beyond Law

By locating justice elsewhere – that is, 'outside' law or 'beyond law' or indeed 'against law'[11] – it is possible to frame a conception of the law as just one conceptual resource amongst many for imagining justice (Brunnegger forthcoming). This does not entail a refusal to acknowledge that justice is often made manifest, as a category of practice, through the law; and that justice is shaped in relation to law. The point is rather that there is a need to explore justice beyond law to work against the presumption of law's (supposed) dominance over justice, and over justice's other relationships with morality, norms, kinships, and so on, that also shape it (see Jennings 2006: 19).

SANDRA BRUNNEGGER

To specify justice as beyond law is therefore to remain open to how justice is expressed conceptually in other registers, not least those of morality and religion. Most chapters in this volume do in fact reflect on the law as justice's most essential/natural arena. However, without denying that justice is usually framed as a matter of legal imperatives, they also illustrate how it is appropriate to note that various discourses concerning justice are at the same time inscribed in other registers, and may periodically attach to and detach from specific reference points.

Furthermore, to think normatively about justice is not necessarily to think in terms of the law. As Greenhouse cautions in the Afterword, 'normative thinking is easily conflated with legal thinking – as if the subjective interiority of the social is the result of the a priori effectiveness of some external legal entity'. In their own ways, all the contributors to this volume resist any assumption that justice is solely a matter of law.

In her treatment of wage migrants in Singapore and their precarious status, Kathiravelu questions fixed rights-based epistemological (and ontological) starting points in determining what is fair, equitable, and just. For Houghton, social relations matter even in the law's self-understanding. Niezen, for his part, sees the graffiti he describes as making claims about justice, which are oriented towards an ambiguous relation to the law. Graffiti is usually illegal because it is correlated with vandalism and crime; but without being legally subversive, graffiti would fail in its effect. His attention to 'non-professional realm' of justice claims highlights how justice is conceived and articulated outside the law, without being uninfluenced by it. For Niezen, the 'rights-consciousness' of graffiti artists and their audiences rest less on a 'juridical conception of rights' and more on an emotional one, grounded in 'collective senses of injustice'.

Tracing the conflict over the Drakes Estero estuary, Sullivan asks how morality brings shape and meaning to actors' lives by framing the pursuit of justice. Sullivan refers to Sarat and Kearns (1998) to underscore how justice and injustice are moral notions that are embedded in historically and socially situated 'legal-civic orders'. Her chapter lays out several morally positioned narratives, including accounts constructing history as evidence, arguments for conserving the estuary as a 'wilderness', and rationalizations of its economic exploitation. Sullivan queries the forms of civic engagement that developed in the social and legal processes of justice-making that shaped the conflict. Holders of distinct subject positions – in her case, environmentalists, First Peoples, and pro–oyster business campaigners– can express senses of both justice and injustice in distinct ways as they rehearse the close relationships between a moral sense and conceptions of place and belonging.

Imagining justice through modes other than law also allows us to grasp, as Greenhouse argues in this volume's Afterword, the relevance of the state to justice. The apparent imperative of law in relation to justice captures or represents state-centred legal approaches, or 'law's conventional association with the state, and its putative centrality to the state's hegemonic expression and efficacy'. For Greenhouse, 'once law's dominance is called into question, its deceptive place in relation to justice can be seen more clearly'. She suggests that justice may be elusive as a concept because of its association with the 'slippery' state (Abrams 1988).

It becomes clear that additional ethnographic studies are needed to explore justice beyond law and its apparent dominance over justice.

INJUSTICE AND JUSTICE

What's injustice got to do with justice (see Nader 2010)? A sense of injustice can fester within the tissue of people's everyday lives. This volume shows how the experience of injustice plays a role in people's use of and understanding of justice. It also shows how the experience of injustice can spur people's agitation for justice. As a state of being, injustice tends to be materialized (in the actuality of what people are experiencing), while justice can sometimes merely be an aspiration, even in a Derridean sense of something that is to come or the 'experience of the impossible' (Derrida 1990: 947) that often fails to become imminent. At the same time, justice and injustice are not necessarily mutually defining; the relations between justice and injustice are not absolute or fixed, but subject to disjunctive or conflicting spatial and temporal modalities, relations, or logics. As Harvey et al. (2011: 7) state: 'You could have justice here and injustice somewhere else.' Or, as Shklar (1990: 19) expresses more conceptually, 'injustice should not be treated intellectually as a hasty preliminary to the analysis of justice'. As the authors in this volume show, these relations are multifarious, and not simple, symmetrical, or stable.

For Houghton, the parameters of justice cannot be grasped exclusively in the judicial context of a Papuan village court. Instead, the wider range of available fora for resolving disputes needs to figure in any attempt to make sense of how Papuans conceptualize justice.

Additionally, multiple social relationships tend to be drawn into single disputes because of the value people place on crafting and sustaining connections. The village court typically attends to the rights attached to relationships, not to claims made by individuals. Examining a single case in one forum, such as the village court, turns out to be too limited for a complete study of what justice could mean or be in a village. Houghton also suggests the value of focusing on injustice rather than justice. In examining court summonses, she investigates how dispute fora emerge as consequences of disputants' notions and experiences of injustice. The village court, rather than being a location for answers, is used as an instrument to locate particular relationships 'threatened' by disputes and to offer disputants the resources to start to 'repair' them. Houghton's interest is in how injustice becomes framed or materialized; for her, relationality filters the encounter between justice and injustice. However, rather than parse cases in their legal details, her chapter focuses on the 'furnishings of injustice' (such as chairs and flags) that partly form litigants' experiences. These furnishings frame what litigants take as wrong and unjust, which in turn shapes their experience when seeking justice. At the same time, the village court emerges as a space where elements of complex injustices felt by families, clan and kinship groups gain fixed definition and direction, often instead of resolution.

The artists creating the kind of (political) graffiti discussed in Niezen's chapter hope for justice while airing a sense of injustice. Justice is demanded, but not promised, much less enacted; to begin with, graffiti artists cannot know what impact their work will have on the emotions and views of those who see their art. The simplicity of graffiti's creation – spray-painting on a wall – hints at the populism of their advocacy, which is more direct than the organized campaigns of rights groups. Writing in public spaces allows for an understanding of how injustice is understood, and how justice is claimed by the marginalized, including street gang members, sex workers, indigenous peoples displaced from reservations, and others amongst the urban poor. According to Niezen, the ultimate results of graffiti and the online communities that organize their members' works sometimes inspire these artists to break the law 'in the pursuit of higher ideals of justice'. Any assessment of these collective agents' claims to justice needs to consider the context of their message about 'injustice' and the solidarity they hope to forge. In Kathiravelu's chapter, we see a disjunction between everyday understandings of justice and injustice of low-wage migrants in authoritarian city-states, like Singapore, and those of well-intentioned state authorities, volunteers, welfare workers, and nongovernmental organisations. She explores two essential aspects of everyday justice crucial to the lives of migrants: respect and freedom of mobility. When justice is conceived of as having multiple dimensions, or taking plural forms, in an authoritarian regime, rather than a liberal democracy, 'the basis for political equality' once again, she argues, becomes a subject for interrogation.

MAKING VISIBLE

All the authors in this volume are motivated by an urge to account for the complexity of justice in the everyday, which is an impulse that compels them to interrupt any essentializing construal of justice as an idea or practice, whether epistemologically or ontologically. The chapters show how justice is constantly imagined and negotiated in everyday life and interactions. Ethnography can be seductive when it suggests that its insights into everyday lives are essential for understanding how concepts such as justice are articulated and how they demonstrate ethnographic potential.

By using ethnographic studies from various locations and putting into play a range of approaches, the contributors to this volume argue for a plural outlook (not excluding an ontological starting point) with respect to the theorization of everyday justice. This takes everyday practices of justice as just one expression of what justice means for people in their realities. Far from merely filling an ethnographic lacuna, this book is intended, at the very least, to inform conceptualizations of justice as categories of practice and analysis in sharply reflexive ways. Sullivan, for example, deals with the substantial role of the courts and with the contentious role of law in legally constituting place. Amietta directs attention to the court and its processes of enacting justice by examining the summoning of lay jurors to decide cases. The authors in this volume also show that temporal and spatial registers are so innate to social, political, and legal discourses as to constitute them; and they show the need to study temporal and spatial logics in tandem. They remind readers, too, that senses of justice or injustice change over time through the reconfiguration of social, political, and economic conjunctures at various scales, as well as through shifts in relationships, as shown by Mora's treatment of the contingency of conflicting senses of justice on one another. Niezen's treatment of graffiti as a 'message-in-a-bottle' mode of communication highlights, for instance, how it may connect strangers separated by time; equally, Wastell reminds readers that temporality may be fractured and manipulated by various actions and actors.

The everyday is also the medium of appropriation and re-designation, as well as of continuity; everyday objects, like the chairs in the Papuan court, are re-signified by being drawn into the ambit of law and relations. Kathiravelu shows how migrants' sense of justice claims an equal right to the city, regardless of citizenship and individuals' possibility of participating in 'the formal consumption economy'.

This volume renders a series of social anatomies, cutting deep into the social, political, and legal fabrics and textures of different societies. Its narratives are not abstractly philosophical, often vying with the self-contained ahistorical fictions and speculations of metaphysics and their economy of 'scale-free abstraction' (Candea 2012). Justice, as an idea or practice, is grasped here within the places of judicialization and other sites of everyday actions, with their different kinds of possibilities and horizons of *im*/possibilities.

The anthropologies *of* justice in this volume shed light on how people work every day to bring justice's future promise (if it is accepted that justice holds such a promise) into the present. This may engender anthropologies *as* justice. But before we can reflect on what anthropologies *as* justice might resemble, we need to give further ethnographic consideration to the very nature of the anthropologies *of* justice approach to reveal the forces, modalities, and institutions engaged in giving form to people's 'justicescapes'.

For too long, we have conceded these concepts to philosophers or submerged them within the apparently ephemeral circumstantial details of subjects' lives. There is a now need to make concepts and experiences of justice analytically visible for anthropological endeavours – indeed, for all endeavours, including social, political, and legal ones – which seek to render justice ever more realizable and present.

Notes

[1] Brubaker and Cooper (2000: 4) pick up this broad bifurcation of 'category of analysis' and 'category of practice' from an understanding of Bourdieu's categories of practice. For Brubaker and Cooper, there are 'categories of everyday social experience', yet it is the 'categories ... [that are] distant' from the experience of participants that are 'used by social analysts' (4).

[2] Due to constraints of space, I do not treat here other influences on debates of justice, such as different theological traditions.

[3] Recent empirical research has addressed the question of the meanings people attach to the concept of justice. This emphasis has certain affinities with the study of transitional and international justice. Scholarship on transitional justice often lays particular importance on studying memory, violence, personhood, and truth-in-justice-making processes, rather than on justice as a *central* analytical category (e.g. Wilson 2001; Ross 2003). A notable exception is Clarke's 2009 monograph, which also focuses on competing international and local notions of justice.

[4] I thank Rachel Sieder for her suggestions in helping make my point clearer.

[5] This opens up the issue of ontological understandings because as Mol (2014: para. 2) says: 'There are not just many ways of knowing "an object", but rather many ways of practising it. Each way of practising stages – performs, does, enacts – a different version of "the" object. Hence, it is not "an object" but more than one. An object multiple.'

[6] Here, I use the suffix '-scape' loosely along lines suggested by Appadurai (1990: 297), who developed the term as a play on 'landscape' to highlight the scalar, amorphous, 'fluid', and 'irregular shapes' of certain global flows (it has been deployed in such terms as ethnoscape, ideoscape, and finan-cescape). Appadurai's use of -scape indicates that these terms are 'perspectival constructs, inflected very much by the historical, linguistic, and political situatedness of different sorts of actors' (296).

[7] Lefebvre ([1947] 1991) and de Certeau (1984), amongst others, offer powerful critical accounts of everyday life.

[8] Valverde (2003: 95), too, claims the 'concreteness of everyday life' can be mistakenly raised as 'an ideological banner'. While she emphasizes the significance of recording people's experiences, she also notes that there is a temptation for researchers 'to use their research to engage in grand polemics against "dead" systems, rules, or doctrines, and even against standardization as such. In such polemics, "experience" and "concreteness" function as abstractions – interestingly, in the same way that "legal equality" functions as an abstraction in conventional legal and political discourse' (95).

[9] A critic of Derrida, Litowitz (2009: para. 7) says that Derrida does not explore 'why a person should choose justice over injustice', or 'whether justice evolves', or what establishes 'who can decide what is just'.

[10] The term 'relational discontinuities' picks up differences between registers and normative understandings and draws attention to the 'mutual influences between local, national, and transnational formulations of justice' (Wilson 2000: 83).

[11] I take these terms from Derrida, but not his conceptual understanding of justice as transcending the realm of the state. For Derrida (1990), even as justice is called on – and takes place – outside and beyond the state law, it slips free of the realm of the state (see also Bankovsky 2012: 11). But, for anthropologists, very little can exist outside the realm, sphere, or entailment of the state; the dichotomy of outside/inside needs to be conceptually transgressed. Philippopoulos-Mihalopoulos (2004: 178–179) is clear that Derrida supposes that the law aims at justice; and that although its decisions are contingent and not always ideal, law is motivated by a desire to

achieve justice: 'Justice is prioritised over law. . . . Justice is beyond law but operates from within law, through and in spite of law.' This does not reflect much openness for other registers.

References
Abrams, Philip. 1988. 'Notes on the Difficulty of Studying the State (1977)'. *Journal of Historical Sociology* 1: 58–89.
Agnew, John. 2011. 'Space and Place'. In John A. Agnew and David N. Livingstone (eds.), *The Sage Handbook of Geographical Knowledge*. London: Sage, 316–331.
Altamirano, Marco. 2013. Review of Jack Reynolds, *Chronopathologies: Time and Politics in Deleuze, Derrida, Analytic Philosophy, and Phenomenology*, *Notre Dame Philosophical Reviews*. http://ndpr.nd.edu/news/chronopathol ogies-time-and-politics-in-deleuze-derrida-analytic-philosophy-and-phe nomenology/.
Appadurai, Arjun. 1990. 'Disjuncture and Difference in the Global Cultural Economy'. In Mike Featherstone (ed.), *Global Culture, Nationalism, Globalization and Modernity*. London: Sage, 295–310.
Bakhtin, Mikhail M. 1981. *The Dialogic Imagination: Four Essays*. Ed. Michael Holquist. Trans. Caryl Emerson and Michael Holquist. Austin: University of Texas Press.
Balkin, Jack M. 2009. 'Critical Legal Theory Today'. In Francis J. Mootz (ed.), *On Philosophy in American Law*. New York: Cambridge University Press, 64–72.
Bankovsky, Miriam. 2012. *Perfecting Justice in Rawls, Habermas and Honneth: A Deconstructive Perspective*. London: Continuum.
Besky, Sarah. 2014. *The Darjeeling Distinction: Labor and Justice on Fair-Trade Tea Plantations in India*. Berkeley: University of California Press.
Biehl, João. 2013. 'Ethnography in the Way of Theory'. *Cultural Anthropology* 28(4): 573–597.
Borneman, John. 1999. 'Can Public Apologies Contribute to Peace? An Argument for Retribution'. *Anthropology of East Europe Review* 17(1): 7–20.
Borneman, John, and Abdellah Hammoudi (eds.). 2009. *Being There: The Fieldwork Encounter and the Making of Truth*. Berkeley: University of California Press.
Bourdieu, Pierre. 1977. *Outline of a Theory of Practice*. Richard Nice, trans. Cambridge Studies in Social Anthropology, 16. London: Cambridge University Press.
Boyarin, Jonathan (ed.). 1994. *Remapping Memory: The Politics of TimeSpace*. Minneapolis: University of Minnesota Press.
Bromberg, Ava, Morrow, Gregory, and Deirdre Pfeiffer. 2007. 'Why Spatial Justice?'. *Critical Planning* 14: 1–4.

30

Brubaker, Rogers. 2012. 'Categories of Analysis and Categories of Practice: A Note on the Study of Muslims in European Countries of Immigration'. *Ethnic and Racial Studies* 36: 1–8.

Brubaker, Rogers, and Frederick Cooper. 2000. 'Beyond "Identity"'. *Theory and Society* 29: 1–47.

Brunnegger, Sandra. 2016. 'The Craft of Justice-Making through the Permanent Peoples' Tribunal in Colombia'. In Sandra Brunnegger and Karen A. Faulk (eds.), *A Sense of Justice: Legal Knowledge and Lived Experience in Latin America.* Stanford, CA: Stanford University Press, 123–147.

Forthcoming. 'Ethnographies of Justice: Possibilities of Justice and Law'. *PoLAR: Political and Legal Anthropology Review.*

Brunnegger, Sandra, and Karen A. Faulk (eds.). 2016. *A Sense of Justice: Legal Knowledge and Lived Experience in Latin America.* Stanford, CA: Stanford University Press.

Cahn, Edmond. 1949. *The Sense of Injustice: An Anthropocentric View of Law.* New York: New York University Press.

Candea, Matei. 2012. 'Derrida en Corse? Hospitality as Scale-Free Abstraction'. *Journal of the Royal Anthropological Institute* 18: 34–48.

Cassatella, Andrea. 2015. 'Jacques Derrida and the Theologico-Political Complex'. PhD thesis, University of Toronto.

Clarke, Kamari M. 2009. *Fictions of Justice: The International Criminal Court and the Challenge of Legal Pluralism.* Cambridge: Cambridge University Press.

Clarke, Kamari M., and Mark Goodale (eds.). 2010. *Mirrors of Justice: Law and Power in the Post–Cold War Era.* Cambridge: Cambridge University Press.

Das, Veena, Michael Jackson, Arthur Kleinman, and Bhrigupati Singh (eds.). 2014. *The Ground Between: Anthropologists Engage Philosophy.* Durham, NC: Duke University Press.

De Certeau, Michel. 1984. *The Practice of Everyday Life*, trans. Steven Rendall. Berkeley: University of California Press.

Demian, Melissa. 2016. 'Court in Between: The Spaces of Relational Justice in Papua New Guinea'. *Australian Feminist Law Journal* 42(1): 13–30.

Derrida, Jacques. 1990. 'Force of Law: The Mystical Foundation of Authority', trans. Mary Quaintance. *Cardozo Law Review* 11: 921–1046.

Epstein, Andrew. 2008. 'Critiquing "La Vie Quotidienne": Contemporary Approaches to the Everyday'. *Contemporary Literature* 49(3): 4.

Ferguson, James. 2007. 'Power Topographies'. In David Nugent and Joan Vincent (eds.), *A Companion to the Anthropology of Politics.* Oxford: Blackwell, 383–399.

Fortun, Kim. 2012. 'Ethnography in Late Industrialism'. *Cultural Anthropology* 27: 446–464.

Fraser, Nancy, and Axel Honneth. 2003. *Redistribution or Recognition? A Political-Philosophical Exchange.* London: Verso.

Goodale, Mark. 2017. *Anthropology and Law: A Critical Introduction*. New York: NYU Press.

Goodale, Mark, and Kamari M. Clarke. 2010. 'Introduction: Understanding the Multiplicity of Justice'. In Kamari M. Clarke and Mark Goodale, *Mirrors of Justice: Law and Power in the Post–Cold War Era*. New York: Cambridge University Press, 1–27.

Green, Sarah, Penny Harvey, and Hannah Knox. 2005. 'Scales of Place and Networks: An Ethnography of the Imperative to Connect through Information and Communications Technologies'. *Current Anthropology* 46: 805–26.

Greenhouse, Carol. 1996. *A Moment's Notice: Time Politics across Cultures*. Ithaca, NY: Cornell University Press.

Harvey, David. 1973. *Social Justice and the City*. Baltimore: Johns Hopkins University Press.

2003. 'The Right to the City'. *International Journal of Urban and Regional Research* 27 (4): 939–941.

Harvey, David, et al. 2011. 'On territorial justice, human flourishing and geographical strategies of liberation: an interview with David Harvey' [Justice territoriale, épanouissement humain et stratégies géographiques de libération: un entretien avec David Harvey, translation: Henri Desbois]. *Justice spatiale | Spatial Justice*, no. 4, December, www.jssj.org.

James, Deborah, and Christina Toren. 2013. 'Introduction: Culture, Context and Anthropologists' Accounts'. In Deborah James, Evelyn Plaice, and Christina Toren (eds.), *Culture Wars: Context, Models and Anthropologists' Accounts*. Oxford: Berghahn, 1–18.

Jennings, Theodore W. 2006. *Reading Derrida/Thinking Paul: On Justice*. Stanford, CA: Stanford University Press.

Kearns, Thomas R., and Austin Sarat. 1998. 'Legal Justice and Injustice: Toward a Situated Perspective'. In Austin Sarat and Thomas R. Kearns (eds.), *Justice and Injustice in Law and Legal Theory*. Ann Arbor: University of Michigan Press, 1–18.

Kim, Young. 2015. *Justice as Right Actions: An Original Theory of Justice in Conversation with Major Contemporary Accounts*. Lanham, MD: Lexington Books.

Lefebvre, Henri. [1947] 1991. *Critique of Everyday Life*. London: Verso.

Litowitz, Douglas. 2009. Review of *Derrida and Legal Philosophy*. Peter Goodrich, Florian Hoffmann, Michel Rosenfeld, and Cornelia Vismann (eds.), *Notre Dame Philosophical Reviews*, http://Ndpr.Nd.Edu/News/23897-Derrida-And-Legal-Philosophy/.

Marcus, George. 1993. 'Mass Toxic Torts and the End of Everyday Life'. In Austin Sarat and Thomas Kearns (eds.), *Law in Everyday Life*. Ann Arbor: University of Michigan Press, 237–274.

Merry, Sally. 1990. *Getting Justice and Getting Even: Legal Consciousness among Working-Class Americans*. Chicago: Chicago University Press.

Merry, Sally E. 2017. 'Foreword'. In Mark Goodale (ed.), *Anthropology and Law: A Critical Introduction*. New York: NYU Press, ix–xii.

Mitchell, Don. 2003. *The Right for the City: Social Justice and the Fight for Public Space*. New York: Guilford.

Mol, Annemarie. 2014. 'A Reader's Guide to the "Ontological Turn" – Part 4'. http://somatosphere.net/2014/a-readers-guide-to-the-ontological-turn-part-4.html/.

Moody-Adams, Michele M. 2014. Review of Veena Das, Michael Jackson, Arthur Kleinman, and Bhrigupati Singh (eds.), *The Ground between: Anthropologists Engage Philosophy*, Durham: Duke University Press. https://ndpr.nd.edu/news/the-ground-between-anthropologists-engage-philosophy/.

Munn, Nancy. 1990. 'Constructing Regional Worlds in Experience: Kula Exchange, Witchcraft and Gawan Local Events'. *Man*, (n.s.) 25: 1–17.

Nader, Laura. 2010. 'Epilogue: The Words We Use: Justice, Human Rights, and the Sense of Injustice'. In Kamari Maxine Clarke and Mark Goodale (eds.), Mirrors of Justice: Law and Power in the Post–Cold War Era. New York: Cambridge University Press.

Nader, Laura, and Andrée Sursock. 1986. 'Anthropology and Justice'. In R. L. Cohen (ed.), *Justice: Views from the Social Science*. New York: Plenum Press, 205–234.

Orford, Anne. 2012. 'In Praise of Description'. *Leiden Journal of International Law* 25(3): 609–625.

Paasi, Anssi, and Kaj Zimmerbauer. 2011. 'Theory and Practice of the Region: A Contextual Analysis of the Transformation of Finnish Regions'. *Treballs de la Societat Catalana de Geografia* 71–72: 163–178.

Philippopoulos-Mihalopoulos, Andreas. 2004. 'Between Law and Justice: A Connection of No-Connection in Luhmann and Derrida'. In Kenneth Einar Himma (ed.), *Law, Morality, and Legal Positivism: Proceedings of the 21st World Congress of the International Association for Philosophy of Law and Social Philosophy (IVR)*. Stuttgart: Franz Steiner Verlag, 175–183.

Rawls, John. 1971. *A Theory of Justice*. Cambridge, MA: Belknap Press of Harvard University Press.

1989. 'The Domain of the Political and Overlapping Consensus'. *New York University Law Review* 64: 233–255.

Robbins, Joel. 2010. 'Recognition, Reciprocity, and Justice: Melanesian Reflections on the Rights of Relationships'. In Kamari M. Clarke and Mark Goodale (eds.), *Mirrors of Justice: Law and Power in the Post–Cold War Era*. Cambridge: Cambridge University Press, 171–190.

Roohi, Sanam. 2015. 'Space, Place and the Social Sciences'. Presented at Insights Meeting on SPACE, organized by the NIAS Consciousness

Studies Programme, Bangalore, 4 July 2015. http://niasconsciousness centre.org/Insights/sroohi-space.pdf.

Rosen, Lawrence. 1989. *The Anthropology of Justice: Law as Culture in Islamic Society*. Cambridge: Cambridge University Press.

2000. *The Justice of Islam: Comparative Perspectives on Islamic Law and Society*. Oxford: Oxford University Press

Ross, Fiona C. 2003. *Bearing Witness: Women and the South African TRC*. London: Pluto Press.

Rousseau, Benedicta. 2008. '"This Is a Court of Law, Not a Court of Morality": Kastom and Custom in Vanuatu State Courts'. *Journal of South Pacific Law* 12(2): 15–27.

Salamanca Villamizar, Carlos, and Francisco Astudillo Pizarro. 2016. 'Justicia(s) espacial(es) y tensiones socio-ambientales. Desafíos y posibilidades para la etnografía de un problema transdisciplinario'. *Etnografías Contemporáneas* 2(3): 24–54.

Sapignoli, Marie. 2018. *Hunting Justice: Development, Law, and Activism in the Kalahari*. Cambridge: Cambridge University Press.

Sarat, Austin, and Thomas R. Kearns (eds.). 1998. *Justice and Injustice in Law and Legal Theory*. Ann Arbor: University of Michigan Press.

(eds.). 2009. *Law in Everyday Life*. University of Michigan Press.

Sen, Amartya. 1999. *Development as Freedom*. Oxford: Oxford University Press.

Shklar, Judith N. 1990. *The Faces of Injustice*. New Haven, CT: Yale University Press.

Sieder, Rachel. 2017. *Demanding Justice and Security: Indigenous Women and Legal Pluralities in Latin America*. New Brunswick, NJ: Rutgers University Press.

Soja, Edward W. 2010. *Seeking Spatial Justice*. Minneapolis: University of Minnesota Press.

Teubner, Gunther 2009. 'Self-Subversive Justice: Contingency or Transcendence Formula of Law'. *Modern Law Review* 72(1): 1–23.

Valverde, Mariana. 2003. '"Which Side Are You On?" Uses of the Everyday in Sociolegal Scholarship'. *POLAR* 26(1): 86–98.

2015. *Chronotopes of Law: Jurisdiction, Scale and Governance*. Abingdon, Oxon: Routledge.

Weszkalnys, Gisa. 2010. *Berlin, Alexanderplatz: Transforming Place in a Unified Germany*. Oxford: Berghahn Books.

Wilson, Richard A. 2000. 'Reconciliation and Revenge in Post-Apartheid South Africa: Rethinking Legal Pluralism and Human Rights'. *Current Anthropology* 41(1): 75–98.

2001. *The Politics of Truth and Reconciliation in South Africa: Legitimising the Post-Apartheid State*. New York: Cambridge University Press.

Young, Iris Marion. 1990. *Justice and the Politics of Difference*. Princeton, NJ: Princeton University Press.

PART ONE

IM/POSSIBILITIES OF
EVERYDAY JUSTICE

CHAPTER TWO

STREET JUSTICE

Graffiti and Claims-Making in Urban Public Space

Ronald Niezen

THE SENSE OF (IN)JUSTICE

It is getting increasingly difficult to avoid the notion that justice claims are not limited to the formal venues of law or even the public account-ability processes of journalism, but are also expressed in everyday activities of public outreach. We can see this outreach in informal efforts toward mass communication, in graffiti and Internet communi-cation (and connections between the two, as we will see) oriented toward passers-by and browsers, consumers of information, the possible-to-convince sympathizers of the plights of others. This nonprofessional realm of justice tells us something about the extent to which justice is experienced and expressed outside the law, but at the same time through the influence of law (see discussion on justice beyond law in Chapter 1). Human rights in particular can be seen as a source of inspiration and expression of new and emerging forms of rights-consciousness and the public expression of grievance. This conscious-ness, in turn, relates to the popular dynamics of human rights lobbying and a corresponding awareness of humanity as a reference point for what is fair, equitable, and honourable, grounded as they are in the 'soft' processes of persuasion and mass influence (see Chapter 3).

The impetus behind public expressions of claims and grievances seems to come not only from the persuasive power of ideas about rights and to whom they should apply but also from new pathways of empowerment. Advocacy efforts that closely involve those who are most affected by rights abuses and that are strategically oriented toward the formation of diverse partnerships are now firmly established as part of the human rights movement. Such advocacy, Jo Becker (2013: 1) argues, is responsible for establishing new international laws and resulting in changes to the policies and practices of those states that are responsible for some of the worst human rights abuses. Partly as a consequence of these forms of activism, the legislative powers of international law have deformalized and devolved during the post–Cold War period, to the point of being taken up even by NGOs like Amnesty International, Greenpeace, or Human Rights Watch. Such extensions of transnational legislative procedures to nonjudicial bodies, Klaus Günther argues, 'create new norms by their own practice which gain transnational binding force in the long run' (Günther 2008: 6). This new, more diffuse institutional normativity, in turn, is inspired by popular ideas or currents of opinion about justice and the ways to achieve it, in which, as Brunnegger and Falk put it, 'the sense of what is fair, or what is owed, feeds into the construction of formal systems' (2016: 8).

While much of the literature on human rights advocacy movements emphasizes the organizational dimension, the more marginal, solitary forms of activism have been largely overlooked. This chapter is an exploration of such 'ordinary' public consciousness, conveyed in outreach motivated by a basic sense of fairness and obligation. My goal is to go beyond the organized networks and strategically oriented justice campaigns, to look for signs of the rights-consciousness that is quite possibly a source of energy of these campaigns. I am looking for its expression quite literally in the everyday, in the world around me where I live and travel. Without actively seeking them out, I have made note of justice claims when they catch my attention, where they are not just visible but calling out to be noticed. This exercise tells us, very simply, that a pervasive, persistent, and popular sense of justice is there before us, if we care to notice it, quite literally in the writing on the wall.

As a medium for justice claims, graffiti has an ambiguous relationship with law. It is usually the result of an illegal act, closely associated with vandalism and crime. At the same time, however, it often expresses a call for justice, a claim for something owed, a reform or fair application of the law. In some cases, which I discuss below, it acts as a kind of vigilantism, with the spray can used to apply an immediate sanction relating to a law that is otherwise unlikely to be enforced.

The association of graffiti writing with vandalism and crime is not always a disadvantage for claimants of rights. In a certain sense, the illegality of the call for justice is what gives it effect, what brings attention to the message, in a way that is impossible in other venues. Members of the public – the graffiti authors' anonymous, unknown passers-by or viewers of their images posted on social media – are in a certain sense drawn to illegality, which they use as one point of reference as they perceive and measure the world around them, giving particular attention to acts or artefacts that seem somehow 'not right'. Hence, the technique used by Greenpeace and others of hanging massive banners from buildings and bridges or, even more daring, Mount Rushmore or the Christ the Redeemer statue in Rio de Janeiro. To make a message stand out by the way it is presented is to bring greater attention and impact to the thoughts it expresses.

I rely here on what others have said about graffiti artists, as members of the hip hop subculture that originated in the Bronx and expanded first to Puerto Rico and then worldwide in the 1980s (Ferrell 1993); or as a subculture of mural painters, those like Chagall and Malévich, who began their work in Russia after 1918, or the artists of Mexico (Rivera, Siqueiros, Orozco, etc.) who in the 1920s reflected the new order of the Revolution and inspired a Latin American tradition of political mural art (Tessier and Lemoine 2015: 10); or those from areas of concentrated artistic-political expression, such as the mural artists from the village of Orgosolo, Sardinia (Cozzolino 2017). My focus in this chapter is not on the graffiti 'artists' – those who dedicate their lives to illegal artistic expression in public space, priding themselves on a certain athleticism, assessing risk, running, hiding, and painting in the dark – nor is it on the authors of 'gang tags', those who mark territory as part of gang activity, and sometimes risk their lives trespassing into rival areas with their spray cans.[1] I am mainly interested in one facet of graffiti, a relatively small proportion of the messages on walls, sidewalks, and lampposts that use simple media: those that convey legally and politic-ally inspired justice claims. I begin my discussion here with a focus on a marginal subgenre of graffiti, occasional side events to the usual pre-occupations of those who put their mark on public space: the calls for justice, expressed in writing (brushed or sprayed), 'stencil graffiti' and 'sticker graffiti', united by their audience, their outreach to public consumers of justice causes, connected to networks and points of assembly online, based on shared understandings of universal norms and indignation at their violation.

We cannot be certain that these claims are consistently made by a particular segment of society – in fact it could well be entirely misleading to try to identify a 'subculture' defined by such things as gender, age, or family income as the source of the writing that makes claims to justice. There is every indication from the messages themselves that the authors vary, and include members of gangs, sex workers, students, and representatives of start-up NGOs – as is clear from the fact that these writings are in a variety of places, using media that vary from the familiar loosely applied spray paint to the more unusual uses of markers or repeated messages done with stencils or stickers. Rather than focus on one category of author, my aim here is to focus on the messages themselves, what they say to me as a reader or consumer and, in turn, what reflections they inspire that might tell us something about the processes of outreach and the hope that is being found (or sought in vain) in rights-oriented campaigns of public outreach.

PUBLIC MINDS

Vienna has a reputation as one of the world's historic cities, with its centre reflecting its grandeur as former capital of the Hapsburg Empire, but it is incongruously also known by a much smaller number of people as one of the world's notable places for graffiti art. I had come here to attend an anthropology conference and, during a walk in a free afternoon, found myself following the Danube canal, with its wide walkways on both sides near the water line, below the streets and sidewalks that run parallel to it. Here graffiti art and writing flourishes on the walls along some five kilometres through the central part of the city. It was only when a tourist asked me for directions to an official *Wienerwand*, or 'Vienna wall' (which, I had to admit, I had never heard of and had no idea where to find) that I realized there was an intended design to the apparent chaos of images and writing along the canal.[2] The city, I was to learn, had passed an ordinance designating particular walls along the canal as freely intended for graffiti, indicated by the symbol of a pigeon. Of course, the boundaries between the 'legal' walls and the 'illegal' spaces next to them are wilfully ignored, and graffiti flourishes along the entire length of the canal. All the same, the city's goal has been mostly accomplished and graffiti rarely intrudes into the historic city centre.

This wall space gives us an opportunity to reflect on the idea of the audience, which in this case might include a certain number of tourists, including a scattering of graffiti connoisseurs (like the one who asked me for directions). Let us begin with a simple example. When someone wrote 'Happy Birthday Anna + Laura', followed by a heart shape, with half-metre-high letters under a bridge along the canal (outside the designated graffiti areas), they were in part making a public statement. It is true that Anna and Laura would probably have been overjoyed to come down to the canal and see all the effort their friends put into making such a prominent display of their birthday, and we can easily imagine that they would have felt good to be part of a group of such close friends. This message was clearly meant to go beyond the usual card and cake. But what, more precisely, makes it different? For one thing, it is the very *publicness* of the display that gives it added significance, stemming from the fact that almost everyone walking along the canal will see that Anna and Laura have friends who think of them on their shared birthday, to the point of committing an illegal act to commemorate their friendship. We attach positive emotion to being recognized, not just by friends but – even in the abstract – by strangers.

The same principles of public outreach apply to the justice claims we find in graffiti art and writing, except that the messages and emotions involved are entirely different. When someone wrote NATIVE LAND in red uppercase letters, with each letter occupying a window on the top two floors of an abandoned building next to Autoroute 15 in Montreal, they were similarly trying to impress their readers by combining a simple message with flouting the city's laws in its execution (in this case laws against 'mischief' and trespass). They were at the same time, in two simple words, drawing attention to aboriginal land claims, with the Mohawk communities on the doorsteps of Toronto and Montreal asserting unrecognized claims, and with frustration occasionally resulting in clashes (in addition to the well-known 1990 siege in Oka, Quebec) between aboriginal claimants and nonindigenous residents (*The Economist* 2006). This graffiti in the windows of an abandoned building was a public expression of these unresolved claims. (The fact that more recently someone broke the windows and eliminated the 'native land' message was an expression of resistance to them.) The motorists and their passengers who drove along the autoroute were the subjects of an act of persuasion, of an effort to bring the claim to their attention, in the much the same space and with the same basic intention as the billboards that line the roadway.

The idea of public audiences as abstract consumers of ideas has an illustrious history, from which several points are worth touching on here. Public opinion in political theory is closely associated with the legitimation of political domination by states of their own citizens, with the idea of a critically debating citizenry acting as a necessary part of politics based on mass preference (see Habermas 1989: 236–44). With new tools of communication and organization available to activists, however, we have seen in recent decades a dramatic increase in the use of public opinion in the exercise of dissent, accompanied not only by increased connectivity, but also, to an unexpected degree, the influence of algorithms as filters of networking and sources of communities united around common opinion, a phenomenon sometimes referred to as the 'filter bubble' (Pariser 2012) or 'echo chamber' (Vaidhyanathan 2018). Mass communication, ranging in terms of technological sophistication from graffiti to Google, is part of widely available tools of outreach and persuasion, oriented to a transnational, rights-conscious public.[3]

It may be useful to consider a communications-based approach to public opinion that is more in keeping with the outreach strategies of the marginal or unconventional activism that we see in street writing. In its qualities of public outreach, graffiti is consistent with the thinking of Gabriel Tarde, who more than a century ago made connections between mass media and public opinion. The basic premise of his work on publics (he pluralized the term intentionally in recognition of their variety) was the influence from a distance on people who, in common with others, have no personal connection with the sources of information they receive and share independently of one another, with communications in 'civilized societies' less and less based on physical proximity (1969: 278). Publics, in these circumstances, are becoming unknown arbiters of opinion, 'impersonal personages' that are, as he put it, 'in the midst of becoming, in the contemporary theatre, like the chorus in a Greek tragedy, the principal interlocutor that one addresses and who then responds to you – or doesn't respond to you' (Tarde 1893: 120). Public communication and influence, according to Tarde, are the basic features of an emerging, global society. He was especially prescient in drawing attention to the connection between technology and mass persuasion as a foundation of new forms of social belonging.

Around the time that Tarde wrote these observations, the possibilities inherent in currents of opinion, and above all the influence that follows from shaping them, had also been noted by activists. For example, the extension of public communication to techniques of protest was captured succinctly by Anna Maria Mozzoni, a founder of the women's movement in Italy:

> Your protest should not be individual, whispered from one ear to another. That has been done time and again, without any result. It

should be collective, made with voices raised, to everyone, on every occasion, to all the constitutional bodies that oppress us, that exclude us, that diminish us. Gather yourselves into associations, and let your banners carry slogans on the two sides of the resistance, that of the workers and that of women.

(quoted in Sarogni 2004: 39–40)

While Mozzoni's campaign for women's rights in the late nineteenth century provides insight into the development of collective justice lobbying, with its ultimate origins in the French Revolution (Baker 1990: ch. 8), it was some time before there was a corresponding awareness of the power of media as a means to convey knowledge of justice causes and to broadly influence public opinion.

This awareness was eventually to become a significant part of the phenomenon sometimes known as the human rights revolution. It was not until the late twentieth century, when new media were used by a burgeoning number of human rights nongovernmental organizations to engage in global campaigns of consciousness-raising, that we see the full effect of 'voices raised' to public audiences.

It is this involvement in the opinions of others that is key to the claims making that we see painted on the surfaces of urban public space. There is in these words and images a message-in-a-bottle aspect of communication between strangers who are separated by time. Graffiti is often a form of public communication, in which the intended audience is an abstraction. In this sense it is not entirely unlike Internet postings, in which there is a similar freedom from journalistic filters, and in which consumers of the communication are often intentionally unknown to the Facebook member, blogger, or web designer, except that writing on a wall limits the audience to those who are in physical proximity to the message (unless, of course, it is photographed and posted on the web). In some cases, as I will discuss, there is a blurring of the boundary between wall writings and blogs, with the Internet manifesting itself, even recruiting participation from 'networked publics' (Collins et al. 2013: 359) in the mechanisms and messages of urban space.

Just who are these anonymous publics that the equally anonymous authors of wall messages are trying to reach? On the face of it, this may be an impossible question to answer. Publics are, after all, unknown almost by definition. Their members appear only occasionally in such things as rallies, opinion editorials, and blogs. But not everyone has been inhibited by the unknowable nature of publics to the point of

43

refusing to speculate on their effect. One of the central tasks of 'public anthropologists' is to interrogate the concept of the public, not so much as an analytical concept but to understand whether and how the messages of activism are getting through to them, above all by asking: 'Are we reaching the groups we would like to reach? Are we networked effectively?' (Collins et al. 2013: 358). Politicians similarly make it their business to try to know what they can about public opinion. Election and referendum campaigns are covered by mainstream media with detailed and sometimes seemingly desperate attempts to gauge the intentions of registered voters. There is also a sizable literature that considers the influence of opinion on criminal justice, with arguments variously emphasizing the public's tendencies toward apathy and wilful ignorance on justice issues or their habit of making pragmatic cognitive shortcuts (Roberts and Stalans 2000: 13–14). Others have pointed to the essential qualities of media themselves, such as the tendency for media to commodify information, and in so doing to compromise rationality in favour of the mythical or charismatic qualities of judicial process (Resta 2010: 21). The same applies to the public consumption of human rights abuses and their victims. The 'public mind' in this sense is complex and contradictory. Publics tend to be emotionally reactive, and at the same time jaded and sceptical. They can be critical and try to root out error in the information they receive, but have undesirable tendencies toward oversimplification of complex issues and attraction toward the spectacular, the unusual, and the emotionally affecting aspects of justice (Niezen 2010: ch. 2).

These qualities of public opinion apply particularly to human rights processes, with claimants facing the challenge of collective self-representation to NGO activists, UN 'experts', and public consumers (and potential supporters) of their causes. The competition for a limited pool of sympathy and activist support has radically transformed the way that human life is commonly understood. The simplicity of the public mind – a quality sometimes even shared by activists and UN experts as more sophisticated consumers of information – is such that those who are lobbying for rights have to reduce both their claims and their common sources of belonging to their essence, to the kind of superficiality that is readily perceived and possibly acted on. Furthering a collective claim under these circumstances calls for selectivity in public representation. In particular, it calls for words and images to be chosen with a view to their simplicity, appeal, and potential to evoke curiosity and affect in remote, unknown, largely abstract audiences.

SETTING THINGS STRAIGHT

As I recently walked along a path next to Parc Lafontaine in Montreal, my attention was caught by the words 'it is not straigt [*sic*]' written on the pavement in red block letters with an arrow indicating the dividing line between pedestrians and cyclists. A quick glance along the path confirmed that even though the yellow line was painted more or less in the middle of the pathway, it wavered to and fro with little precision. These painted words with the arrow symbol on the pavement can be understood in several ways: a possible reference to the proximity of Montreal's 'gay village', but also perhaps as a light-hearted observation of the urban environment, as a sardonic commentary on the condition of the road infrastructure in Montreal, with its potholes and decay, a steady source of public scandal, ultimately connected to wider issues of graft and corruption.

Metaphorically, we can see this statement as a broader commentary on the nature of justice. 'It is not straight' is a pure reflection of the nature of injustice, involving something out of order, out of alignment in the configuration of human relationships, something that invokes a sense of discomfort or indignation, a feeling of wanting to 'set things to right'. The first step toward this correction is often simply drawing attention to the problem, pointing to fact that something in our shared world is not straight, involving others in the sense of injustice, and strategizing toward remedy.

To illustrate this, let us return to the Danube Canal in Vienna, again to a place that is not part of an official *Wienerwand* but some distance away. Here, a few 'tags' next to one another illustrate the occasional legal content of illegal graffiti. One says (in English), 'Disrespect my Colors a . . .' The rest is covered by a poster for a concert series, but we can be reasonably sure that it includes the word 'and' followed by some sort of threat – a 'gang tag' in other words. In fact, this tag is making explicit what many tags do, marking territory, making it known that this part of town is occupied by such and such gang whose colours and claim to territory one had better not violate. This is not so much a public rights claim as a legal marker, an act of legal pluralism in the form of a nonstate law that is the outcome of a collective decision or legislative process, put into writing and reinforced by the threat of force.

Next to it is another kind of legal statement, 'Free Fahad!' with Fahad's name underscored. This is a fairly straightforward example of a public justice claim. Fahad, it would seem to the reader/passer-by, is in prison. The author of this tag thinks that the imprisonment is wrong, wants Fahad free, and is making this known to a public audience (myself included). The reader is being invited to do anything in their power to bring about Fahad's release, much in the manner of the well-known 'Free Leonard Peltier' bumper stickers that display support for a case of wrongful conviction in the United States. That is to say, the words 'free Fahad' express solidarity with someone in prison, but they are also strategic (however ineffectually, lost in the communicative chaos of a graffiti-filled wall), calling the imprisonment to the attention of a public audience in the hope that something can be done, that the injustice will come to the attention of a public, and in turn (through that public) to those in authority who may have some responsibility for the injustice and/or authority to act to remedy it. 'Free Fahad!' is in this sense a public justice claim.

I later followed up on this tag, which turned out to be not quite as simple as it seemed. An Internet search using the keywords 'free Fahad' uncovered an online movement centred on the case of Syed Fahad Hashmi, who, at the age of twenty-seven, was extradited from the United Kingdom to the United States based on charges that he conspired to support a terror group overseas. One article describes Fahad as 'a loving, caring, deeply religious man' who grew up and lived in New York and who travelled to London to enter a master's program in political science. Those who support Fahad online argue that his arrest and extradition was unjust, based solely on the testimony of one individual, described as a government witness 'globetrotter', who travelled to England and Canada 'to testify against Muslims'. An address is provided at the bottom of the page for sending donations (Free Fahad 2007). What we find here, then, is an imperative statement, almost lost in the communicative chaos of a graffiti-filled wall, connected to an online social movement that has formed a single justice cause, as representative of wider concerns about policing and the rise of despotism in response to the threat of terrorism in Europe and North America. The tag is thus both an expression of public outreach and a name given to a social justice cause that has become a source of collective identity.

The use of English in this justice claim in Vienna provokes another reflection. This was one of many messages along the canal written in English, which seems odd in a German-speaking country. This was probably not so much an indication of the origins of the authors – very likely few among those out in the streets at night have greater compe-tence in English than they do in German. Rather, it suggests an effort to reach a wider public than the residents of Vienna, to be visible to and legible by the city's many tourists, some who come to see the canal and its *Wand* as a tourist attraction. This is possibly related to the fact that English has become the global language of claims making. Street protesters acting on such varied issues as cartoons depicting the prophet, which brought people into the streets and in front of the cameras in Pakistan, or the Catalonian claims for independence in a 2015 referendum, can be seen online in photographs taken by the global press, acting as intermediaries between those displaying promin-ent signs in English and their online publics, sometimes in a way that seems at odds with the religious and national sentiments at the origin of their protest.

Once I became aware of the element of claims making in some of the graffiti where I lived and travelled, I began to see examples of it nearly everywhere I went. A tag written in differently coloured markers in block letters on a black wall in the northern part of rue Saint-Laurent in Montreal – 'Street harassment is getting old . . . Get with the times and leave my body alone' – tells us something more about the intended audience of graffiti. In this case the author has written as though their readers are personally known. The invocation of a failure to 'get with the times' implies that the author/artist is aware of a movement of moral progress, a sense that they have rights to bodily integrity that have come into being at least within living memory, rights that are now part of a wider understanding of the meaning and consequences of sexual harassment. At the same time, they could well be making a wider point, a human rights claim, reaching people who walk along rue Saint-Laurent who might be provoked into sympathy by a carefully worded plea.

These last examples are fairly straightforward in expressing a sense of injustice or a rights claim, but it can often happen that the only way to see the connection to rights or a sense of legal solidarity with others is to take the context of the message into careful consideration. For example, the words 'let's build a boat' in blue block letters on a white stucco wall on a side street in Montreal's 'gay village' seemed intended to make one wonder why on earth someone (singly or in a group) would want to break the law by defacing a building to communicate such an ordinary message. Perhaps it was an effort at humour, with the commonplaceness of the message juxtaposing oddly with the illegality of the medium, a playful, defiance-of-authority style of humour that makes us sympathize with rebels who avoid violence and refuse to take themselves too seriously. Perhaps it was something more.

When I had a chance to look carefully at the photograph I had taken of this tag, I noticed another, much smaller one next to it on a parking meter, which read simply '1017'. This piqued my curiosity and I went back to the site to have a closer look. Taking the context of this odd message into account, it was obvious that someone had tagged all the parking meters up the block with a signature, and, using the same marker, had written '1017' on this one parking meter before continuing. What would motivate someone to change from a signature to a number? And what did the number mean?

A possible answer to this brings us to the politics of language in Quebec. The piece of legislation regulating the public expression of languages other than French is 'law 101', the Charter of the French Language (*La charte de la langue française*). Chapter 7 of the charter, concerning 'the language of commerce and business', states: 'Public signs and posters and commercial advertising must be in French. They may also be both in French and in another language provided that French is markedly predominant.' The law is administered by the Office québécois de la langue française (OQLF) (Quebec Board of the French Language), whose officials are sometimes referred to as 'tongue troopers' or 'language police'. If we look carefully at the background of the '1017' graffiti we see a sign in the window of a business with the words 'piazzetta', meaning a small plaza or public square in Italian, in other words, a violation of law 101, chapter 7. The number 1017 is therefore quite possibly a version of a tag that is immediately recognizable to anyone who has lived in Quebec, at least anyone who is aware of their surroundings and the politics of language in the province. The tag '101' or '*loi 101*' applied to signs in English is a common way to draw attention to violations of the Charter of the French Language.

(The 'Let's Build a Boat' tag in this context could therefore be another statement in the politics of language, a defiance of the limits on the public expression of English, adding a language law to the violations inherent in self-expression on private property with a spray can. We can only speculate.)

An Internet search of '*loi 101*' provides another example of the online inspiration for graffiti, making it clear that much of the writing we see in urban public space is not isolated, not written by individuals in acts of public outreach, but can be acts of communication inspired or sponsored by organizations, networks, or social movements. Online information on Quebec's Language Charter is closely linked with the Saint-Jean-Baptiste Society, an organization dedicated to the protection of the French language and the promotion of Quebec sovereignty. Clearly the connection between graffiti and online activism, between the material and the digital, is closer than it might initially seem in the urban space of Europe and North America and deserves to be considered further.

FROM GRAFFITI TO MASS ONLINE COMMUNICATION

An advertisement I recently came across in a Montreal metro car for a breath-freshening chewing gum ('Arctic bubbles') included a photo of a young couple embracing and kissing, with the caption '*rapprochements sans risques*' (encounters without risk). The implicit connection between chewing gum and condom use in this poster of was course meant to draw the viewers' attention, perhaps motivate their spending habits, but what drew my attention even more was the fact that it was partly covered (leaving the faces and touching lips still visible, ostensibly so that viewers could see the outrage) by a fifteen-centimetre-square sticker with a red 'X' – the universal symbol for prohibition and eradication – and the words in block capitals, '*SALE PUB SEXISTE*' (dirty sexist ad). I had earlier seen the same 'sticker graffiti' applied to other ads in the city, targeting images that were clearer in their objectification of women. In this case, though, the 'sexism' to which the sticker-wielding protester was objecting seemed to be less about gender stereotyping and more about the commercialization of sex itself. The protester was apparently trying to raise awareness of a particular kind of harm, the way that advertising agencies calibrate the images they use in order to draw upon and promote sexuality. The sticker was calling attention to this practice as an illegitimate objectification of a realm of life that should be off-limits to the imaginations and manipulations of 'ad-men'.

A web search of the key terms 'sale pub sexiste' brings up a women's student organization, the Association pour une Solidarité Syndicale Étudiante (ASSÉ) (the acronym sounds identical to the French word 'assez' – enough). An online brochure (*dépliant*) explains its '*sale pub sexiste*' campaign in the following terms: 'Advertising is one of the direct and violent vectors of sexism. Sexualized norms are hammered into our spirits every day. Advertising participates in the construction of female and male genders, real social constraints imposed on individuals as a function of their biological sex' (ASSÉ 2013).[4] The sticker on the poster in the metro is therefore (as I expected) one of many placed strategically on offending advertisements, part of an organized campaign of public outreach, or 'continuing the combat', in solidarity with others.

In this example we therefore see something more than the wall writings of a disempowered underclass. There are indications here of a more coordinated and strategic collective purpose, using tools of mass communication, in this case imaging software, a printer, and paper with adhesive backing. The strategy associated with this technology is the simple one of message repetition, creating a 'meme' or a simple message that communicates easily from mind to mind, to make it impossible for any sentient, literate being to avoid at least some encounter in their daily lives with the message being communicated.[5] In other words, the protest targets the *ethics* of advertising by using the *methods* of advertising.

When I was recently in Germany (to make use of the state library), I noticed that this quality of mass communication had been taken a step further by a sticker on a pedestrian walk signal in Potsdamer Platz, Berlin. (This just happened to be not twenty meters from a monument featuring a three-meter-high remnant of the Berlin Wall – the historic reference point for political graffiti.) The sticker reads (in English): 'FIGHT FOR YOUR DIGITAL RIGHTS!' with a barely visible URL (www.netzpolitik.org) below. If we take the trouble to follow this up with a search (as the distributors of the sticker no doubt hope we do) we find ourselves at a web site that describes its purpose as follows:

> netzpolitik.org is a platform for digital civil liberties ... Through netzpolitik.org we describe how politics is changing the Internet through regulation and how the Net is changing policy, publics and everything else. We see ourselves as offering journalism, but are not neutral. Our position is: We are committed to rights of digital freedom and their political implementation.
>
> (netzpolitik 2015)[6]

Here, as with the *sale pub sexiste* campaign, the connection between the words posted in urban public space and those posted online was direct and, more significantly, *strategic*. This strategy takes the form of what we might refer to as 'teasers', simple messages or 'memes' in public postings intended to attract online follow-up, in much the same way that Hollywood's advertisers use trailers to attract audiences to the complete product in the cinema.

Another way this can be done takes the form of stencil graffiti, a recognized graffiti style, in which the artist can take the time to produce a cut-out image that then becomes the template for street art and writing that can be quickly spray-painted in multiple locations. (One of its appeals is that it gives a certain precision to the sprayed imagery, much like silk-screening.) Even though there are material limits to the amount of written information that can be included in them, these stencils often have simple message content in addition to imagery.

One such stencil, which I came across not far from where I live, consisted of the words 'Stop Chemtrail' with an irregular seven-pointed star, sprayed on the sidewalk along Avenue René Levesque in Montreal. An Internet search of the keyword 'chemtrail' reveals that the author/artist had inadvertently omitted the plural 's' and was intending to draw attention to the environmental threat of 'chemtrails', which had a substantial online presence. One of the principle sites, among many, dedicated to this phenomenon can be found under the banner 'World Gathering; Stop! Stop Chemtrails!' which defines the issue as follows:

> 'Chemtrails' or 'Chem Trails' or 'Bioweapon Trails' is a massive global spraying operation using a large fleet of many hundreds of aircraft which seem to operate over most countries of the world. This outside-of-big-media worldwide aerial aerosol-discharging operation became severe around the year 2000, and by now must be severely damaging **all life** on Earth. There are, according to a large number of reports over the past several years, babies, children and adults going to hospital with breathing problems and chronic and acute severe sickness all over the world because of this massive, aerial discharging of **bioweapons**, chemicals and metals.
>
> (World Gathering 2015)

The list of problems associated with this issue includes almost every conceivable health crisis, including what is described as 'The Chemtrail and Swine Flu/H1N1 Connection', and 'The WHOLE WORLD Has CHEMTRAIL ALZHEIMERS.' Where drawing attention to this vast conspiracy becomes a kind of rights claim is through the invocation of law, making the phenomenon of 'chemtrails' not only catastrophically harmful, but illegal under international standards. The online information thus includes headlines such as 'United Nations Bans Chemtrails' and 'Chemtrails Banned under Geneva Convention', making reference to various moratoriums and prohibitions in international law concerning air pollution and chemical warfare. One of the striking things about this invocation of international law is that by referencing it the authors are not only objecting to a condition of crisis, but attempting to give it greater reality. After all, if chemtrails are universally abhorred and illegal in the community of nations under the authority of something as significant as a Geneva Convention, then they *must be real*. At the same time, the law gives a sense of justice undone, of perpetrators who are powerful enough to escape the consequences of their illegal actions, of remedy denied or, more hopefully, pending, remedy that can be applied only when enough people are aware of the harm being done and are ready to stand up in defence of their rights to political transparency and environmental justice.

Another aspect of this campaign that stands out is the fact that its participants appear to be mostly unknown to one another, much like the audiences to which they are reaching out. The stencil graffiti on the sidewalk that caught my attention is an expression of a community of affirmation, an online meeting place for those who support one another in ideas and life choices that are not accepted in a 'real' social world of diverse and debated opinions (Niezen 2013). Unlike the members of the student union group ASSÉ and the organizers of the netzpolitik website, which seem to be in control of their outreach from a core group of participants, the 'stop chemtrails' website seems to be less centralized, more of a loosely organized movement. It is 'virtual', not in the sense of being exotic, inauthentic, or unmoored, but in the sense that it is 'a genuine site of human activity supported by crafted objects' (Nardi 2015: 19), but with the proviso here that the crafted objects of the 'virtual' world spill out into 'offline' everyday life. The stencil graffiti that I encountered on Avenue René Levesque in this sense represents something that was unknown to Gabriel Tarde in the turn of the nineteenth and early twentieth centuries: a public engaging in ideological recruitment among a wider public.

CONCLUSION

If there is a demarcation between the solitary wall writing that draws attention to a cause that affects the writer personally and the justice claims oriented toward mass persuasion, it is in the technology used to convey the message. Something as simple as a stencil or sticker allows the message to be precisely repeated, inhibits spontaneity, and by virtue of these qualities is oriented toward a basic strategy of mass persuasion: the infiltration into public consciousness of a simple message multiplied many times over, a meme.

What I have tried to show by exploring examples of public outreach is that there is clear continuity between the single, unique pleas for justice written by individuals or small groups and the repeated messages connected to organized campaigns. What we call graffiti is sometimes aspiring toward the same thing as the media outreach of NGOs or political parties. Each is trying to achieve the same kind of exposure, the same influence on the emotions and opinions of unknown others. The main difference between them is that the graffiti artists' means are often more limited. There are usually fewer resources available to those who are holding a spray can or marker or fixing a sticker to a lamppost, which partly explains their chosen technologies of communication.

This simplicity of technology points to the populism of rights consciousness, taking us beyond the organized campaigns and transnational networks of advocacy groups. It allows us to see the extent to which rights are understood and acted on by those who are well and truly marginalized: the street gang members, sex workers, indigenous people displaced from reserves, and others among the urban poor. Rights consciousness does not stop at the door of prominent advocacy-oriented NGOs, but extends to those with far fewer resources and organizational capacities.

Then again, street writing can also be connected to fairly well-organized campaigns of consciousness-raising. If we follow the simple messages we encounter on the street through Internet searches using their key words or sometimes directly with a URL provided in the messages, we can often find their online assembly points. The most important source of meaning behind message repetition is not just the justice cause, but the community that gathers in support of it. This underscores the fact that we cannot properly understand much of what we see in the world around us without following it into the Internet. This is a bit like Freud's idea of the manifest content of dreams leading toward the repressed desires of the unconscious – except that once we find ourselves looking for justice causes online there is little that is repressed or concealed – aside of course from the algorithms that contribute to shaping how social media communities are formed in the first place. Here we find the complete representation of opinion, the amplified messages behind the 'teasers' put out on the street. Participation by posting a comment or a blog feeds seamlessly into site membership. To varying degrees, opinion in these social justice sites is controlled. The expression of views and values within a certain bandwidth is supported, rewarded with a sense of belonging. The ultimate sources of this kind of low-technology, mass-produced graffiti (if we can still call it that), the stickers, stencils, flags, banners, and posters we see in the streets, are the online communities that coordinate their members' efforts, sometimes motivating them to break the law in the pursuit of higher ideals of justice.

Perhaps the appeal of justice-oriented graffiti often lies in its connection to online spaces – through direct representation of those spaces. The limits of geography, of the fact that a message can be reproduced and posted in only so many physical places and spaces, constitute a major impediment to the reach of graffiti messages. At the same time, however, its appeal could be as a supplement and countermeasure to the prioritization of content that takes place behind the scenes in online space. Graffiti could well be in part an antidote to the algorithms that prioritize and tailor messages for particular audiences, or at least another way for those caught in the market logic of limited public attention to reach an audience and acquire from it more of the limited good of sympathy. It is in this sense a quintessentially 'popular' or 'democratic' form of media, cutting through all journalistic, commercial, and algorithmic filters by communicating directly to its (albeit limited) audiences.

The examples of outreach I encountered as a member of the authors' public give us a glimpse into the rights consciousness that is so often alluded to as a defining feature of the post–Cold War era. This is not a juridical conception of rights, but more an emotional one, based on collective senses of injustice, actively and strategically promoted. Indignation over the violations or incompleteness of law is not only shared within groups online, it is also communicated to unknown others in vast networks of persuasion and sympathy. Expanding the community of the committed is a strategy oriented toward empowerment, with 'voices raised' (or websites built) serving to persuade publics and gather members, acting as a deterrent to political abuse and an impetus toward political and legal reform.

Members of online communities are clearly aware of the significance of influencing a wider swath of public opinion and recruiting others to their chosen cause. Raising voices is in this sense a legal remedy in itself, with access to justice almost universal. In this phenomenon there is no stark digital divide between those with the privilege of access and those without. Starting out on this path to consciousness-raising requires only the wherewithal for a can of paint – and the cover of darkness to use it.

Notes

1 See Farkas (2012) for a series of interviews with Toronto-based graffiti artists, which chronicles their aspirations and activities.
2 The basic rules of the designated graffiti walls are explained in a city-sponsored web page next to a smiling photo of the mayor, Dr. Michael Häupl (himself the subject of satirical graffiti on the walls he sponsors). The site promotes the idea of legal walls for graffiti artists, which are indicated by the symbol of a pigeon. www.wienerwand.at. Accessed December 2, 2015.
3 Herman and Chomsky (2002), in *Manufacturing Consent*, are pessimistic about the possibilities for the propaganda functions of mass media to be overcome by an unregulated Internet, an early iteration of an idea that has since received support from those who emphasize the influence of advertising and algorithms in social media (see Pariser 2012).
4 '*La publicité est l'un des vecteurs directs et violents du sexisme. Des normes sexuées sont chaque jour martelées dans les esprits. La publicité participe à la construction du genre féminin et masculin, véritables contraintes sociales impo-sées aux individus en fonction de leur sexe biologique.*' My translation.
5 The concept of the meme in Richard Dawkins's *The Selfish Gene* is under-stood in terms of evolutionary biology. The viral phenomenon in the ideas being expressed by activists is intended to go beyond the meme, to attract viewers and readers to more complex ideas for legal and political reform.
6 '*netzpolitik.org ist eine Plattform für digitale Freiheitsrechte. Wir thematisieren die wichtigen Fragestellungen rund um Internet, Gesellschaft und Politik und zeigen Wege auf, wie man sich auch selbst mit Hilfe des Netzes für digitale Freiheiten und Offenheit engagieren kann. Mit netzpolitik.org beschreiben wir, wie die Politik das Internet durch Regulation verändert und wie das Netz Politik, Öffen-tlichkeiten und alles andere verändert. Wir verstehen uns als journalistisches Angebot, sind jedoch nicht neutral. Unsere Haltung ist: Wir engagieren uns für digitale Freiheitsrechte und ihre politische Umsetzung.*' My translation.

References

ASSÉ. 2013. 'Dépliant Explicatif Sale Pub Sexiste'. www.asse-solidarite.qc.ca/wp-content/uploads/2013/03/depliant-sales-pubs-sexistes-2010.pdf. Accessed 6 December 2015.
Baker, Keith. 1990. *Inventing the French Revolution*. Cambridge: Cambridge University Press.
Becker, Jo. 2013. *Campaigning for Justice: Human Rights Advocacy in Practice*. Stanford, CA: Stanford University Press.

Brunnegger, Sandra, and Karen Faulk (eds.). 2016. *A Sense of Justice: Legal Knowledge and Lived Experience in Latin America*. Stanford, CA: Stanford University Press.

Collins, Samuel, Matthew Durington, Glenn Daniels, Natalie Demyan, David Rico, Julian Beckles, and Cara Heasley. 2013. 'Tagging Culture: Building a Public Anthropology through Social Media'. *Human Organization* 72 (4): 358–368.

Cozzolino, Francesca. 2017. *Peindre pour agir: Muralisme et politique en Sardaigne*. Paris: Karthala.

Dawkins, Richard 2006 [1976]. *The Selfish Gene*. Oxford: Oxford University Press.

The Economist. 2006. 'This Land Is My Land: Yet Another Land-Claim Dispute Turns Ugly and Sheds a Spotlight on the Failure of Canada's Policies toward Its Aboriginal People'. 14 September. www.economist.com/node/7911293. Accessed 6 December 2015.

Farkas, Yvette, ed. 2012. *Toronto Graffiti: The Human behind the Wall*. Toronto, ON. www.torontograffiti.ca.

Ferrell, Jeff. 1993. *Crimes of Style: Urban Graffiti and the Politics of Criminality*. Boston: Northeastern University Press.

Free Fahad. 2007. 'Free Fahad: The Untold Story of Syed Fahad Hashmi'. https://freefahad.wordpress.com/2007/06/07/hello-world/. Accessed 4 December 2015.

Günther, Klaus. 2008. 'Legal Pluralism or Dominant Concept of Law: Globalization as a Problem of Legal Theory'. *No Foundations* 5: 5–21.

Habermas, Jürgen. 1989 [1962]. *The Structural Transformation of the Public Sphere: An Inquiry into a Category of Bourgeois Society*. Thomas Burger and Frederick Lawrence, trans. Cambridge, MA: MIT Press.

Herman, Edward, and Noam Chomsky. 2002. *Manufacturing Consent: The Political Economy of the Mass Media*. New York: Pantheon.

Macdonald, Nancy. 2003. *The Graffiti Subculture: Youth, Masculinity, and Identity in London and New York*. London: Palgrave Macmillan.

Nardi, Bonnie. 2015. 'Virtuality'. *Annual Review of Anthropology* 44: 15–31.

netzpolitik.com. 2015. 'Über uns'. https://netzpolitik.org/about-this-blog/. Accessed 1 December 2015.

Niezen, Ronald. 2010. *Public Justice and the Anthropology of Law*. Cambridge: Cambridge University Press.

Niezen, Ronald. 2013. 'Internet Suicide: Communities of Affirmation and the Lethality of Communication'. *Transcultural Psychiatry* 50(2): 303–322.

Pariser, Eli. 2012. *The Filter Bubble: How the New Personalized Web Is Changing What We Read and How We Think*. New York: Penguin.

Resta, Giorgio. 2010. 'Il problema dei processi mediatici nella prospettiva del diritto comparator'. In Giorgio Resta (ed.), *Il rapporto tra giustizia e mass media: quali regole per quali soggetti*. Naples: Editoriale Scientifica.

Roberts, Julian, and Loretta Stalans. 2000. *Public Opinion, Crime, and Criminal Justice*. Boulder, CO: Westview.

Sarogni, Emilia. 2004. *La donna italiana: 1861–2000 Il lungo cammino verso i diritti*. Milan: Gruppo editoriale il Saggiatore.

Société Saint-Jean-Baptiste de Montréal. 2015. 'Société Saint-Jean-Baptiste de Montréal: Entêtée d'Avenir ... Depuis 1834'. *Ssjb.com*. Accessed 4 December 2015.

Tarde, Gabriel. 1893. *Les Transformations du droit: étude sociologique*. Paris: Félix Alcan.

Tarde, Gabriel. 1969. *On Communication and Social Influence*. T. Clark, trans. and ed. Chicago: University of Chicago Press.

Tessier, Yvan, and Stéphanie Lemoine. 2015. *Les Murs révoltés: Quand le street art parle social et politique*. Paris: Gallimard.

Vaidhyanathan, Siva. 2018. *Anti-Social Media: How Facebook Disconnects Us and Undermines Democracy*. Oxford: Oxford University Press.

World Gathering. n.d. 'Stop! Stop Chemtrails! Stop! Stop Chemtrails – Introduction'. www.worldgathering.net/stop/. Accessed 7 October 2015.

CHAPTER THREE

SEEKING RESPECT, FAIRNESS, AND COMMUNITY

Low-Wage Migrants, Authoritarian Regimes, and the Everyday Urban

Laavanya Kathiravelu

In December 2013, a violent riot broke out in the Little India district of Singapore. Public vehicles such police cars and an ambulance were set on fire and dozens of law enforcement officers were called in to quell the situation. The level of destruction and chaos during the incident was unprecedented in a city-state that is known for its strong rule of law, and that hadn't seen similar public unrest of a similar scale in more than forty years. The violence was sparked off by the acci-dental running-over of a low-wage Tamil migrant man by a bus chartered by a private transport agency. While the man lay dying amid the chaos caused by the accident, ambulances took more than thirty minutes to reach the scene – by which time the Indian migrant was dead.

According to narratives of low-wage Indian migrants interviewed after the incident, it was not the accident itself that incited the crowd of migrants to start a riot, but the fact that the ambulance did not arrive in time. In a state known for its rigid efficiency, the delay of an ambulance to the scene was interpreted as a clear indication of neglect of migrant workers' welfare. This man's life, it was collectively felt, was seen as unimportant because of his status as a low-wage migrant worker, a category of labour that the state conceives of as easily replaceable and transient, and therefore of little political or social consequence (Yeoh 2006). The injustice that this unfortunate migrant was perceived to be a victim of became a shared and collective affect, that then took on a violent life of its own.

The gross injustice of perceived unequal and unjust treatment, here, was felt viscerally and piercingly by the surrounding crowd of co-ethnic Tamil migrants in Little India, who typically gather around the Race Course Road area of the neighbourhood every Sunday. This was not an organized or pre-planned attack on the state (represented by police officers and state vehicles like police cars and ambulances) for sustaining structural abuses through an unfair migration system. It was an immediate reaction to the apparent neglect and unfair treatment of a co-ethnic and fellow marginalized migrant. Drawing from this incident and the everyday lives of Indian low-wage migrants in Singapore, this chapter explores how the conditions of injustice engender an environment and latent circumstances for the emergence of a form of 'everyday justice'. While not necessarily overtly or consciously expressed in those terms, these notions of everyday justice permeate low-wage migrants' conceptions of what is fair and just in terms of their treatment as guest workers and urban residents. These ideas are inevitably shaped by state structures that regulate migrant bodies, but also run counter to more expansive discourses of 'human rights'. In doing so, this research aims to demonstrate the disjunctures between everyday understandings of justice (and injustice) that low-wage migrants in authoritarian city-states like Singapore develop, on the one hand, and that of well-meaning state authorities, volunteers, welfare workers, and even (international) non-governmental organizations (NGOs), on the other. These misalignments will be discussed in relation to the embedded and contextual nature of the form of everyday justice that these migrant men seek. In this vein, this chapter offers insights to notions of justice and injustice that move beyond legalized conceptualizations, as well as how ontologically distinct notions of justice work in relational ways, particularly under urban circumstances which involve tight and dense city living.

The chapter first discusses the empirical context of the research project. After an interrogation of the plural and competing definitions of justice that are at play in the site, the chapter discusses two key aspects of everyday justice that are central to low-wage migrant lives – respect, and freedom of mobility and association. The conclusion suggests that when conceptualizations of plural everyday forms of justice are considered within the context of soft authoritarian regimes rather than liberal democracies, the basis for political equality needs to be reconsidered.[1]

DEFINING JUSTICE

Justice is an extremely broad concept that can take on both legal and everyday forms that are not necessarily recognized through state mechanisms and laws (see Chapter 1). Here, I am suggesting that legally delineated and top-down forms of social justice, particularly within paternalistic and authoritarian regimes, may not be coherent with everyday notions of what is just. This disjuncture is the starting point for the explorations of this chapter. My concern in this chapter is to delineate a conceptualization of justice that is drawn primarily from marginalized migrants' own understandings of what counts as just. In dealing here primarily with Tamil low-wage migrants' experiences of injustice and understandings of what is just, their linguistic and associated conceptual life worlds must be taken into account.[2] In doing so, it becomes apparent that justice is a notion that cannot be easily translated without losing the conceptual richness of the term. The word for justice in Tamil, *neethi*, primarily connotes a mode of law that is associated with and enforceable by the state or state actors. This can be seen as closer to conceptualizations of judicial process and the law. For the low-wage Tamil migrants who were the informants in this project, notions of fairness (*neirmai*) and what is right, appropriate, or respectful (*mariyaathai*) were more often invoked as ways of articulating non-legal and quotidian understandings of justice, as it affects the mundane and banal aspects of migrants' lives. Such articulations of respect and of what is fair are situated within everyday and regular relations with employers, state entities, and other urban dwellers.

In this chapter, I adopt Nina Glick-Schiller's (2012) notion of a scholarship of relationalities as way of understanding the unequal relations between low wage migrants, welfare workers, and agencies of the state that are all players within a discourse of social justice that is co-created. This articulation of relationalities is especially useful here as it brings in a notion of the political that does not centre on identity politics but is one that connects the personal to larger structures of dominance. This perspective foregrounds an analytical stance that acknowledges that power is embedded at every level of interaction, including the everyday, while also allowing for the possibility of a truly plural conceptualization of justice. This politics of relationality understands subjectivities as shifting, dependent on the dynamism of changing contexts and culture, but also structurally determined by historical hierarchies and contemporary prejudices. Relationships of exploitation and those of equality and social justice can thus be differentiated through a scholarship of relationalities. This notion of relationality speaks to more 'practical and grounded notions of justice, that draw upon the importance of choice, human agency and diversity' in everyday lives of people, especially those who are poor and marginalized (Brunnegger and Faulk 2016: 2–3). I see these conceptualizations of justice as productive in conversation with a contemporary urban politics of 'right to the city' (Harvey 2003) in illuminating a relational mode of justice not always grounded in the provision of legal rights and entitlements. In particular, this chapter demonstrates how what is fair varies depending on the temporal surroundings of, for example, a time-space of post-riot Singapore, but is also specific to a highly urbanized context where high levels of urban density dictate metropolitan living conditions that are often tight and intimate, and relations within this space dictated by a politics of dependency.

JUSTICE AND THE EVERYDAY

There is a developed literature on the 'everyday' or quotidian particularly in studies of multicultural and diverse societies (e.g., Wessendorf 2014; Vertovec 2015). Here I draw from perspectives of the everyday as mundane, banal, and grounded in everyday practice to inform my analysis of migrant workers and everyday justice. This approach is ethnographically driven and situated within scholarly perspectives of everyday life. What is key to understandings of the everyday is to see larger structural and macro factors as always intertwined and involved in the shaping of the quotidian, ordinary, and routine (Wise and Velayutham 2009). Clarke and Goodale (2010: 18) draw a similar conclusion, asserting that 'contemporary local justice making is always refracted – at least in part – through broader frames of meaning and praxis'.

In relational terms, everyday justice that low-wage migrants seek is divergent from the larger social justice agendas advocated by rights activists, which seek to eliminate institutionalized forms of discrimination and oppression such as debt bondage, unfree labour, and under-payment of wages. While these structural changes are acknowledged as important, for migrants who often fall in the gaps between how laws are conceptualized and implemented, such higher-level initiatives are viewed as far removed from their lives. However, this does not imply that these are opposing agendas. Labour justice issues championed by international organizations like the International Labour Organization (ILO) that champion decent work for all, and emphasize that migrant labour should be seen as more than just workers, are closer to the calls made by migrants themselves. In this Singaporean case, the notions of fairness and respect that low-wage migrants drew on were linked to the very mundane rights of being able to access city spaces easily and without restriction, in order to build community and social networks and to perform cultural identity. To enable and allow such mobilities was seen as fair – in terms of the rights and privileges that temporary non-citizens should have access to. Fairness here does not necessarily imply identical conditions for all urban citizens or residents, but recognizes a diversity and plurality of lives and aspirations.

In adopting an inter-scalar and relational approach, the rioting incident in Little India described at the beginning of this chapter needs to be contextualized within larger structural circumstances and contextual detail in order to better understand the significance of such an episode within our discussions of justice and marginalized migrants. Indian migrant men, like the ones who started the riot, form the majority component of the more than 1 million low-wage migrants that live and work in Singapore. They labour on sites such as construction projects, shipyards, and in light industrial factories. These are jobs that local Singaporeans are reluctant to do. They pay poorly and hold very low social status and are thus seen as undesirable, especially in a nation that only relatively recently achieved 'developed' or 'first-world' status, where social mobility even for the working class is measured by the ability to land a white-collar 'desk' job. Singaporeans in such industries are typically supervisors, or in higher-level positions dealing with the management of low-wage labour, in itself constituting imbalanced and unequal relations between local and migrant.

The recent rise of precarious work in industrial societies (i.e., work that is insecure and uncertain, often low paying and dead-end, and in which the risks of work are shifted from employers and the government to workers) can also be seen in Singapore, where low-wage temporary migrants overwhelmingly take on these types of jobs. Low-wage migrants, defined by the state and civil society as those whose monthly salary is below a certain amount, are unable to legally bring their dependent spouses and children when they migrate. Instead, they live as bachelors, often in dormitory-style accommodation at the edges of the city. This engenders socio-spatial disaffiliations (Kathiravelu 2015) that translate into larger dislocations between Singaporean middle classes and migrant working classes. This issue of everyday urban mobility will be further developed in this chapter.

In gathering data for this project, interviews and ethnographic observations were conducted with shopkeepers, with Singaporean and immigrant residents, and with low-wage South Asian migrants who frequented the area of Little India. While the majority of informants were of Tamil ethnicity and Indian nationality, Singaporean Chinese and Bangladeshi migrant men also formed important informant groups as co-users of the space. Participant observation across different sites was primarily undertaken on Sundays, the most common day off for migrant workers, and the busiest day in the Little India neighbourhood.

STATIST NOTIONS OF JUSTICE

> When we look at the migrant workers' issue, we are not looking at it from the perspective of human rights. We are looking at it on a need basis.... Like it or not, we need to sustain and grow an economy that is able to generate an annual per capita [GDP] of US$35,000. At the end of the day, whatever factors would be able to help us to sustain the growth of the economy for the benefit of our countrymen, for the benefit of our country; we will definitely go for it.
> —Yeo Guat Kwang, Member of the Singaporean Parliament, National Trade Union Congress official, and Co-Chairman of the NTUC-SNEF Migrant Workers Centre (Chan 2011)

Structural forms of inequality such as limiting family reunification and spatial disaffiliation are indicative of the state's conceptualizations of justice – in terms, for example, of which category of classed and raced migrant is allowed more civil liberties and rights within the host country. The neoliberal state, in the Singaporean case, is a strong one, and as enactor and enabler of institutionalized forms of structural violence and injustice toward low-wage migrants, it engages in 'worlding' practices that rely on new assemblages of governance that bring all social life into the purview of the market (Roy and Ong 2011; Burte and Kamath 2017). These relations translate into ways in which low-wage migrants are treated by supervisors, employers, and fellow urban residents. Activists point out that these structural inequalities and abuses have now become normalized and are unquestioned by a majority of the public (Chok 2017). Most significantly, this is internalized by migrants and results in subjective shifts in terms of how they conceive self-worth, masculinity, and their identity as entrepreneurial selves, as a means of countering state and popular constructions of them as dirty, dangerous sexual predators and as only economic agents (Kathiravelu 2016). This chapter builds and extends from such understandings of low-wage South Asian migrants in the Global South, delving into how subjective and everyday constructions of justice are informed by marginalized and transient subjectivities.

Within the context of the riot that was mentioned at the opening of the chapter, justice, as decided and meted out by the state, took the form of deportations without proper trial of fifty-seven Indian men on work permits who had been at the scene of the riots.[3] Singapore's Minister of Law explained the decision as an 'administrative' rather than judicial one (Lim 2013), justifying the lack of transparency and due process as an unnecessary drain on the resources of the state. The implicit implication here is that these migrant workers needed to be deported, not as the outcome of judicial process, but to send a public message about how the Singaporean state deals with public disturbances caused by marginal populations. Legally enforced 'justice', in this sense, becomes a bureaucratic procedure, masking its role as a disciplinary tool of the state. It is a resource that is unequally accessible, especially within regimes where there is little discernible distinction between the government and the state (Rajah 2012). This can also be seen as an example of 'legalized pluralism', where 'multiple legal systems exist for people in the same social' world (Clarke and Goodale 2010: 9).

As a direct result of the riots, there was also a ban placed on public consumption of alcohol in the Little India district, as conclusions of a public inquiry determined that alcohol was the primary reason for the riots. The invocation of the alcohol-fuelled unskilled male migrant is one that caught the public imagination, as well as that of Singaporean employers. Indian migrants' informants reported the additional precautions that employers were taking, as Indian workers were replaced by Bangladeshi or Chinese nationals, particularly those from the villages surrounding Chattiram, the South Indian village where the migrant whose death sparked the riots was from. These punitive measures served to further engender discrimination and fear of members of a group who were already seen as dangerous, hyper-masculine, and threatening sexual predators.

In addition to the alcohol consumption ban, there was a rapid construction of bus shelters, designed such that they allowed for the containment and control of low-wage migrants within public space. These bus shelters were built specifically for private bus services catering only to low-wage migrants, transporting them to and from their dormitories at the edges of the island and which were often badly connected to the public transport system. Police presence in the area also became far more visible. This performance of policing serves to create a climate of fear that discourages Indian migrants from inhabiting and occupying public spaces that had previously been seen as acceptable zones where they could socialize and gather (Yeo et al. 2012). This reduces the already limited public space available to this group and pushes them further to the margins of the city where they are confined to the zones of dormitories, minimizing interactions with the rest of the urban population.

As one local resident commented, 'Yeah there's certainly greater police presence now.... Yes. They make more patrols but I think it's just them showing their presence, to let the workers know that you know the police are here, somebody is watching them? But the amount of the interaction between them and police I think is still somewhat the same.'

It is less the paternalism of the restriction of mobility that low-wage migrants react to; it is the brusque and rude manner with which law enforcement officers treat them that they express unhappiness about. It is the lack of respect that such actions convey that is seen as unjust and undeserving. In describing the injustice of banning alcohol in the area of Little India just because of one incident in the decades in which that space had been used as a meeting place for the South Asian migrant worker population, a local resident says: 'All these years, how many thousand people have come, just because of one incident.... Let's say one incident happen. A fight happen in one coffeeshop. The guy runs into the chicken rice stall and takes the chopper and chop. So what? Chicken rice stall cannot use chopper ah?' The sentiment expressed here expresses sympathy for the disproportionate way in which the state meted out justice, reflecting shifting attitudes of the local population, a development taken up in the following section.

NGOS AS MEDIATORS BETWEEN STATE AND MIGRANTS

Within more authoritarian and paternalistic regimes such as Singapore, the presence of NGOs is fraught. They function primarily in a space that is allowed to them by the state and are often restricted in their ability to affect large-scale or significant social change. However, Singaporean NGOs that cater to the welfare of low-wage migrants have been, in recent years, one of the most successful civil society entities within the city-state, raising awareness of the plight of this marginalized and often invisible community, as well as effecting incremental change. In recent years, there has been a large amount of attention and sympathy from the general public directed at the low-wage migrant worker, both the male migrant who takes on hard physical labour and the female domestic who does care work within the family.

In addition to soup kitchens and shelters, NGOs take on the work of advocating for low-wage migrant rights at the national level, but also on a case-by-case basis at local courts, such as when migrants haven't been paid wages on time, or when employers refuse to foot medical expenses, as required by law. Part of the work of the organizations and individuals has been to humanize these low-wage migrants and to counter notions engendered through state policies of demarcating such employment as disposable, refuting that low-wage migrants can be reduced to units of biological labour, a unit of 'bare life' (Agamben 1998). This is central to the claiming of respect and acknowledgement by migrants, a topic that will be further developed in the next section of the chapter.

Given the focus on everyday and relational notions of justice, legal or formal law-based notions of justice are less a concern of this chapter. However, we must acknowledge the complex relation between formal legal and everyday forms of justice (defined in terms of everyday banal practices). They inform one another through the uneven implementation of laws that protect the rights and interests of low-wage migrants in Singapore. In a recent report by the non-governmental migrant welfare organization HOME (Humanitarian Organization for Migrant Economics), it was found that only 50 per cent of companies that were demonstrated to have paid workers late or failed to have paid workers were persecuted (Chok and Ng 2017). Low-wage migrants who had failed to claim their due wages even after initiating procedures against these companies were asked to take the action to the public courts, an almost impossible undertaking for these migrants who have little economic and cultural capital. Many return to their home countries without obtaining many months' wages due for work done. Other examples of the uneven implementation of justice are to do with policy around working hours and overtime pay. Under Singapore's labour laws, workers are mandated a minimum of one day off per week. However, many low-wage migrants in the construction sector, conforming to tight timelines, are often required to work every day of the week. These men typically get only two days off in the entire year, on the first of January and on the first day of the Lunar New Year. For domestic workers employed to live and work within employers' homes, there is no obligation on the part of employers to grant time off, as domestic workers, classified under the domestic sphere, are not covered under local labour laws. In 2014, however, after years of campaigning by Singaporean migrant welfare organizations, employers have now a contractual obligation to provide domestic workers a day off per week. This has not, however, been translated into legally binding legislation and is not enforced. Off days are also often seen by employers as an opportunity for foreign domestic workers (FDWs) to engage in entrepreneurial activities. Participating in 'productive' leisure activities such as taking hair-cutting classes and money management courses on their days off is seen as desirable and appropriate, and often a pre-condition for time off. This paternalism stems from a lack of being able to see the differently classed and migrant Other as having similar desires for leisure and consumption. Despite these shortcomings, the victories over the mandatory 'day off' in Singapore for foreign domestic workers is one that is celebrated as indicative of the shifts that the state is taking in terms of catering to the welfare of the temporary population.

Quality of food and nutrition of temporary low-wage migrants has been another topic that has come under scrutiny by Singaporean NGOs. Low-wage migrants who labour on construction sites are particularly vulnerable in this instance as they often do not have the time or resources to cook their own food, and must rely on their employing companies to provide pre-packaged meals. Social workers have brought to the attention of labour ministry authorities that this food is often old, of poor quality, and lacking in protein and other elements necessary for a well-balanced diet. Everyday issues such as ensuring an adequate diet or clean and sanitary living conditions are the types of issues that NGOs also advocate for on behalf of marginalized migrants. These are other important aspects of the forms of everyday justice that improve the quality of migrant lives, and have direct and immediate consequences on heath and ability to perform work. However, they are often not included in abstract and high-level discussions of rights or reforms.

There has also been a recent surge in the number of one-off activities that have sought to involve low-wage migrants, acknowledging their contributions to growing and building the city. These take the form of days out, where migrants and locals engage in photography tours of local neighbourhoods, church-led healings of injured migrant workers, or yoga sessions, that see this firmly middle-class activity as one that should be extended also to the less privileged among the urban population. Public holidays such as National Day or Labour Day then also become opportunities where the mainstream media celebrate the contributions of low-wage migrants, and the ways in which Singaporeans are being inclusive to this population. While well intentioned, they amount to little more than symbolic gestures, doing little to alter the structural position of the exploited and underpaid. However, these acts, seen in sum, are indicative of a shifting politics and ethics of seeing the Other as more than just a 'worker' and worthy of individual respect, a key component of the kind of justice that low-wage migrants seek.

FREEDOM OF MOBILITY AND ASSOCIATION

Thus far, I have attempted to present various competing and intersecting notions of justice in relation to low-wage migrants in Singapore. The following section unpacks everyday notions of justice from low-wage migrants' perspectives. These narratives are situated within the socio-spatial changes that have marked a key South Asian migrant enclave – Singapore's Little India.

David Harvey's (2003) seminal work on urban social justice and the 'Right to the City' has led to multiple and myriad discussions of the claims of disenfranchised groups in large metropolitan areas. This section is situated within the context of such formulations, where quotidian rights to the city are dependent on the ability to access freely zones of the city, but also social, economic, and affective resources necessary for the reproduction of everyday life. Engaging in social relations and the ability to move freely without coercion and threat are important components of the basic functioning that makes up the tenets of what migrants themselves think is fair and just.

Notions of everyday justice for marginalized communities such as women in parts of rural and urban India have started taking into account the importance and significance of freedom of mobility (Phadke et al. 2011). For many of these women, being able to move without fear and coercion across public areas and between private spaces is an important aspect of negotiating daily routines such as performing ablutions, accessing water for household consumption, and caring for children. For urban migrant and minority men, however, these issues of quotidian mobility can also be significant, as they are most often the target of violent crimes, suspicion, and have a higher propensity to be stopped and arrested by law enforcement officers. In relatively safe Singapore, however, the issues around mobility are primarily to do with the tight and tough controls imposed by the state. Because of the ever-present threat of deportation, migrant men conceive of their position in the city-state as extremely precarious. This is increasingly so in a climate where low-wage Indian migrants are looked upon with suspicion and as potential criminals. The presence of dark-skinned South Asian migrant men on sidewalks and streets during weekends is followed by a discourse of danger and (sexual) threat. The loitering and unproductive occupation of public spaces is seen as undesirable. Migrant workers articulate this latent climate of fear overtly; the lack of agency in their migrant status dependent on the largesse of the employer and the state is apparent. Mechanisms of self-policing are now internalized: 'Because now everybody is scared. If happen anything then can catch police then can sent back. Then because we come in Singapore for earn money, want to work and earn money. So in Singapore have any problem, because it is not our country, we cannot solve. So everybody is very scared. They also don't want to make any problems.'[4]

The importance of being able to 'sit down', 'hang out', or loiter in public spaces such as parks, pavements, and squares is central to the social networks and socialities practised by low-wage migrant men in Singapore (cf. Kathiravelu 2012). In a city where much public space is consumption space such as shopping malls, these non-commercial zones act as spaces of exception where low-wage marginalized migrants feel that they can participate in city life without having to be members of the consuming middle class.

Singaporeans who live and work in the area are also viscerally cognizant about the socio-spatial changes that mark the space since the riots of December 2013. These changes are generally welcome by middle- and working-class residents; however, there is also an acknowledgement that this outcome is not a completely fair or just one for low-wage South Asian migrants:

> It feels somewhat safer but I wouldn't say to a very big extent. Because I lived here for such a long time and of course I have accustomed to living amongst them. But I think my girlfriend who comes here quite often, she would feel somewhat safer because of the greater police presence. And because of the less rowdy behaviour of the Indians around here. Because generally the crowd is better behaved and of

course as a resident that makes me feel safer lah.[5] And they used to overflow onto the roads during the weekends but now it is more controlled, so it's somewhat a good thing for drivers around here as well.

A shopkeeper describes the importance of Little India as a social, emotional, and communal space for low-wage Indian migrants. He relates from his own experience as a low-wage migrant a few decades ago. The shared affinities of language and religion are highlighted here as important elements of social life for low-wage migrants within a multilingual and multicultural city.

> Oh when I came in 1993, then I used to live in various places, but on the weekends, because in my construction site, the engineer and I had around fifty to sixty construction workers, so I used to go with them and stay with them, and so, I personally felt how they feel, and yeah I have directly felt that pleasure of being in a crowd on a Sunday, who belongs to same community or same religion. You feel like, you see, you were three thousand miles away from home, and still, there is a society to talk, to share, you know, to vent your feelings. That part is really interesting and everybody in my opinion needs that.

Another key development in the area in addition to increased policing, surveillance, and the alcohol ban is the stoppage of private bus services to worker dormitories at 9 PM. (One of these types of buses was the one that caused the death of the Indian man and sparked off the riots.) This coincided with the building of the bus shelters mentioned in the beginning of the chapter, and can be seen as part of attempts by state authorities to control the mobility of migrants. The limiting of private bus routes to Little India on Sundays has meant that most migrant workers can no longer stay late in the neighbourhood on their day off, as they would not have a means of transport to reach their far-flung dormitories.

One migrant man describes how it no longer makes sense to come to Little India after a day's work, because of the ending of bus services at 9 PM. 'Yeah, this way you come in, five o'clock finish, you bathe already, you come in, is seven or eight o'clock already. Eight o'clock come in, that's why people don't want to come in. Last time, one o'clock, two o'clock bus have.'

The lack of transport options has greatly reduced the numbers of South Asian men who frequent Little India, reducing its centre as an ethnic enclave and migrant economy. This has been aided by the dispersion of services and specialist economies to other parts of the island, typically within worker dormitories or Housing Development Board estates, where the majority of Singaporeans live.[6] Yet Little India continues to be an important symbolic space for social, cultural, and economic life for low-wage South Asian men.

Another shopkeeper, commenting on the large reduction in numbers, comments: 'If on a Sunday three years back, it'll be at least two hundred thousand people concentrating in an area of one-half-square kilometre, at least two hundred thousand in half-square kilometre. Now, it should be only, erm, twenty-five thousand.' Even if his estimates are wrong, the perception of decreased usage of the space is prevalent. Shopkeepers in the Little India shopkeepers' association (LISHA) have also made complaints to state authorities that their revenues have fallen drastically with the reduction of migrant patrons to the area. Accumulatively, the changes to zoning and alterations to connectivity emphasize that the importance of the space as a functioning migrant enclave is secondary to the maintenance of its image as a safe and attractive 'heritage district' for consumption by tourists.

The neoliberalization of public spaces in Little India has meant not only that there has been increasing gentrification encouraged, with the sprouting of boutique hotels and craft beer bars, but has also involved a greater presence of security personnel within the neighbourhood, and most visibly on weekends. These uniformed security personnel are composed of men and women who form a private security force, representing an outsourcing of the surveillance and control of the space of Little India. Many of these private police are of Malaysian nationality, migrant workers themselves. Most are also of Indian or Tamil ethnicity, possibly chosen for that particular assignment because of the linguistic and cultural affinities they share with the migrants who congregate in Little India. This acknowledgement for the need of a police force that can communicate effectively with the migrant population is an important justice outcome, as these auxiliary police are the most visible and direct mediators of the state that low-wage migrants encounter. Their presence has now become a visible and largely accepted part of the landscape of the neighbourhood.

> The people actually are now used to it. Sad to say, but they're actually used to it after the riot. But after this, there was nothing like this. There was no such thing as the police never come. They would not interfere, they would do their business and just move on. But now they are worried and the Singaporeans are really ... they are cautious people. They don't want to make the same mistake again. So once this has happened, they

71

make sure it doesn't happen over again. This is when maybe the residents of the places they call up the police and ask for their help. They don't want to repeat the same mistake.

Reactions of Indian low-wage migrants to measures that clamp down on public drinking and association have been matter-of-fact and muted. We can read this within the context of their precarious positions within the Singaporean state, and their inability to contest these curbs on social and cultural needs. Many migrants in fact interpreted these paternalistic discourses in positive terms, saying that the money they would have spent on alcohol they now save, and remit back to their home countries. Such calculations that do not take into account a need for leisure activities or space are indicative of how the caricature of the Indian migrant as only 'worker' has been internalized effectively, and how statist notions of the neoliberal self-governing subject have been, to a large extent, reified. Readings of migrant men as needing only to accumulate capital and not meet other social or emotional needs as residents of the city are thus reinforced through these clamp-downs on physical mobility, and ability to maintain ethnic and cultural relations and networks.

The prevalence of cheap phone calls and social media access has, on the other hand, made the necessity of physical interactions less significant (Thompson 2009; Platt et al. 2016). Many networks both back home in India and with fellow migrants in Singapore are maintained through frequent phone calls and text messages.

One observer, a store owner in Little India, comments, 'Now there is a cell phone, email, Facebook communication right, so they don't need the support of fellow workers. Only they need, the, you know, emotional support, so when they want to talk something, somebody to hear. So that is all they want, and they will get in the dormitory.' Despite increased restrictions on movements within the city, low-wage migrant men continue to find ways to make and maintain networks and cultural life. However, beyond relations between migrants themselves, a key concern in issues of social justice for migrants is the need for respect from co-urban dwellers with whom they 'rub along' every day.

RESPECT

Grounded, embodied notions of everyday justice centred around movement and mobility are not the only ways in which low-wage South

Asian migrants conceived of everyday justice. Abstract and highly intangible notions of respect were articulated as one of the most significant ways in which justice and fairness were perceived.

Although respect is an abstract notion – you can't eat respect, and respect does not provide shelter – it was repeatedly highlighted as one of the most important qualities to migrants who spoke about how they would like to be treated as guest workers. In addition to the routine forms of discrimination that they face due to their race, class, and immigration status, after the association of low-wage Indian workers with alcoholism and riots,[7] these men also now are burdened with the additional label of being unruly, ill-disciplined, and disruptors of a social order that is so highly valued in Singapore. Respect meant even more within this context as migrants then could see themselves as being acknowledged as individuals rather than merely part of a disposable population. Respect was articulated as significant particularly in interpersonal interactions within the everyday city spaces that they inhabited. In traversing through urban public spaces, the lack of eye contact and not acknowledging their presence in shared spaces were seen as indicators of their lack of status and inherent undesirability.

> First, you don't have the feeling of belongingness. Second, you live a subhuman life. Third, when it comes to your home away from home, then here you don't get treated like a person. You are treated like an intruder. Then why should I be coming here? I want to be where I have my dignity and my peace but I cannot have this dignity because money is the triggering factor here. Only for money, people are still coming here. They [are] working.

Interactions with superiors such as employers or site supervisors were highlighted as a key dealing through which respect and acknowledgement were desired, as these were some of the primary relationships that low-wage migrants invested in on an everyday basis. Demeaning treatment included being treated rudely and discourteously as underlings or subordinates, and scolded or chastised publicly and aggressively for work not done to the satisfaction of superiors. The lack of professionalism in communications was underscored especially in relation to being humiliated in front of co-ethnics or co-workers of a different nationality: 'You feel ... the word should be "insulted". In front of your friends and peers, you are being interrogated like you have done a crime for mingling with your friends. You feel bad. You feel low.' In addition to the dehumanizing treatment by employers and immediate supervisors, low-wage migrants read the practice of late and non-payment of wages as unfair and unjust, a tangible relation to the more intangible ways in which they are shown a lack of respect. Constant reminders of their replicability and precarity through these delays also reinforce the lack of respect for their work.

CONCLUSION: CONTEXTUALIZING NOTIONS OF EVERYDAY JUSTICE

This chapter has attempted to demonstrate competing and complementary notions of everyday justice that play out in relation to low-wage (South Asian, but predominantly Tamil) male migrants in Singapore. This final section of the chapter will draw on earlier discussions to extend ideas of everyday justice, arguing for a context-specific and ontologically grounded understanding of the idea, especially in relation to a normative and universalizing human rights or labour rights discourse and within non-Western authoritarian states.

The allure of a human rights discourse is its supposed internationalism. Presented as universal, it speaks to a mode of cosmopolitan ideal that is appealing as a kind of global standard to aspire and live up to. In states such as Singapore, which have faced harsh international criticism of their treatment of low-wage migrants, particularly from the West, coming from a 'human rights' perspective, such frameworks are viewed with reserve and suspicion. The Singaporean state, in turn, has previously used 'Asian values' (Birch 1998) as an appropriate discourse to engage with in order to counter such claims, critiquing human rights as a Eurocentric paradigm, unsuitable for understanding and governance in social democracies in Asia, which are based on more collective (as opposed to individualistic) notions of citizenship and the polity. These tussles over the definition and practice of social justice are important to consider within discussions of pluralization.

Here I am not advocating for a culturalist reading, where the low-wage migrants' cultural understandings of what is fair or just is different to what natives or the middle class perceive. Rather than an issue of cultural difference, the issue here is more due to a lack of attention and neglect of the priorities and subjective experiences of low-wage migrant populations. This is where advocating for migrant rights within a larger human rights framework fails to achieve an equitable justice agenda. The perspective that conjoins and even equates to some extent a human rights discourse to justice is one that is critiqued by Clarke and Goodale (2010) for being blind to the abstract and de-contextualized nature in which justice in discussed by transnational entities such as international NGOs. Instead, they advocate for a more grounded perspective that sees human rights and justice as diametrically opposed to one another – the former as a universal ideal and the latter vernacularized through social and political struggle. In drawing from such perspectives in this chapter, I have attempted to extend understandings of justice to consider the vernacular element as also central to its quotidian definition, through foregrounding the mundane and banal aspects of migrants' lives, such as the access to freedom of mobility and association, the ability to recreate community and identity, and the right to be respected for the work they do. Linking plural and ground-up ideas of justice with notions of urban rights (Harvey 2003) brings us to conceptualizations of social justice that are embedded in the everyday metropolitan spaces of the urban. Everyday forms of justice must also incorporate an equal right to the city, regardless of citizenship status, ability to participate in the formal consumption economy, or phenotype.

The significance of a pluralization of justice perspective has been acknowledged by scholars such as Clarke and Goodale (2010). This chapter has attempted to demonstrate, with ethnographic and interview evidence, that understandings of justice as essentially plural must also take into account different and relational ontological starting points that may also lead to disparate and unequal political outcomes. Plurality, in a non-Cartesian sense, must rely on an acknowledgement of ontological difference that is not based on a Self/Other distinction, but that acknowledges difference as multiple and diverse. Here is where the agenda of social justice must begin, and where existing schemas have failed to accommodate multiplicities of difference and combinations of relationalities (Glick Schiller 2012), where competing social justice agendas occupy the same national and discursive space. There is thus a need for a reconceptualization of social justice that does not see outcomes only as equality of opportunity or the ability to achieve social mobility (within the host country context, for instance, through achieving a higher socioeconomic status or legalized citizenship status). In an authoritarian space like Singapore where limits on inclusion into the polity and citizenry are imposed by law and accepted by the electorate, the claims of social justice must be different. Understanding economically and socially marginalized groups such as migrant workers as cultural minorities is one possible perspective. The notions of plural and differentiated citizenship – and rights – proposed by Iris Marion Young (1990) provide us tools with which to think about how the continually shifting and dynamic population of migrants can be understood within the larger city and polity.

The plurality of justice perspective then must also acknowledge the competing of justice agendas, priorities, and, ultimately, outcomes. One problematic then can be seen as that of scale. Systematic and structural change can often be obscured by the inability to recognize the importance of smaller and more achievable agendas, and ones that migrants themselves may see as primary. This chapter has demonstrated that the everyday realm in which low-wage migrants themselves conceive of justice – in terms of the quotidian notions of fair pay, fair treatment, and respect – is not necessarily taken into account into larger definitions of justice by NGO discourse, law enforcement, and even the international activist community.

Theorists and activists working from a Eurocentric paradigm of assuming liberal democracies as the primary ontological and historical basis of social justice agendas neglect other forms of actually functioning democracies and governance models (Grewal 2016). Moving away from neocolonial to more pluralist modes of how justice is conceptualized (Clarke 2009), this chapter contributes to non-Western and 'Southern' (Connell 2007) notions of migrant rights, social justice, and rights to the city. Here is where methodological nationalism and context-specific analysis has its place in contesting non-endogenous conceptualizations of everyday justice. Within more controlled, authoritarian and post-developmentalist states, social justice agendas are best fought not at the level of formal political participation and party policy, or even civil society agitations, but in the everyday. This is the realm where most direct and tangible social change is possible, but also where migrants themselves seek recognition, inclusion, and respect. When the realm of formal party politics or policy is one that is inaccessible, the quotidian realm is where citizens and city residents can enact social change and resistance to dominant moral, political, and economic orders most rapidly, visibly, and easily.

Notes

1 This research draws on ongoing engagement with low-wage migrant communities in Singapore since 2011, but particularly draws on

in-depth and spot interviews and ethnography conducted in late 2014 and early 2015 around the Little India neighbourhood in the city-state of Singapore.

2 It is important here to take into account the significance of the Tamil language for aspects of culture, practices for regulating religious practice and social relations, as well as more generally for a way of 'being in the world' (Merleau-Ponty 1962).

3 Twenty-eight of these fifty-seven were charged in court, and more than 200 additional men were given warnings by the Singaporean police.

4 Many of the interviews and conversations were conducted in English, not the first language of many low-wage migrants, nor one that they are particularly comfortable speaking. The interview transcripts have been left uncorrected in their original form.

5 'Lah' is a common suffix in Singlish, a Singaporean creole that low-wage migrants also use colloquially.

6 Eighty per cent of Singaporeans live in Housing Development Board estates. They comprised overwhelmingly of good quality high-rise apartments, built and leased by the state. There are also a significant proportion of these apartments surrounding the Little India area.

7 The association of Indian men with alcoholism (and spousal abuse) is one that is a recurrent trope in Singapore, and also extends to include Singaporean Indian men.

References

Agamben, Giorgio. 1998. *Homo Sacer: Sovereign Power and Bare Life*. Stanford, CA: Stanford University Press.

Birch, David. 1998. 'Constructing Asian Values: National Identities and 'Responsible Citizens'. *Social Semiotics* 8 (2–3): 177–201. doi: 10.1080/10350339809360407.

Brunnegger, Sandra, and Karen Ann Faulk (eds.). 2016. *A Sense of Justice: Legal Knowledge and Lived Experience in Latin America*. Stanford, CA: Stanford University Press.

Burte, Himanshu, and Lalitha Kamath. 2017. 'The Violence of Worlding: Producing Space in Neo-Liberal Durban, Mumbai and Rio de Janerio'. *Review of Urban Affairs* 52(7): 66–74.

Chan, Aris. 2011. Hired on Sufferance: China's Migrant Workers in Singapore. In *Hong Kong: China Labour Bulletin*.

Chok, Stephanie. 2017. *Labour Justice and Low-Paid Migrant Workers in Singapore: Ethics, Faith and Social Justice*. Singapore: Ethos Institute for Public Christianity.

Chok, Stephanie, and Jevon Ng. 2017. *Wage Theft and Exploitation among Singapore's Migrant Workers*. Singapore: Humanitarian Organization for Migration Economics (HOME).

Clarke, Kamari Maxine. 2009. *Fictions of Justice: The International Criminal Court and the Challenge of Legal Pluralism in Sub-Saharan Africa*. Cambridge: Cambridge University Press.

Clarke, Kamari Maxine, and Mark Goodale (eds.). 2010. *Mirrors of Justice: Law and Power in the Post–Cold War Era*. Cambridge: Cambridge University Press.

Connell, Raewyn. 2007. *Southern Theory: Social Science and the Global Dynamics of Knowledge*. London: Polity.

Glick Schiller, Nina. 2012. 'Situating Identities: Towards an Identities Studies without Binaries of Difference'. *Identities: Global Studies in Culture and Power* 19(4): 520–532.

Grewal, Kiran. 2016. *The Socio-political Practice of Human Rights: Between the Universal and the Particular*. London: Routledge.

Harvey, David. 2003. 'The Right to the City'. *International Journal of Urban and Regional Research* 27(4): 939–941.

Kathiravelu, Laavanya. 2012. 'Social Networks in Dubai: Informal Solidarities in an Uncaring State'. *Journal of Intercultural Studies* 33(1): 103–119.

2015. 'Encounter, Transport and Transitory Spaces.' In Steven Vertovec (ed.), *Diversities Old and New: Migration and Socio-Spatial Patterns in New York, Singapore and Johannesburg*. London: Palgrave, 120–134.

2016. *Migrant Dubai: Low Wage Workers and the Construction of a Global City*. London: Palgrave.

Lim, Yan Liang. 2013. 'Little India Riot: Repatriation of 53 Workers under Way'. *The Straits Times*. www.straitstimes.com/singapore/little-india-riot-repatriation-of-53-workers-under-way.

Phadke, Shilpa, Sameera Khan, and Shilpa Ranade. 2011. *Why Loiter? Women and Risk on Mumbai Streets*. Delhi: Penguin Books.

Platt, Maria, Brenda S. A. Yeoh, Kristel Anne Acedera, Choon Yen Khoo, Grace Baey, and Theodora Lam. 2016. 'Renegotiating Migration Experiences: Indonesian Domestic Workers in Singapore and Use of Information Communication Technologies'. *New Media & Society* 18(10): 2207–2223.

Rajah, Jothie. 2012. *Authoritarian Rule of Law: Legislation, Discourse and Legitimacy in Singapore*. Cambridge: Cambridge University Press.

Roy, A., and Aihwa Ong (eds.). 2011. *Worlding Cities: Asian Experiments and the Art of Being Global*. Oxford: John Wiley & Sons.

Thompson, Eric C. 2009. 'Mobile Phones, Communities and Social Networks among Foreign Workers in Singapore'. *Global Networks* 9(3): 359–380.

Vertovec, Steven, ed. 2015. *Diversities Old and New: Migration and Socio-Spatial Patterns in New York, Singapore and Johannesburg*. London: Palgrave.

Wessendorf, Susanne. 2014. '"Being open but sometimes closed": Conviviality in a Super-Diverse London Neighbourhood'. *European Journal of Cultural Studies* 17(4): 392–405.

Wise, Amanda, and Selvaraj Velayutham. 2009. 'Introduction: Multiculturalism and Everyday Life'. In Amanda Wise and Selvaraj Velayutham (eds.), *Everyday Multiculturalism*. New York: Palgrave Macmillan, 1–20.

Yeo, Su-Jan, Limin Hee, and Chye Kiang Heng. 2012. 'Urban Informality and Everyday (Night)life: A Field Study in Singapore'. *International Development Planning Review* 34(4): 369–390.

Yeoh, Brenda. 2006. 'Bifurcated Labour: The Unequal Incorporaton of Trans-migrants in Singapore'. *Tijdschrift voor economische en sociale geografie* 97(1): 26–37.

Young, Iris Marion. 1990. *Justice and the Politics of Difference*. Princeton, NJ: Princeton University Press.

PART TWO

THE FORCE OF EVERYDAY JUSTICE

CHAPTER FOUR

'WE DON'T WORK FOR THE SERBS, WE WORK FOR HUMAN RIGHTS'

Justice and Impartiality in Transitional Kosovo

Agathe Mora[1]

INTRODUCTION

In this chapter I look at competing notions of justice deployed by lawyers at the Kosovo Property Agency (KPA) to make sense of the seeming contradiction between Kosovo Albanian lawyers' institutional, professional duty of impartiality and their profound nationalist convictions and sentiments of historical wrongs done to 'their people'. The KPA is a quasi-judicial institution, put in place by the United Nations Interim Administration Mission in Kosovo (UNMIK) to 'resolve' war-related property claims and thereby restitute property rights to, for a great majority of claims, Kosovo Serbian displaced persons.

Impartiality is at the heart of the ideal of procedural justice as embodied in the allegory of the blind 'Lady Justice' (see, e.g., Storme 2014: 67). By asking how impartiality can be guaranteed in a context as fraught and highly politicized as post-war Kosovo, I explore how impartiality is produced in the everyday. I argue that impartiality is produced and made possible by different, seemingly contradictory repertoires of justice that are acted out in everyday practice by the national lawyers of the agency. Contrary to standard, black letter law arguments that frame international law and human rights as the 'pure' norms against which the messiness of local legal practice can only fall short,[2] I aim to demonstrate that it is rather the messiness of the 'local' context and the plurality of notions of justice at play that socially produce impartiality. I argue that, in the specific political landscape of post-war Kosovo, it is the 'nationalistic bias' of Kosovo Albanian lawyers that ensures due diligence and respect for rule of law principles.

My argument is based on fourteen months of ethnographic fieldwork as a research intern at the KPA between 2012 and 2013, and is articulated in four steps. I open with a thick description of events that took place at the KPA around the 100th anniversary of Albania's independence. Despite the apparent pro-Albanian bias that this vignette reveals, the KPA is in Kosovo and Serbia widely seen as impartial and one of the few efficient institutions. To explain that ethnographic puzzle, I explain in a second step the institutional set-up of the KPA, which is deeply shaped by an international imaginary of justice as human rights, and which reads the history of Kosovo (and ex-Yugoslavia in general) as a problem of ethnic minority rights. Indeed, due to the international oversight of Kosovo's autonomy (and subsequently its de facto independence), Kosovo was envisioned as a multi-ethnic state with a premium on rule of law and respect for minority rights. Accordingly, property rights were considered one of the most pressing issues to be resolved to establish the rule of law in Kosovo. This ideology of property rights as human rights fundamentally underpinned the establishment of the KPA.

In the third section, I look at how impartiality is being implemented at the KPA at a procedural level. Here I describe the institutional mechanisms that were put in place specifically to safeguard the impartiality of the lawyers' work. However, as I show, this impartiality is limited to technical-procedural issues and does little to mitigate potential political and ideological biases. I thus posit that, even in an institution set up under international rule where standards of impartiality are enshrined in the procedures themselves, technocratic mechanisms and the ideal of 'justice as human rights' alone cannot ensure impartiality.

In order to make sense of how lawyers deal with these contradictory and seemingly irreconcilable institutional and personal notions of (in)justice, I finally probe the tenets of the dialectic between 'global' ideals and 'local' practice, and ethnographically demonstrate the limits of an anthropology of human rights that sees vernacularization and meaning-making as the only analytical tools available. In this last part, I argue that it is a sense of distance from the 'local' that gives human rights their social and political force. I describe how the discourse of human rights is invoked rather than applied, and legitimating in itself rather than vernacularized into locally meaningful legal and moral instruments. It is precisely because the national lawyers are so deeply rooted in the 'local' context that they are able to simultaneously uphold ideals of procedural justice enshrined in international law and a personal sense of distributive justice stemming from nationalistic sentiments, and therefore to act impartially. Through this I suggest that it is by looking at the two different, irreconcilable repertoires of justice that are deployed by the national lawyers in the everyday that we can begin to understand how impartiality is achieved at the KPA. This approach resonates with Wastell's and Sullivan's insights (Chapters 5 and 6) that where different registers of justice coexist, these might be incommensurable.

'GËZUAR 100 VJETORIN E PAVARËSISË' – 'HAPPY 100 YEARS OF ALBANIAN INDEPENDENCE'

On Wednesday, 28 November 2012, Albania marked the 100th anniversary of its independence. Although it was not an official holiday in Kosovo, most public institutions and private companies had given their employees the day off, and many had plans to take off Thursday and Friday, too, and make it a long weekend. Rumour had it that the government had sponsored a thousand lambs to be slaughtered in public festivities. In the run-up to Independence Day, many shop windows had been decorated in the Albanian national colours, red and black. The main thoroughfares of Kosovo's capital, Pristina, had been bedecked in flags with the Albanian eagle, and people were gearing up for four days of festivities and were sporting Albanian colours at work on the preceding days.

At the KPA, where I had been interning as an embedded researcher since June of that same year, office spaces were also decorated with Albanian flags and banners. The national deputy director led by example, with flags on all of his office walls. Some of the international staff participated in the merriment, donning the red-and-black shirts they had been given by their Kosovo Albanian colleagues during the coffee break on the 26th.

On Monday morning, the 26th, the excitement was palpable in the corridors of the agency. Clocking in, KPA officers were discussing their holiday plans. Valmira, a Kosovo Albanian woman in her late twenties, was about to enter the building. I waited for at the lift and we rode up to the third floor of the building together.

At the time, I was observing the work of the legal officers directly working with the three commissioners of the Kosovo Property Claims

Commission (KPCC), the KPA's adjudicatory body. Valmira was one of the legal officers (or 'lawyers' as the KPA legal officers call themselves) of the Case Processing Team (CPT), the unit that carries out the legal analysis of claims before they reach the KPCC office. She had started working for the Housing and Property Directorate (HPD, the first property restitution mechanism set up by the UN) six years previously, and had continued with the KPA at the close of the first mandate. In the lift, as I was feeling somewhat out of place as the only person not wearing red and black, she responded to my inquiring gaze at their outfits, with the rest of the lift passengers nodding their heads in approval:

> We are Albanians. We fought together many times in history; we are one blood, one language. And we have the same flag. My flag is black and red, not blue and yellow [the flag of Independent Kosovo]. I cannot change that. This land is Kosovo, but it's Albanian land. We've been here for centuries. We're Illyrian. My nationality is Albanian because I belong to the Albanian nation.

With these words, the lift doors opened on the small corridor full of metal cabinets containing archived files. While Valmira continued straight to the CPT office, I followed the KPCC team to theirs, on the left-hand side. Inside the crammed office, a national lawyer and one of the international staff were in heated debate. When entering the office, the international legal officer had commented on the flag above her national colleague's desk, asking the reason for this bold display of nationalism at the workplace. The language used by the international staff member must have seemed offensive to her national colleagues, and the tone became ever more glacial. The international officer was commenting on the need to remain impartial, while her national colleagues simply told her she couldn't understand as she was 'not from here', a foreigner. The international officer afterward confessed she hadn't known it was Albanian Independence Day on the 28th.

Fortunately, the coffee break gave me an excuse to get out. Every morning at 9:30, most staff members head out for a delicious *makiato* in one of the nearby cafés. Sitting beside Valmira next to a warm open fire, an older colleague from the CPT unit continued the conversation that had started in the lift:

> As Albanian people, we suffered a lot. For years we suffered under Serbian occupation. From 1989, because of the repression of the Serbian authorities, everybody [the Kosovo Albanians] was fired. Some of us

here were taught law not at the university but in secret, in private houses, because the university was only in Serbian. During the war, my family and I, as many others, we went to Macedonia for three months to escape. I was afraid for my children. All six of us slept in the car . . . for days. We heard horrible stories from Kosovo. Women, old people and children forced to walk for days across the country and used as human shields, men starving in Serbian camps. So you understand why it's important for us to celebrate that we are Albanian publicly today. What Serbs say about the conflict and what happened before, it's not the truth. I hope you read books written by Albanians about Kosovo history, and not by Serbs, because you must know the truth.

Checking my Facebook page a few days later, I found a post by a colleague from the eviction unit.[3] In his post, liked and commented on by other KPA staff, the eviction officer explicitly referred to the horrors of the war experienced by Kosovo Albanians with a picture of the forced marches I was told about by the older lawyer. The Facebook post read: 'It makes me feel sad when I see scenes like this one in the photo, thanks GOD I have not experienced this horror, but pain and terror what this people faced it is really hard to FORGET IT . . .!!!'[4]

As the international officer I mentioned above noticed, leading to the argument with her national colleagues, there appeared to be a very visible contradiction between the KPA national staff's personal, 'nationalist' convictions and their duty of impartiality.

Impartiality, in this context, is best understood in reference to article 14(1)[5] of the International Covenant on Civil and Political Rights, which stipulates, according to the Human Rights Committee, 'that judges must not harbour preconceptions about the matter put before them, and that they must not act in ways that promote the interests of one of the parties' (OHCHR 2003: 120).[6] The European Court of Human Rights, moreover, sees impartiality as containing both a 'subjective' and an 'objective' component (OHCHR 2003, 120):

> Not only must the tribunal be impartial, in that 'no member of the tribunal should hold any personal prejudice or bias', but it must also 'be impartial from an objective viewpoint', in that 'it must offer guarantees to exclude any legitimate doubt in this respect'.[7]

In this view, impartiality, a complex social fact, is produced in relation to the parties and to the issues at stake (the 'subjective' element). It must, however, also be rendered explicit through, for example, institutionalized, procedural rules in order for the institution to be in a position to provide the necessary guarantees 'to exclude any legitimate doubt' (the 'objective' element). The international officer was irritated (to put it mildly) by the bold display of the national lawyers' ethnic 'nationalist' sentiments at the workplace, in a supposedly impartial institution abiding by international law standards such as the KPA. In line with the above definitions, she saw the national lawyers' behaviour as counterproductive, jeopardizing the integrity of the institution.

It is not surprising that lawyers – who are a special kind of bureaucrat – have private interests and prejudices that are not necessarily congruent with the type of work they do (see Herzfeld 1993; Handler 1996). In his study of performance in everyday life, Goffman (1959) famously showed that everywhere actors separate their private and professional selves and take on different personae according to the (private or public) spheres in which they find themselves. What is of interest here is that the national staff did not seem to believe that their nationalist behaviour should have remained outside the workplace. They did not appear to think that flaunting their Albanian allegiance at work contradicted their public personae as KPA lawyers, and that this could be detrimental to their professional duty of impartiality, or to the independence of the institution from the perspective of international law (else at least the deputy director, as the national KPA figurehead, probably would have behaved differently).

The nationalist behaviour of my Kosovo Albanian lawyer colleagues at the workplace can partly be explained by the political context of contemporary Kosovo, which is de facto in the hands of its Kosovo Albanian majority, and partly by the long history of the politicization of ethnicity across national borders in the Balkans that normalized everyday nationalism in both the private and the public spheres. But neither victor's politics nor nationalist history can explain the national lawyers' commitment to impartiality, and the general public's perception of the KPA as an actually impartial institution. The ethnic composition of the KPA complicates matters further. The agency is predominantly staffed by Kosovo Albanians, and all the national lawyers of the CPT and KPCC – the two units that directly work on the legal analysis of claims – are Kosovo Albanians. On the other hand, 98 per cent of claimants are Kosovo Serbs, most of whom now live as displaced persons (DPs) in Serbia. Nonetheless, the institution is generally seen – both from within and from the outside in Kosovo as well as in Serbia – as one of the only independent, uncorrupted, and fair institutions in Kosovo. How, then, could Kosovo Albanian lawyers, apparently so secure in their Albanian nationalist convictions, work impartially for the benefit of predominantly Kosovo Serbian claimants? What makes this impartiality possible is the question I wish to explore in this chapter.

'PROPERTY RIGHTS ARE HUMAN RIGHTS'

Besky (2014: 13) argues that 'we can begin to trace the act of doing justice anthropologically by studying whose imaginaries of injustice gain political traction, and why'. Because of the way the conflict in Kosovo was 'resolved' – the NATO military intervention followed by international oversight of the autonomous province of Kosovo – it is the international human rights imaginary of justice that gained political traction rather than the nationalist Albanian history of suffering I sketched out above (see Pandolfi 2003). Writing on the protracted 'end of human rights', Douzinas (2000: 129) describes the Kosovo war as '[t]he first war officially conducted to protect human rights. According to Tony Blair, this was a just war, promoting the doctrine of intervention based on values, while [the then UK Foreign Secretary] Robin Cook declared that NATO was a "humanitarian alliance"'.

Accordingly, international actors also framed Kosovo's post-war situation as a humanitarian emergency, with the 'restoration' of human rights – property rights in particular – as a top priority. A logic of humanitarian intervention thus guided UNMIK in its drive to restore a peaceful status quo at the end of the war. In early 2000, it created the first property dispute resolution mechanism. The Housing and Property Directorate (HPD) was set up with international funding to remedy what was basically a humanitarian emergency, as a majority of Kosovo's population had been displaced by the conflict. Clarifying property relations was seen as a decisive step toward addressing the population's most pressing needs and restoring the basic human right of housing.

The HPD's modus operandi was thus from the outset fundamentally shaped by the conception of property as a human right, the logic of humanitarian intervention underpinning its set-up as well as the funding landscape. However, only residential property fell under the HPD's purview. This caused obvious problems when, as happened often, the title to a house was restored but the surrounding field was left in legal limbo and tilled by 'illegal occupants'. UNMIK therefore mandated a report to analyse these shortcomings and come up with policy recommendations to improve the property restitution mechanism. The report diagnosed that the return of DPs and refugees – at the time of the assessment in 2004 predominantly Kosovo Serbs – and economic development were impossible without the regularization of private immovable property, including agricultural and commercial property:

> To regularise the situation, strengthen the rule of law, and secure property rights, something must be done. The system as it presently stands cannot resolve these disputes. Until they are resolved, neither IDPs and refugees nor the population at large can expect greater investment and economic development.
>
> (Moratti et al. 2004: 4–5)

The KPA was thus conceived as the successor to the HPD in 2006 with a mandate including agricultural, residential, and commercial private immovable property but narrowing disputes down to those that were a direct result of the 1998–99 war, defined by the cut-off dates of 27 February 1998 and 20 June 1999.[8] The same discourse of property rights as human rights and funding logic that had shaped the HPD also underpinned and strongly informed the ideological foundation of the KPA.

As evidenced in the United Nations' 2005 comprehensive review of the situation in Kosovo, known as the Kai Eide Report (Eide 2005: 15), the return of Serbian DPs was seen as paramount to the creation of a multi-ethnic state, and safeguarding their human rights to property became essential. In order to quickly re-establish legal certainty about property relations, it was argued that it was impossible to take into account earlier changes to property rights due to the historical succession of different property regimes. Narrowing down the definition of property loss to such a short period of time (sixteen months) had the consequence that most of the 'victims' that were entitled to claim were Kosovo Serbs; most Kosovo Albanians had lost their property due to discriminatory laws and practices under Milošević during the 1990s in the run-up to the conflict. Of course, many Kosovo Albanians were also displaced and lost their houses to destruction during the war. However, having 'won' the war, they more easily returned to 'liberated' Kosovo, and, in many cases, had no compunction over moving into houses that had previously been inhabited by Kosovo Serbs.

A 'CLASH OF WORKING CULTURES'?

At the time the KPA was created, UNMIK seems to have shared my initial assumption that national lawyers might experience conflicts of interest when working on war-related property disputes, the memory of which was still very raw for many of them. Apparently aware of this, UNMIK devised two strategies that succeeded, at least from a technical point of view, in creating the necessary conditions for the impartiality of national staff. On the one hand, they organized the institution's workflow as a technocratic machine managed by computer applications especially designed by the KPA IT team for each discrete unit. On the other, they called in 'internationals' to supervise the work of the 'local' staff. As in other bureaucratic settings, the technocratic apparatus put in place was 'designed to unify and control individuals conceived as either naturally independent and refractory or entangled in other collectivities' (Hull 2003: 288).

When I started at the KPA, I was introduced by the director to the different heads of unit as an intern who needed to learn 'how the process worked'. Very much like other staff members would be trained when they first arrived at the agency, I was asked to sit next to a lawyer or a coordinator (as the international legal officers are called at the KPA), take notes of the explanations of my colleagues, and read the standard operating procedures for that specific unit. I would then perform the tasks I had learned on my own KPA computer. Each time I moved from one unit to the next, the applications for the previous unit would be deleted from the desktop computer that followed me everywhere (along with a desk and a chair); new ones would be installed, and a similar learning process would start. The explanations I received of 'how the system worked' were always about the workings of the computer applications. My colleagues understood their work through the applications, which framed and dictated the logic of the workflow. That way, complex kinship and property title issues were reduced to the ticking of boxes and the filling-in of forms in a pre-set, technical-legal language made up of abbreviations, following simple, causal chains of actions. Information was made available only according to the applications' settings, ensuring that no one had access to the full database entry for a specific claim. This strict compartmentalization of information, along with the nominative track-change and quality control procedure instituted at each step of the process, succeeded in dividing the messy reality behind the claims into discrete parcels of technical information stripped of their emotionality.

The processing of claims at the KPA was conceived first and foremost as a technical procedure of data entry and data analysis. In de-politicizing claims and rendering information purely technical, UNMIK created a legal decision-making machine detached from everyday life and governed by technocratic rule (see Ferguson 1994; Murray Li 2007). The KPA staff, reduced to the role of technicians of this seemingly omniscient machine, thought the system so strong that there was only very little room for freedom of manoeuvre. 'It is not possible for lawyers not to be objective', I was told, 'because the system is so good'.

Yet, technical conditions for impartiality do not automatically equal impartial work. Therefore, UNMIK set up the institution in a way that the work of the national staff would always be supervised by inter-nationals. As the European Rule of Law mission (EULEX)[9] property coordinator explained: 'the presence of internationals is intended to ensure infection is kept minimal. Internationals are able to access the resources of people speaking the local language[s], but ensure that they [the national staff] don't have the last word'. On top of expressing prejudice about the presupposed impartiality or biases inherent to different categories of persons, the use of the term 'infection' also denotes the perceived importance of fostering a 'healthy' (read: 'modern' and EU-compatible) body politic unpolluted by 'local' influence – reproducing age-old stereotypes about the Balkans such as corruption, inefficiency and ethnic hatred (Todorova 2009 [1997]).

For the technical machine to run smoothly, it had to be administered by technocrats, who could only be internationals, as they were con-ceived of as embodiments of neutrality. Internationals were appointed, in the view of EULEX, to safeguard and further international rule of law standards such as judicial independence and impartiality. In brief, their role was to ensure impartiality where they thought it could only be absent. In this perspective, echoed by many rule of law mission obser-vers (see, e.g., Cady 2012), the national staff were too emotionally involved with the issues at stake, which led to 'biased' justice. And in fact, under UNMIK, it was common for Kosovo Albanian judges in both civil and criminal courts to show ethnic bias against Serbian defendants (Cady 2012: 29).

However, international oversight does not in itself guarantee an impartial stance by the national lawyers. If we return to the European

Court of Human Rights' differentiation between 'subjective' and 'objective' impartiality, the consensus at the KPA was that although the presence of internationals was necessary because it participated in establishing the guarantees for 'objective' impartiality through their technical-legal input, it did not ensure the 'subjective' impartiality of the national staff through a political-legal oversight. I build the following part of my argument on the reflections of both the national and the international staff about the role of the internationals in the institution.

Internationals acknowledged their general lack of knowledge of the 'local' sociopolitical and legal setting. As they told me, when they first arrived at the KPA, they felt they didn't know much about the events covered by the mandate. More problematically in their point of view, they also lacked knowledge of property law (their previous work experience having largely been in other areas of law) and of the applicable laws in Kosovo (a mixture of Yugoslav-era, UNMIK and civil law–oriented legislation). This was also a source of irritation for the national lawyers, as a national colleague expressed: '[S]ometimes I have my doubts if internationals do actually have a degree in law. The kind of questions they ask — how would a lawyer ask this?'

This is not to say that the KPA coordinators were incompetent or 'bad lawyers', but it was assumed in the set-up of the institution that their international-ness and their technical skills as jurists educated abroad were the essential requirements for the job, and that further knowledge of the historical and legal context was not necessary. In fact, as Coles (2007) argues, the cultivation of this sense of ignorance is what makes them neutral experts in the eyes of the international community and got them their jobs in the first place. In post-war Bosnia, as in transitional Kosovo, internationals were hired for their 'international bod[ies] and the skills [presumed to be] attached to th[ese] bod[ies]' (p. 97). 'The international-as-tool held within his or her body the authority of the international community as well as an assumed set of particularly defined and produced skills or values: expertise ..., democracy, and neutrality' (p. 100). Coles deploys the concept of 'mere presence' to define the role of the 'international's bodily tool kit' (p. 100). She describes how, however passive the role of some internationals actually was, their presence was seen as necessary, as it evoked, among other things, 'goodwill and post-war reconciliation' and an implicit enforcement of 'rules and proper conduct' (p. 100). And, indeed, one of the coordinators at the KPA echoed this idea almost verbatim when he told me: 'It's not us; we are not such amazing lawyers. It's more our presence which might help them be more neutral.' Their 'mere presence' was also seen as indispensable for the sake of the Serbian claimants who, I was repeatedly told by KPA staff, believed in the impartiality of the KPA because of the presence of internationals.

However, beyond their 'mere presence', KPA coordinators did not always seem very conscious of their role as supposed impartial overseers: as the earlier vignette shows, some of them were unaware of the potential political implications of wearing Albanian colours on Independence Day. When I expressed surprise at their choice of outfit, they told me they just wanted to please their Albanian colleagues who had offered them the T-shirts, and did not seem to think that their actions could have a negative impact on their authority as coordinators. This is probably because, in everyday practice, the coordinators' role is mainly a formal and technical 'quality control', based on their 'commitment to bureaucratic and technical rationality' (Coles 2007: 106).

At the CPT, for example, they made sure that reports drafted by national lawyers were formatted in accordance with the guidelines of the KPCC, and cleared up the 'messiness' of some of the legal analyses, rather than simply verifying whether the lawyer showed any bias or not. As I was told by one CPT national lawyer:

> Coordinators interfere in your language. But they don't have the credentials of translators or language specialists. Their duty is to look at the claims to make sure they are understandable, impartial and that the procedural steps are fulfilled.... They should work on impartiality, not on language. They focus on language and forget to check all the steps. So lawyers feel frustrated. If [the legal reasoning] is understandable and clear, why the need for cosmetic changes?... They are obsessed with changing everything.

For the international staff, however, this thorough, technical, 'quality check' was indispensable to make up for what was described to me as a skills gap. Indeed, a common complaint of the international staff (coordinators, KPCC commissioners and EULEX civil judges alike) was that the legal education of Kosovo Albanian lawyers did not train them to interpret the law and write clear, black-letter law analysis. As a EULEX civil judge told me: 'the reasoning for them is equal to the facts of the case. There is no legal reasoning in their analysis. You can take somebody from the street and they would express themselves in the same way.'

Beyond this 'clash of working cultures', as these tensions were coined by an international coordinator, both the coordinators and the national lawyers seemed to agree that in practice the work of the coordinators was not dedicated to ensuring subjective impartiality first and foremost. During my time at the KPA I often observed disagreements between coordinators and lawyers about the legal outcome of some cases. The grounds for these disagreements were mostly technical-legal, and not ideological or political. From an internal perspective, the institutional structure was designed to promote international standards of impartiality. The international presence, moreover, (arguably) improved the quality of the legal work. However, both strategies only created technical conditions for objective impartiality. If coordinators limited their input to technical-legal matters, it signifies that the legal reasoning performed by the national lawyers before the cases reached the coordinators showed no apparent bias. What, then, ensured the subjective impartiality of the work of the Kosovo Albanian lawyers?

'WE DON'T WORK FOR THE SERBS, WE WORK FOR HUMAN RIGHTS'

The self-definition of the KPA as an 'institution providing human rights' has far-reaching consequences. The 'human rights ideology' that underpinned the mandate of the KPA was invoked by legal practitioners at the institution to legitimize their legal work, which, because of the narrowness of its mandate, did not encompass their personal understanding of the kind of justice they thought would be appropriate for a 'real' peace and reconciliation process. I thus propose that it is by looking at the lawyers' different understandings of justice that we can begin to understand how they themselves acted out their duty of impartiality.

A week after the celebration of the 100th year of Albanian independence, I met for lunch with Valmira. While we ate, I asked Valmira how she felt as an Albanian woman and a lawyer to be working for an institution mandated to restitute property rights to Kosovo Serbian DPs. Her answer was exemplary for the kind of answers I received:

> Justice is justice. For all. Personally it's not easy. But I keep my personal point of view for myself.... For me as a lawyer, it is important to know

95

that people could claim their rights.... The KPA mandate is difficult to accept for the [Kosovo] Albanians. But it is necessary to be in accordance with the Human Rights Convention.

Valmira's statement shows that she differentiated between her personal point of view and the perspective she adopted in her work and in her understanding of property restitution as defined and acted out in the KPA mandate. It is by invoking and acting on different registers of justice that my informants made sense of their work, navigated the political pitfalls of Kosovo's transitional landscape, and reconciled the tensions they experienced on a daily basis.

Justice is a vague and malleable concept which, through its 'aspirational quality and substantive openness', derives its potency from the variety of ideals it evokes (Merry 2010: 28). Two ideals of justice are in tension in Valmira's statement: procedural ideals of justice as enshrined in international law, and notions of distributive justice that would encompass Albanians' grievances; the success of the KPA is to insist on the first, despite the second.

The first, the normative and relatively narrow procedural understanding of justice, sees it as the ideal outcome of legal proceedings – that is, decisions reached through procedural correctness – through which seemingly universal conceptions of morality are deployed, as in the application of the human rights legal system. The second sense of justice at play here is the ideal of distributive justice. It refers to 'broad political and social aspirations related to [among other things] accountability, stability, fairness' and the distribution of wealth (Dembour and Kelly 2007: 17). These aspirations of distributive (but also of retributive) justice often come to life not through rational or normative explanations, but through the realm of emotions and lived, very tangible forms of injustice and suffering (see Nader 2010; Niezen 2013). Therefore, while justice remains a distant ideal, it is made actionable through its opposite, injustice. Valmira's description reveals the inner tensions she feels between the normative conception of procedural justice she adheres to and reproduces as a lawyer, and her feeling of injustice over the narrowness of the KPA mandate that 'only' provides legal avenues for distributive justice to Kosovo Serbs. She and other lawyer colleagues think it is unfair that there is no dedicated legal mechanism for reparations for 'her people', who suffered at least as much as the Kosovo Serbs during the war.[10] Meanwhile the Serbs, from Valmira's perspective the perpetrators of war crimes, are rewarded with

a property restitution mechanism. As she explained to me: 'the Albanians only have the [regular] courts', which, in the view of many, do
not work. This in contrast to the KPA, seen as one of the only efficient
and uncorrupted legal bodies in Kosovo.

The other element in Valmira's statement is the emphasis on an
ideology of justice that is 'legitimated by its grounding in transnational
space and is constrained by the texts and practices of the human rights
legal system' (Merry 2010: 28). Lawyers repeatedly stressed the idea of
justice for all, and framed their work as 'for human rights' and 'not for
the Serbs'. Thereby, they invoked an ideal of universal justice to
provide some sort of reconciling framework to justify their work and
the restitution process to themselves, their families, and the Kosovo
Albanian public at large. As another colleague stated, 'We give legal
aid and human rights to parties.' This way, Kosovo Serbian claimants
can fall under the universalizing category of victims of human rights
violations, defined as such as the legal beneficiaries of the restitution
process while at the same time bracketing out any other sense of (in)
justice experienced by the Kosovo Albanians. In this sense, human
rights represent universal standards and abstract ideals that are legitimating in themselves. They articulate powerful ideals of justice because
they remain distant and abstract, 'even if the possibility of enforcement
is merely theoretical' (Pirie 2013: 215).

Anthropological literature looking at the 'translation' of the transnational human rights discourse into 'local' practice has identified a
'need for contextualization' (Jensen 2014: 463), whereby the trans-
plantation of 'rule of law' or 'transitional justice' toolkits into various
local settings is problematized. This literature highlights how, despite
recognizing their failure themselves, policy-oriented actors seem to
believe – bordering on dogmatism – in the positive and transformative
effects of 'best practice' policies that aim at implementing universal
standards of rights in local practice (Goodale and Merry 2007; Shaw
et al. 2010; Garth and Dezalay 2011). Authors such as Goodale (2007)
and Speed (2007) ethnographically document moments of 'translation', or of local appropriation of transnational principles of human
rights in 'local' practice. Both argue that informants adopt a globalized
language of rights as a form of political contestation, as a vernacularized
appropriation of 'legalism', which is otherwise seen as a 'regulatory'
instrument of 'neoliberalizing' state domination (Speed 2007: 164,
178). In Goodale's words, the human rights discourse 'both transforms
the terms of reference through which the legal mediates social,

political, and economic relations, which is to be expected, but, even more, creates new conditions in which individuals or groups can organise social resistance' (2007: 158). In a later publication, Goodale and Clarke continue this line of argument by positing that the 'transnational' or 'global' notions of 'justice' and 'human rights' can *only* be understood, and become meaningful for actors, through vernacularization, in the 'local' (Clarke and Goodale 2010: 9). By focusing on the encounters themselves, the diversity of processes of vernacularization (and its opposite process, 'back translation'; see, e.g., Englund 2012) comes to light. In this understanding, vernacularization – or the process through which transnational discourses such as the discourse of human rights is made meaningful as it is implemented locally – is essential to comprehend the significance of refracted notions of justice that 'local' actors deploy in the everyday (Clarke and Goodale 2010: 9).

From a methodological point of view it is useful to adopt an approach that renders visible the multifaceted encounters between the 'global' and the 'local' (Shaw et al. 2010: 5, see also Anders and Zenker 2014); however, articulating universal ideals as necessarily ill-fitting, or 'doing violence to' (Pirie 2013: 215) localized practices and priorities *unless* they are made meaningful through vernacularization is problematic. In fact, sometimes, vernacularization falls short of explaining the 'global'–'local' dialectic. On a continuum ranging from 'replication' to 'hybridization', Merry describes vernacularization as a process by which 'symbols, ideologies, and organizational forms generated in one locality [merge, to varying degrees] with those of other localities to produce new, hybrid institutions' thanks to the intermediary work of translators (2006: 46).

This presupposes that the transnational discourse is actually applied – at least to a certain degree – in local terms. A specificity of the legal system in Kosovo is that, according to Article 22 of its constitution, all the international standards are directly applicable. Despite this, however, the language of international law is not actually used by KPA legal officers in their daily casework. The human rights discourse is invoked for its moral weight rather than its technical–legal force of law.

For example, one CPT coordinator called a special meeting to discuss KPA's position on a matter of Yugoslav-era property law that had never been dealt with before, and for which no jurisprudence or legal commentaries could be found. Five national colleagues were chosen by the coordinator to elucidate the issue and draft an 'Internal Memo' determining the KPA position on the matter. The national lawyers felt that their role was to provide for the lacking jurisprudence: by drawing on pragmatic examples of how things were done in the past, they hoped to show how the language of the law should be interpreted in practice so that 'justice' could be done. One of them said:

> From my own experience, even under the Serbs, when the father died, the family was not expelled from the flat. If the user right is extinguished when the person dies, it would be against the convention on Human Rights. You cannot deprive someone of one's property, that would be unjust.

As this example shows, lawyers mention human rights with reference to making justice, both as means and as ends, but not as a specific corpus of applicable legislation: 'the human rights declaration is a guide, a star in the dark night', stated the national judge of the Supreme Court KPA Appeals panel. Human rights are ubiquitous at the KPA, as the mandate is entrenched in the ideology of universal rights to property. Yet the discourse never engages with the details, it remains non-specific. Therefore, I do not think that the lawyers of the KPA could be said to act as translators of the human rights legal system into context-specific meanings and legal actions. I suggest that human rights do not get 'vernacularized' through their work; there is no 're-appropriation' of the core meaning of the transnational human rights discourse through the use of local vocabularies. Everyday legal practice and international law stay separate and distinct as no 'translation' takes place. It is precisely because they stay distinct and that the human rights discourse remains non-specific and abstract that it is such a powerful repertoire of justice for the national lawyers of the agency.

The dialectic between 'global ideals' and 'local practice' that is mediated by KPA lawyers is perhaps better explained in terms of 'framing' whereby sensitive legal work is made sensible through the invocation – not the application – of the doctrine of human rights in its transnational dimension. In her analysis of the use of expert knowledge at the European Commission, Boswell (2008) makes a similar point: policy makers use research to legitimize their work, but not to inform it. Contrary to the 'instrumentalist' standpoint according to which policy makers use research findings to improve their policy outputs, Boswell explains the exponential use of research in policy for its 'legitimizing' quality: 'the use of knowledge can endow government agencies with what has been described as "epistemic authority"' (p. 472). Moreover, not unlike my analysis of the national lawyers' legitimizing invocation of human rights, Boswell describes how policy positions based on a commitment to international human rights law are especially appropriate to back 'technocratic modes of justification' as they 'ground policies in more rational and universalistic principles, which transcend populist or nationalistic perspectives' (Bosewell 2008: 479; see also Pirie 2013: 214–215). Invoking a discourse is not the same as adapting and implementing it. In fact, rather than acting as a meaning-making medium, here, the human rights discourse is powerful because it remains an ideal, universal 'star in the dark night'.

The 'global' is often opposed to the 'local' following a 'language and practice of scale' that creates 'hierarchical distinction between forms of action' (Dembour and Kelly 2007: 16). However, in compartmentalizing 'my personal point of view' and 'for me as a lawyer', Valmira implies a distinctive combination of 'global' and 'local'. Likewise, the lawyer's explanation of a certain Yugoslav-era legal practice combines the invocation of human rights with a rights-based judgmental evaluation of what would or would not have been 'just', 'even under the Serbs'. Therefore, while Valmira's statement and the two quotes above show that legal officers see the human rights discourse as an abstract set of ideals they articulate in terms of rendering justice for all, this does not necessarily mean that they see the 'global' as overarching and above the 'local'. In other words, the fact that lawyers do not participate in the vernacularization of the human rights discourse does not prevent Valmira and her colleagues from concretely grounding this universalistic sense of justice in the locality of their everyday life as lawyers.

In the present context, human rights as the institutional, normative narrative of procedural justice that acts as both a framing and legitimizing device, and the nationalistic repertoire of justice so boldly embodied by the national lawyers re-enforce one another. In fact, they are mutually constitutive *in* their contradictions. The Kosovo Albanian lawyers, as biased as they might be in their personal opinions, are, indeed, perhaps even more diligent than Serbian lawyers would be when carrying out their professional duties, again due to the importance given to the rule of law as one of the key preconditions for Kosovo's sovereignty. The national lawyers' commitment to identifying fake documents is a telling example. In the complex legal environment of contemporary Kosovo, characterized by multiple, pluralistic sources of law and contested legal institutions, an important part of lawyers' everyday work at the KPA is to distinguish 'genuine' from 'fake' documents that take the form of uncertified documents, 'simple' forgeries, but also of documents issued by unrecognized, 'parallel' Serbian institutions. As a coordinator expressed: '[National] lawyers are very good at not accepting parallel institutions' documents because it is part of their battle for independence from Serbia as [Kosovo] Albanians in Kosovo'.

CONCLUDING REMARKS

At the KPA, conditions for objective impartiality created by the two institutional strategies – compartmentalization and international 'oversight' – derive from a notion of procedural justice allegorized as the blind 'Lady Justice', and in this perspective, they work. This echoes processes of rendering technical that have been described in the anthropology of development and that depoliticize processes that are, at their heart, deeply political (Ferguson 1994; Scott 1998; Murray Li 2007). However, as I have shown, there is more to it than that. As the events around the celebration of Albanian independence illustrate, a disconnect persists between the personal sense of injustice of national lawyers and the impartiality that the institution requires of its staff, and that they are very conscious of the political, very sensitive nature of their work. Nonetheless, they see themselves as, and are perceived as, impartial.

Encounters between 'local' practice and 'global' rule are generally analysed in anthropology in terms of vernacularization whereby the 'global' is incorporated into, and given meaning by and in, the 'local'. However, in this context, the language of transnational law is invoked, but not used in practice as a corpus of applicable legislation. International law is the institutional subtext, the mandate's frame. But beyond defining the technocratic tenets of the procedure, the frame does not necessarily dictate the way lawyers act in the everyday. In other words, international law is enshrined in the institutional procedures themselves, but remains a distant set of ideals for the national lawyers. They actively endorse and mobilize the ideology of justice as human rights to legitimize their work to both themselves and the society at large. Framing Serbs under the universalizing category of human rights victims allows lawyers to work diligently 'for human rights', and to accept and manage the technical rule of law toolkit imposed on them. Yet doing so cannot simply be explained in terms of 'local' appropriation of 'global', transnational neoliberal ideals. Likewise, the bold display of nationalistic sentiments at the workplace is not simply a manifestation of 'local' resistance to international, 'neutral' rule. 'Local' and 'global' repertoires of justice deployed invoke divergent but complementary moral values entrenched in the complex environ- ment of transitional Kosovo. And it is because these irreconcilable moral and legal values are experienced together that impartiality is made possible in the everyday.

Impartiality, then, would be about not stepping back but consciously reinforcing and embracing the inherent contradictions of the 'global' and the 'local' repertoires of justice acted out by the national lawyers of the KPA, as they relate to what it means to be a Kosovan citizen within Kosovo's transitional regime. In contrast to the initial contradiction the international legal officer had highlighted in the opening vignette, my ethnography illustrates not only how different senses of justice that are not always reconcilable can coexist but also how these irreconcilable senses of justice depend on one another to create the social conditions leading to the subjective enactment of impartiality.

Notes

1 I am grateful to Toby Kelly, Anthony Good, Fernanda Pirie, Jon Schubert, Hadas Weiss, and Sandra Brunnegger for their generous comments.
2 See, for example, the Preamble of the Basic Principles on the Independ- ence of the Judiciary (1985).
3 As its name states, the eviction unit is in charge of evicting 'illegal occupants' from successful claimants' adjudicated properties.
4 I have not been able to include the screenshot of my Facebook page for copyright reasons. The image of the marches shared by my colleague is available at: www.flickr.com/photos/un_photo/4417554258.
5 Its second sentence states: 'In the determination of any criminal charge against him, or of his rights and obligations in a suit at law, everyone shall be entitled to a fair and public hearing by a competent, independent and impartial tribunal established by law.'
6 Communication No. 387/1989, *Arvo O. Karttunen* v. *Finland* (Views adopted on 23 October 1992), in UN doc. GAOR, A/48/40 (vol. II), p. 120, para. 7.2.
7 *Eur. Court HR, Case of Daktaras* v. *Lithuania*, judgment of 10 October 2000, para. 30.
8 This period has been defined as the most intense phase of the conflict. Why exactly these dates were chosen, however, is the subject of much speculation. At the KPA itself, no one ever really queries the significance of the cut-off dates.
9 UNMIK's successor since 2008.
10 Actually much more, if we follow the OSCE (1999) report on the Kosovo war.

References

Anders, Gerhard, and Olaf Zenker. 2014. 'Transition and Justice: An Introduction'. *Development & Change* 45(3): 395–414.

Besky, Sarah. 2014. *The Darjeeling Distinction: Labor and Justice on Fair-Trade Tea Plantations in India*. Berkeley: University of California Press.

Boswell, Christina. 2008. 'The Political Functions of Expert Knowledge: Knowledge and Legitimation in European Union Immigration Policy'. *Journal of European Public Policy* 15(4): 471–488.

Cady, Jean-Christian. 2012. 'Establishing the Rule of Law: The UN Challenge in Kosovo'. *Focus Stratégique* 34 bis.

Clarke, Kamari Maxine, and Mark Goodale, eds. 2010. *Mirrors of Justice: Law and Power in the Post–Cold War Era*. New York: Cambridge University Press.

Coles, Kimberley. 2007. *Democratic Designs: International Intervention and Electoral Practices in Postwar Bosnia-Herzegovina*. Ann Arbor: University of Michigan Press.

Dezalay, Yves, and Bryant G. Garth. 2011. *Lawyers and the Rule of Law in an Era of Globalization*. Oxon: Routledge.

Dembour, Marie-Bénédicte, and Tobias Kelly, eds. 2007. *Paths to International Justice: Social and Legal Perspectives*. Cambridge: Cambridge University Press.

Douzinas, Costas. 2000. *The End of Human Rights*. Oxford: Hart.

Eide, Kai. 2005. *A Comprehensive Review of the Situation in Kosovo*. New York: United Nations Security Council.

Englund, Harri. 2012. 'Human Rights and Village Headmen in Malawi: Translation beyond Vernacularization'. In Julia Eckert, Brian Donahoe, Christian Strumpell, and Zerrin Ozlem Biner (eds.), *Law against the State: Ethnographic Forays into Law's Transformations*. Cambridge: Cambridge University Press.

Ferguson, James. 1994. *The Anti-Politics Machine: 'Development', Depoliticization, and Bureaucratic Power in Lesotho*. Minneapolis: University of Minnesota Press.

Goffman, E. 1959. *The Presentation of Self in Everyday Life*. New York: Doubleday.

Goodale, Mark. 2007. 'The Power of Right(s): Tracking Empires of Law and New Modes of Social Resistance in Bolivia (and Elsewhere)'. In Mark Goodale and Sally Engle Merry (eds.), *The Practice of Human Rights: Tracking Law between the Global and the Local*. Cambridge: Cambridge University Press.

Goodale, Mark, and Sally Engle Merry, eds. 2007. *The Practice of Human Rights: Tracking Law between the Global and the Local*. Cambridge: Cambridge University Press.

Handler, Joel. 1996. *Down from Bureaucracy: The Ambiguity of Empowerment and Privatization*. Princeton, NJ: Princeton University Press.

Herzfeld, Michael. 1993. *The Social Production of Indifference: Exploring the Symbolic Roots of Western Bureaucracy*. Chicago: University of Chicago Press.

Hull, Matthew. 2003. 'The File: Agency, Authority and Autography in a Pakistani Bureaucracy'. *Language and Communication* 23: 287–314.

Jensen, Steffen. 2014. 'Conflicting Logics of Exceptionality: New Beginnings and the Problem of Police Violence in Post-Apartheid South Africa'. *Development & Change* 45(3): 458–478.

Merry, Sally Engle. 2006. 'Transnational Human Rights and Local Activism'. *American Anthropologist* 108(1): 38–51.

———. 2010. 'Beyond Compliance: Toward an Anthropological Understanding of International Justice'. In Kamari Maxine Clarke and Mark Goodale (eds.), *Mirrors of Justice: Law and Power in the Post–Cold War Era*. New York: Cambridge University Press.

Moratti, Massimo, Charles Philpott, and Brian Wicklin. 2004. *Feasibility Study to Assess the Scope and Nature of Work for an Alternative Dispute Resolution Mechanism for Land and Private Commercial Properties in Kosovo*. Pristina: European Agency for Reconstruction.

Murray Li, Tania. 2007. *The Will to Improve: Governmentality, Development and the Practice of Politics*. Durham, NC: Duke University Press.

Nader, Laura. 2010. 'Epilogue: The Words We Use: Justice, Human Rights, and the Sense of Injustice'. In Kamari Maxine Clarke and Mark Goodale (eds.), *Mirrors of Justice: Law and Power in the Post–Cold War Era*. New York: Cambridge University Press.

Niezen, Ronald. 2013. *Truth and Indignation: Canada's Truth and Reconciliation Commission on Indian Residential Schools*. Toronto: University of Toronto Press.

OHCHR. 2003. 'Independence and Impartiality of Judges, Prosecutors and Lawyers'. In OHCHR and IBA (eds.), *Human Rights in the Administration of Justice: A Manual on Human Rights for Judges, Prosecutors and Lawyers*. Geneva: United Nations.

OSCE. 1999. *Kosovo/Kosova: As Seen, as Told: An Analysis of the Human Rights Findings of the OSCE Kosovo Verification Mission, October 1998 to June 1999*. Warsaw: OSCE.

Pandolfi, Mariella. 2003. 'Contract of Mutual (In)difference: Government and the Humanitarian Apparatus in Contemporary Albania and Kosovo'. *Indiana Journal of Global Legal Studies* 10(1).

Pirie, Fernanda. 2013. *The Anthropology of Law*. Oxford: Oxford University Press.

Scott, James C. 1998. *Seeing like a State: How Certain Schemes to Improve the Human Condition Have Failed*. New Haven: Yale University Press.

Shaw, Rosalind, Lars Waldorf, and Pierre Hazan, eds. 2010. *Localizing Transitional Justice: Interventions and Priorities after Mass Violence*. Stanford, CA: Stanford University Press.

Speed, Shannon. 2007. 'Exercising Rights and Reconfiguring Resistance in the Zapatista Juntas de Buen Gobierno'. In Mark Goodale and Sally Engle Merry (eds.), *The Practice of Human Rights: Tracking Law between the Global and the Local*. Cambridge: Cambridge University Press.

Storme, Marcel. 2014. 'Reflections on Judicial Independence: Past Achievements and Future Agenda'. In Simon Shetreet (ed.), *The Culture of Judicial Independence: Rule of Law and World Peace*. Leiden: Brill.

Todorova, Maria. 2009 [1997]. *Imagining the Balkans*. New York: Oxford University Press.

CHAPTER FIVE

THE ENDURING TRANSITION

Temporality, Human Security, and Competing Notions of Justice Inside and Outside the Law in Bosnia and Herzegovina

Sari Wastell

> *We are in the waiting room of history and justice. And let me tell you, that train is not just delayed. It isn't coming.*
> —Academic from Tuzla[1]

INTRODUCTION

February 2014 saw what was anachronistically referred to as a 'Bosnian Spring'. It was a political uprising that crossed the ethnic lines that were indelibly inscribed during the conflicts of the 1990s to demand accountability from politicians and an end to crony capitalism and extraordinary levels of corruption. In short, it was a heartfelt cry that insisted that injustice be understood as more than the misfortunes of a post-conflict society, but that those injustices be recognized as either passive or orchestrated injustices (Shklar 1990). These injustices, the ethics of governance that were being interrogated by the uprising, were perceived as an outcome not only of national governance but of a political ontology wrought by global governance (see Chapter 4, this volume). From factory workers to student activists, from pensioners to ex-conscripts, the perceptions of where to site the sources of injustice was not as localized as some might have hoped it would have been. It betrayed what Dabashi has elsewhere called 'the Goliath of a world so mercilessly cast in the logic of its own madness' (2015: 53) that 'imperial cosmopolitanism' (p. 288) had rendered injustice and trauma the norm – a simple state of affairs to be managed (Husanović 2015), not something to be overcome.

From my previous research across eighteen field sites in the country (in the context of a comparative four-year project with Spain funded by the European Research Council), the Bosnian Spring was not a surprise. 'Transitional justice', pioneered and enacted as a sort of peace-building experiment in Bosnia-Herzegovina, had never sufficiently addressed socioeconomic justice and many of the things that our hundreds of informants claimed would make social reconciliation remotely possible, if indeed that should even be the operative phrase. Instead, a disenfranchised, disillusioned, and demoralized population watched silently as privatization and corrupt ethno-nationalist elites oversaw what I have called here the 'enduring transition'. It is a transition that does not query where history is or should be going, and as a result, a transition without any seeming end. The international community that crafted the post-Yugoslav peace through the Dayton Accord threw money into Bosnia and Herzegovina (BiH) with abandon, but with little concern for citizens' priorities and an unexpected complicity with the politicians who ignored the very people they were elected to serve.

The uprising was a wake-up call. It gave way to the Plenum movement, public assemblies, and the questioning of procedural democracy over actual substantive democracy (Sarajlić 2014). It also queried what the very notion of participation in efforts to realize social justice might possibly look like and the various modalities through which those efforts could be realized, co-opted, subverted, or re-conceptualized. Finally, it put a spotlight on how development – post-conflict reconstruction – had been rather a sham for nearly twenty years.

Then came the floods. Terrible floods. Politicians did little or nothing. In Banja Luka, as the riverbanks were already being breached, some carried on with a scheduled lunch at the finest hotel, just managing to get to their Audis and BMWs before the streets were over-run with water. After nearly half the country was submerged, land mines (120,000 estimated still extant) were shifted by floods and landslides, and nearly a million people affected by the catastrophe, citizens across the former Yugoslavia, found sufficient solidarity to stand in for their government(s). The plenum movement in BiH proved a major platform for the rapid disaster response that the government could not offer. And to those in the country, in the diaspora, and observers long associated with the country and its painful political limbo, there seemed a moment in which the unanticipated confluence of the pro-tests, plenum movement, and floods was beginning to signal a long-awaited sea change that only BiH and its historical and cultural resources might have been able to initiate (Bieber and Brentin 2019). For a brief moment, the misfortune of mass flooding, enunciated in water and mud and re-traumatization, told the story of injustice that would give rise to the call for an 'Un-bribeable Bosnia' (Arsenejević et al. 2014).

The protest movement and the plenums that proceeded them exhibited certain extraordinary characteristics from the outset, charac-teristics that set them apart from other protest movements that have taken place in myriad social settings in recent years. Within days of an explosion of street activity marked at times by violent clashes and the burning of buildings, it became clear that despite precipitous orders of rubber bullets and the bellicose talk of national politicians (and many representatives of the international community alike), it was uniquely within the purview of various members of the protest itself to control the violence and channel frustrations into the creation of public, political fora. Injustice would be channelled in terms of reference not countenanced by the international community, the European Union, or national politicians. In other words, the protesters self-organized and acted like a state, controlling the use of violence and defying the state's classic monopoly on the power to punish by articulating new means for an expression of shared outrage. The movement also quickly took on the resemblance of a social charter – albeit an implicit one. Perhaps the most striking images in the aftermath of the violence that erupted in Tuzla were the news broadcasts the following day, where protesters gathered across the city to – literally – clean up the mess they had made. Both on television interviews and in my own fieldwork, people who had been party to the burning of buildings and cars shrugged and said that as this was *their* city, or *their* country, so it was *their* responsi-bility to return it to order. Poignantly, more than one activist explained to me that this might be the best way to teach corrupt politicians what accountability really looked like. And heartbreakingly and inspiringly (in equal measures), it was that undercurrent of social responsibility and the very sorts of solidarity it could mobilize that would respond most dramatically to the devastating floods of May 2014.

This piece aims to investigate (1) what the 'state of exception' (Agamben 2005) in Bosnia and Herzegovina entails, what is unique about it and the time politics (Greenhouse 1996) to which it gives rise;

(2) the extent to which law over-determines how international and local politicians alike are able to inscribe and misread more 'grassroots' understandings of injustice; (3) how these over-looked or ignored registers of injustice are politically realized and mobilized to further the ends of local political actors; and (4) whether Bosnia and Herzegovina exhibits certain capacities for political improvisation, given its varied past under the socialist Tito regime, the Austro-Hungarian empire, and the Ottoman empire that might suggest how incommensurable political ontologies can reconfigure not only efforts at post-conflict solidarity-building, but new formulations of political, economic, and social imaginaries. Inevitably and admittedly, much of what follows will be more provocative than conclusive.

TAKING EXCEPTION, BUYING TIME

The ascendency of 'transitional justice' as the pre-eminent form of peace-building in post-conflict societies is presumed to be self-evidently linear and progressive. While what one is transitioning from and to often remains un-enunciated, I would argue it is always tacitly presumed to be a move *forward*, away from the affective, 'primordial', and/ or 'ethnic' allegiances that are believed to have sown the seeds of conflict, *toward* the order of the rule of law, market capitalism, and democracy. 'Transitional justice' is, in part, the fantasy of a progressive chronology for civilization and, in that sense, perhaps the newest guise of modernization theory.

In Bosnia and Herzegovina, the limbo of the last twenty-plus years of 'enduring transition' gives the lie to this temporal conceptualization of 'transitional justice' in a number of ways. BiH is often referred to as the laboratory of 'transitional justice,' and the lab rats – those Bosnians who are familiar with the term 'transitional justice' – by and large understand it to be an oxymoron. The sense of stagnation is overwhelming. Despite the constant frenzy of activity on the part of both international actors and local politicians, most people feel that very little changes or improves. The most noticeable change for your average Sarajevan taxi driver is the burgeoning fad for building shopping malls in which the vast majority of Bosnian citizens can ill afford to shop. Indeed, the plethora of shopping malls erected in past years in Sarajevo alone could be said to be an index of how affective the 'orderly' rule of capitalism actually is. As a senior advisor at BiH NATO Headquarters put it in the context of a discussion about human security in BiH, 'Capitalism is equal conditions, not equality. Post war capitalism is the worst one. It isn't either.' Many of the interventions introduced to bring order to a still volatile BiH have had the opposite effect; they have resigned the country to a temporal stalemate. Where war is *supposed* to be the exception and the end of war a return to normalcy (a before/during/after trajectory like the Aristotelian linear arc of action), the stalemate that concluded BiH's war(s) of the 1990s persists, allowing the war to continue by other means indefinitely. If the international community can claim success by the absence of armed conflict in BiH for more than two decades, it has perhaps come at the price of ever realizing the transition either they or the Bosnians envisaged.

Why should this be so? What is so very exceptional about BiH's ongoing 'state of exception'? And how have the practices of 'transitional justice' in BiH unwittingly conspired with the agendas of local elites to consolidate their power in this 'waiting room of justice'?

Gross and Ní Aoláin argue that the very idea of 'exception' is based on a problematic 'assumption of separation' (2006: 171). 'Success here is measured not only in the ability to overcome grave threats and dangers, but also in the ability to confine the application of extraordinary measures to extraordinary times, insulating periods of normalcy from the encroachment of vast emergency powers' (p. 171). This observation seems to settle where the authors stand with respect to two relevant ongoing debates: (1) the debate around Agamben's (2005) use of the term 'exception' and (2) the dispute about the fundamental nature of 'transitional justice' among practitioners and academics alike.

In terms of the former, the authors contend that 'states of exception' are not the absence of law, that is, law suspending itself in favour of the management of the exceptional moment by other means. Rather, it suggests a scenario in which law creates the juridical ground to instantiate a new and enduring version of what counts as 'normal'. Gross and Ní Aoláin (2006) offer numerous examples from around the world, including the United States' 'Patriot Act' of 2001. This act, providing for extraordinary emergency powers in the face of 'the war on terror' post-9/11, had a 'sunset provision', a date on which the law would cease to be in force. However, instead of the act becoming redundant, a further piece of legislation was passed in 2005, abrogating only the part of the act that allowed for the 'sunset provision'. As such, the act remains in force indefinitely, requiring a further piece of legislation to repeal it.

As for the latter, the authors' discussion of 'exception' offers an implicit answer to the fundamental question: Is 'transitional justice' about trying to maintain 'normal' law and order (and the version of 'justice' they underwrite) in extraordinary times, *or* is it about creating extraordinary law and order to suit extraordinary circumstances? The vast majority of commentators on this question tend to agree that the objective is to maintain a measure of normalcy in contexts that mitigate against such a goal. However, when Gross and Ní Aoláin observe that 'as emergencies become more prolonged and less exceptional, it becomes harder to argue for a business as usual approach since it is clear that much is "not usual"' (2006, 173), one can extrapolate from their observation that, equally, what constitutes 'law', 'order', and 'justice' in the wake of mass atrocity might necessarily be subject to changes in the terms of reference that define 'normal' as well.

The prosecution of war crimes under international criminal law, discussed below, seems equivocal on this point. Is it 'ordinary' legal activity applied to extraordinary instances of violence, or is it an extraordinary form of legal activity designed to address the unique needs of unimaginable forms of criminality? On the one hand, these trials see the application of rule of law tenets employed in domestic fora (due process, the principle of legality, no retroactivity, etc.) with reference to international customary law to adjudicate on the existence of criminal transgression and the culpability of the accused. As Mark Drumbl puts it, '[i]n the end, the architecture of the special field of mass violence is little more than an expropriation of domestic methodologies ... already assailed for their suitability to ordinary individual crime and all the more ill-fitting for cases of extraordinary international crime' (2005: 545). However, what actually internationalizes a crime?[2] After all, these are understood to be 'international' crimes, even though the acts involved are already delineated as criminal in 'ordinary' domestic settings. Srebrenica, for example, was not tried in the various cases in front of the International Criminal Tribunal for the Former Yugoslavia (ICTY) as eight thousand 'ordinary' murders, but as genocide carried out through acts of murder. Even in lay terms, one does not think there is much that is 'ordinary' about genocide.

However, Drumbl, although offering a critique of international criminal law and therefore focusing on a different constellation of concerns from Gross and Ní Aoláin, offers a parallel critique to that of Gross and Ní Aoláin on the 'assumption of separation'. He notes that 'the perpetrator of mass atrocity fundamentally differs from the perpetrator of ordinary crime. The fulcrum of this difference is that, whereas ordinary crime tends to be deviant in the times and places it is committed, the extraordinary acts of individual criminality that collectively lead to mass atrocity are not so deviant. In fact, these acts of individual criminality may support a social norm even though they transgress a *jus cogens* norm' (2005: 549–550).

So the belief that what is normal and what is exceptional are objectively distinct is a red herring from the outset. Any anthropologist would expect no less. The law can itself re-configure what is to be recognized as normal, even as flashpoints in history can reshape what a society believes to be normal, requiring legal innovations. Nowhere could such observations prove more salient than in the context of post-conflict BiH.

In BiH, a war was ended in a legally imposed stalemate. Democracy was introduced through a constitutional dispensation that allows for a tripartite presidency along ethnic lines, stalling all forms of politics at the national level, and persisting in contravention to European Human Rights law.[3] Neo-liberalism and capitalism were installed through the privatization of collectively owned apartment blocks and factories, causing massive changes in the disparity of wealth across the population (amplified by an influx of politically motivated foreign investment and the ramifications of war profiteering and ongoing corruption). And the rule of law was established in the midst of a bewildering state of exception that made BiH a protectorate in all but name. As Paula Pickering writes:

> [a]t a meeting of the Peace Implementation Committee in Bonn in December 1997, the UN High Representative won extraordinary powers enabling him to override Bosnian institutions to pass legislation and to remove from domestic office domestic officials obstructing implementation of the peace plan. After Bosnian officials failed to agree on basic decisions – such as a common currency or property laws that comply with international standards – the High Representative decreed the necessary legislation. By one count, the UN High Representative had imposed by fiat more than five hundred decisions between 1997 and the end of 2003.
>
> (citing Knaus and Martin 2003) (2007: 48)

The difficulty is that the Dayton Agreement, like much of the imposed legal changes that followed it, has no 'sunset provision', but created a de-centralized, politically divided state in which the repeal of these laws, much less changes to the country's constitution, are all but impossible.

The Dayton Accord was an effort at buying time that now allows the ethno-nationalist politicians to buy time in perpetuity. What I want to argue in this chapter is that international crisis management in BiH turns on an ahistorical dyad of the time of affect versus the time of order. This temporal rendering mistakes the aims of the war and its modus operandi for the cause of the war. In so doing, it helps to complete the work of the conflict and plays into the hands of ethno-nationalist politicians who benefit tremendously from a transition without end. I also want to suggest that it is the very practices of securitization – and their decoupling from issues of development, where European security sector reform has increasingly viewed the two as mutually constitutive (Albrecht et al. 2010) – that creates this temporal caesura. This is not misfortune; this is injustice that is felt in the variety of registers that are unique to the history of Bosnia and Herzegovina. Those registers index both exceptional constraints and striking potential for re-fashioning both the country's history and acting as an exemplar for 'local', national authorship of post-conflict transition elsewhere.

LEGAL INSCRIPTIONS

The Dayton Accord created a territorially disjointed country that would be reflected in its political and juridical systems. It comprises two entities, Republika Srpska and the Federation of BiH, together with the anomaly of Brčko District, as no agreement could be reached about it back in 1995 (Bose 2002). Inside of the Federation, there also exist ten cantons, and in each territorial sub-division there is usually a clear ethnic bias that translates into ethnic political representations. Because the peace-makers clearly believed that these age-old enmities were the cause of the conflict(s), the peace designed was meant to offer sovereignty to each of the three 'constitutive' nations. One was no longer 'Bosnian', but rather Serb-Bosnian (presumed to be Orthodox), Croat-Bosnian (presumed Catholic), or Bosniak-Bosnian (presumed Muslim). Each nation would elect a president and send their representative to Sarajevo, where political gridlock would be inevitable. Changes to the constitution would never prove in the best interests of any of the three nations, as these politicians have only their constituencies to whom they must answer, not an entire post-conflict nation-state. There are no national interests in the politics of BiH; there are only local interests over-determined by the ethnic majority that resides there. As the author Aleksandar Hemon commented, 'the country is divided, both as a territory and as a state, among nationalist bureaucrats that bargain over and trade its broken parts, its unenforceable laws, the debris of its future.... What appears as inept madness is in fact a method' (2012). All the rulers have to do is evidence the extent to which they can hold onto power inside of their constituencies. Thus Dayton, and the constitutional dispensation that it ushered in, acts as the founding moment when law inscribed the fusion of the ethnic/religious/political and materialized them into social forms of politico-juridical rule – the very forms that preclude the transition from war-torn country to functioning nation-state. 'The war in Bosnia and Herzegovina was bad, but the peace has turned out to be ridiculous and demeaning' (Hemon 2012).

The 'national' legal system that this created is labyrinthine and inscrutable to most – foreigners and Bosnian citizens alike. There are fourteen separate jurisdictions: one at national level, two at entity level, ten at cantonal level, and then a de facto jurisdiction in Brčko District, which is run by a foreign administrator and has its own ministries and courts, just as the entities and cantons do. As with the multiple parliaments and ministries that mirror the court system, there is very little effective control at the national level.[4] In terms of public provision, the legal system is a sort of postcode lottery. A pregnant woman in the Sarajevo canton might be legally entitled to approximately twice the maternity leave as her counterpart in Zenica canton, some forty minutes away. And such disparities, existing at the entity level (both Sarajevo and Zenica cantons are inside the Federation of BiH), are exacerbated between entities, where law in Republika Srpska resists any harmonization with the Federation. The sum result is a burgeoning number of human rights violations and a paucity of confidence in the legal 'system' on the part of almost all of the BiH population. Courts will not enforce decisions taken on the same matter by other courts (including appeals to the European Court of Human Rights). There is no integrated and hierarchical route of appeal that would contribute to a coherent rule of law system in the country. And regular citizens understand their legal system to be more of an impediment to realizing justice than justice's vehicle. The solecistic legal 'system' in BiH is not simply inchoate; it is a fully realized and completed chaos.

114

In fairness, one would be hard pressed to include the Dayton Accord, subsequent accords, and the political and legal systems they instantiated as part of 'transitional justice' efforts in BiH. They were peace-building interventions, and while peace-building shares much common ground with 'transitional justice', each operates under very separate rubrics and each faces a distinct array of challenges. Dayton was simply meant to stop a war and to act as the starting point from which the implementation of 'transitional justice' initiatives might proceed.

However, there is no doubt that one form of legal activity has overshadowed all other elements of 'transitional justice' work in BiH –in terms of both the resources dedicated to it and the extent to which the successes and failures of 'transitional justice' in BiH are often measured. This would be the (some Bosnians would say) disproportionate attention given to the prosecution of war crimes, both nationally and at the International Criminal Tribunal for the former Yugoslavia (ICTY) in The Hague.

Let me say from the outset that these observations are neither congratulatory nor disparaging in terms of the work of the ICTY, its public perception in BiH, or its relationship to 'transitional justice' in that country. There are sufficient texts to which one can refer that offer poignant critical analyses of international criminal law (ICL) generally (e.g., Tallgren 2002; Campbell 2004; 2007; Drumbl 2005; 2007), the work of the ICTY in relation to BiH's still nascent democracy and judicial capacity specifically (Nettlefield 2010; Chehtman 2011), and the possible rationales for many people's disillusionment with the Tribunal inside the country (Hodzić 2010). My commentary is simply to amplify the many appraisals of ICL already out there from an 'extra-legal' perspective and one based on the specificities of long-term field-work in BiH.

The painful reality is that the vast majority of people who survived the conflicts visited upon BiH (and its environs) in the 1990s simply do not feel that this legal activity addressed their sense of injustice and how these injustices were rendered in both the past of the conflicts and the present of the 'enduring transition'. Indeed, many feel the legal frenzy around prosecuting war criminals actually distracted from current injustices with which people had to wrestle and gave license to a commitment to recognize injustice solely in terms of legal infractions – and only those infractions that the law thought worthy of address. What maybe should have been addressed is two-fold: (1) the unhappy truth that in an entirely under-examined fashion, the work of ICL prosecutions could not help but reinscribe ethnic *difference*, which is all too easily elided with ethnic *division*, and (2) that social justice as conceived from the perspective of those deemed the recipients of the munificence of international criminal tribunals was not simply ignored, but perceived as an impediment to an international agenda that was convinced had a corner on the market of knowledge production in the service of building a durable peace in BiH.

It is, to my mind, one of the great tragedies and under-examined short-comings of international humanitarian law, inherent in its definitions, requirements, and real-life practices, that it necessarily undermines one of the four cornerstones of human security – freedom from domination along ethnic, national, racial, or religious grounds. In reiterating the initial violence of the war – imposed and enforced ethnic determination of one's identity and therefore wartime experiences– war crimes trials (at least in the context of BiH) actually ensure that the only way to create 'cultural security' after conflict is to create laws that further entrench the 'objective reality' of ethnic division and allow for shared sovereignty along uncontestable ethnic lines. The aggregation of indictments, testimony, and judgments from the ICTY transform into the congeries of an intractably ethnicized body politic.

One has to ask, where is the justice in that, and very especially in the quotidian experiences of day-in, day-out life? If one's identity as a 'victim' (and the law insists on such categorizations as well) is a matter determined by the subjective gaze of the perpetrator, if that perpetrator might still run the local bakery, if being an ethnicized victim is the only thing that both makes you obscenely vulnerable – politically and economically – and gives you the platform to make any kind of claim, injustice will inevitably take root in the stalls of a trauma market wrought of legal inscriptions. What else can one actually trade on under such circumstances? As Rama Mani noted, 'the task of development in transitional societies has not been viewed by development economists and peace-builders as an issue of justice. This is clear from the way in which post-conflict economic reconstruction packages are drawn up, with concerns of social justice and inequity being almost non-existent' (2008: 264). Put another way, more poignantly by the poet Adisa Basić:

> Aren't you just a victim
> selling your own trauma?
> asked the Harvard blonde

with the brains worth half a million.
I couldn't find the words in English to say
Do you have any idea how right you are?
(as quoted in Arsenejević 2010: 176)

POLITICAL REALIZATIONS

You know when things will change? – when more than 60% in BiH stay hungry. As long as you have something to eat, a quarter of the bread and something to spread over . . . – and they [the political elites] are deliberately keeping us there at the verge.. . . 'Half a metre from the bottom!' If we were at the bottom, we would have pushed ourselves off of it and surfaced somewhere. This way, we just stay half a metre from the bottom.

—Ex-conscript, Nevesinje

It is commonplace in BiH to blame one of two parties – the international community or the cadre of Bosnian politicians and bureaucrats who benefit from the current political impasse. Some blame both, no doubt, but even then, the two respective sources of influence are understood to exist in tension. Each is potentially the other's adversary, even if neither is better than the other.

However, if one takes seriously the proposition that the legal inscriptions discussed above have (and continue to) materialize ethnic *distinctions* and that these distinctions, once realized, are parlayed by local politicians into inveterate *divisions*, then the relationship between the two sources of political influence seems more to fall along a temporal spectrum marked by *shared* practices (Husanović 2011). Rather than imagining the international community and 'local' ethno-nationalist politicians as two radically opposed players pitted against one another in the post-conflict wrestling match to decide BiH's future, it might be better to think of them as relay runners unwittingly running on the same team, the former handing the baton over to the latter in a race without end.

Such a reformulation of the international community–national politics nexus in BiH problematizes the long-standing presumption in human security studies that human security can *either* be pursued in a state-centric fashion, creating robust nation-states that would underpin global governance structures (e.g., Bienefeld 1995) *or* focus on the potential relationship of a global governance structure that protects the security of individuals, bypassing the capacities of the state when and as necessary (e.g., Griffin 1995). 'Transitional justice' in BiH clearly wants to have it both ways, although the once unforeseen ramifications of this continuum approach have been the cause of as many problems as it has solved.

It is little wonder that after the broad expansion of the idea of 'security' introduced by the UNDP's *Human Security Report 1994*, academics and practitioners alike sought to parse what might be the limits of 'human security'. As with the backlash prompted in the decades after the United Nations Declaration on Human Rights, many felt that human security had simply become what Douzinas referred to in the context of human rights as 'the legislation of desire' (2000). Human security, although prompting a yoking of development and security issues (previously conceived in narrow terms, such as territorial defence, military and policing capacity, nuclear deterrence), comes to mean very little if its boundaries remain too elastic and all-encompassing. Somehow, in its ever-expanding remit, human security cannot find a way to countenance the question of context-specific senses of injustice, very especially in post-conflict societies in transition.

In this section of the chapter, I want to explore how the legal inscription of ethnic distinctions has been mobilized by Bosnian politicians and bureaucrats to create disparities in basic provision. Such disparities, always territorially determined by which ethnicity remains dominant in a given area, allow 'majority ethnics' to feel they have a far greater level of provision than they actually do, guaranteeing that their political representatives only have to promise to protect co-ethnic interests in order to maintain fealty. That is the 'human security' side of the coin. At the same time, these politicians leverage the more restrictive conceptualization of 'security' (viz., territorial defence), as disparities in provision fan the flames of potential inter-ethnic unrest. Local politicians, providing little and promising nothing more than to be ready to defend the interests of the 'group', earn plaudits for raising and then dancing with the spectre of revanchism.

The most notorious example of this is probably the OSCE-backed 'two schools under one roof' programme.[5] The logical extension of legal inscription is educational extension to reach and transmit the inevitability of ethnic division in BiH to a new generation. In some parts of Bosnia, children from the same community attend two sets of classes, comprising two different versions of the 'national group of subjects', taught in two separate languages (in post-war BiH, Serbo-Croatian gave way to Bosnian, Croatian, Serbian (B/C/S) as allegedly distinct languages, although they remain mutually intelligible) by two separate sets of teaching staff. In this bizarre educational apartheid, the students are bussed to school separately, have separate classrooms and recreational periods, and often even use separate entrances to the school. Where possible, some schools even try to arrange timetables so the children will take their classes at different times, a bewildering concession to the project of creating ethnic antagonism in a country where most pupils – even in the capital, Sarajevo – attend classes for only half a day due to a lack of classrooms, desks, and basic resources.

Clearly, such an educational model allows for the trans-generational transmission of ethnic division. It also places senses of injustice in a past rather than in the present. Students internalize injustice as a product of the war(s) and not what current political interventions are crafting for their futures. However, speaking with some youths, one realizes that this is not just 'ethnic identity training'. This generation of primary and even secondary school students have no clear memories of the conflict (s) of the 1990s. As such, unlike their elders, they have little inhibition to return to war 'if needs be'. Having never endured the traumas of mass atrocity in their own lifetimes, but inheriting the mantle of trauma that is the inheritance of all Bosnians, the inscription of absolute ethnic incompatibility as a given creates a potential new generation of conscripts, all the more easily manipulated by their leaders than their parents' generation even.

If the 'two schools under one roof' model further concretizes ethnic identity in a new generation, the more mundane practices of political manipulation also address the generation of the parents. In many of these schools, the cost of bussing, school lunches, and extra-curricular activities varies. The municipality can justify it because, although offering one of three versions of the 'national' curricula to students the same age under the same roof, the 'schools' are legally independent institutions. Based on subscription rates, caprice, or mere political mischief, costs for completely similar services will vary depending on which of the schools one attends (i.e., to which ethnic group one belongs).

The Kafkaesque governance of basic service provision often knows no limits. In the small town of Stolac, where our team collected data, interviews, and life histories over two field visits, we asked simple questions about how pensions were provided, legal claims were heard, healthcare ensured. The town was largely mixed before the war, but

'Serb-Bosnians' left early in the conflict and 'Bosniak-Bosnians' were either driven out or interred in the Dretelj concentration camp. At present the town is majority 'Croat-Bosnian' and, like many towns in the region, tends to fly the Croatian national flag from lampposts on the streets and atop the Old Town national monument.

On the subject of pensions, we were informed that things had recently improved. Like the system of health insurance, educational curricula and the like, the pension system remained segregated. This meant that the several hundred retired 'Bosniak-Bosnian' returnees to Stolac had their pensions administered through Mostar, a little less than an hour away. However, Mostar was not able to send retirement checks through the post because Stolac's post office was part of the Croatian postal system (although remember that we are still inside the nation-state of BiH). To collect the cheques, the elderly were required to pay additional fees for special delivery or to travel to Mostar in person.

It is in the banalities of these basic service provision discrepancies, and the accumulated weight they often visit on already vulnerable 'minority ethnic' returnee populations, that local politicians continue to wage the war by other means and maintain undisputed, ethnically biased control. In some instances, even an ethnic majority can fall foul of the ethno-nationalist machine. Take the case of Drvar. Located in the north-western corner of Bosnia almost at the Croatian border, Drvar is testimony to the ravages of post-war inequity. Our team travelled there (and to the very contrasting and vibrant town of Livno) to continue life history work among ex-conscripts. My project manager particularly wanted me to visit there.

Nestled in a site of unparalleled natural beauty sits the ghost town that Drvar has become. Its once thriving timber mills were silent. Factories were closed. The leisure facility, once an attraction to tourists from BiH and Croatia alike, remained decimated. For every store or cafe that we found open, four to five abandoned shopfronts would flank it on either side. The memorial park was overgrown, and its famous monument lay in large pieces surrounded by rubble and the occasional graffiti.

Young people were conspicuously under-represented out on the street or in bars, both during the day and during the night. The out-migration of the younger generation had further exacerbated the town's economic woes and depleted the number of young families willing to live there. The youth football league had recently closed for wont of players.

Drvar has a demographic problem. It is majority 'Serb-Bosnian' in an overwhelmingly majority 'Croat-Bosnian' canton.[6] However, Republika Srpska also has little time for Drvar. Lying outside the entity of Republika Srpska, their votes are inconsequential. The people of Drvar are doubly disenfranchised by the 'shared sovereignty' arrangement that is post-Dayton politics.

The inanition at the belly of Bosnian politics also obscures some of the ethnographic truths of people's lived experiences and memories of the time of conflict versus the current parenthesized time of transition. On the one hand, life history work and interviewing undertaken in eighteen towns and cities across BiH among four different categories of people who would have had particular forms of involvement in the conflict(s) (ex-conscripts and deserters; widows and children of fallen soldiers; medical practitioners; and artists, musicians, and poets whose cultural production responded to the war(s) at the time or whose work currently deals with that past) reveals a startling level of homogeneity in certain respects. Among former soldiers, processes of recruitment, training, wartime conditions, involvement in a grey economy (that sought to redistribute and sometimes profit from access to scarce resources), and de-mobilization show little variance, and by and large, this is to be expected. But their accounts of how their war-time involvement was motivated, the sense of manipulation and betrayal that many express after the fact, their impressions of foreigners and foreign intervention, and the sense of the possibilities and obstacles to social reconciliation across ethnic lines were incredibly similar as well. So too across our other target groups. While many remained scarred and uncertain about how much they could forgive and forget the wartime traumas visited on them by the 'ethnic other', the actual renderings of what they had seen and endured, and their feelings about it after the fact, seemed often to fall into the same register.

On the other hand, where one did see variation in the retelling of these personal histories happened not across ethnic lines but across the vagaries of territorial lines – much like the story of Drvar. For example, to be a 'Croat-Bosnian' in Široki Brijeg during 'their' war was not only an entirely different experience from being a 'Croat-Bosnian' on the northern borders of BiH (perhaps eight to ten hours away), but it was also an entirely different experience from being a 'Croat-Bosnian' in Mostar during their siege – a twenty-minute drive away. The crux of these differences came from mapping the particularities of the contemporary conflict onto much longer, locally specific historical trajectories, where past abuses, prejudices, and misappropriations shaped the contours of current experiences – past traumas and previous emblems of shared local pride informed current senses of aggrievedness or superiority.

It may well be common currency to bemoan the existence of three separate histories of the conflict(s), of three different versions of the 'truth' about what happened. But I submit that accepting that overly facile 'problem' once again capitulates to the ethno-nationalist project of ethnic division. The political realization of materializing ethnic distinctions has been by and large completed in almost every form of governance imaginable in BiH. All that is left to ensure the perpetuation of the 'enduring transition' is a mode of management of memory and of trauma that disallows any breaching of the boundaries of ethnic affect.

TIMES OF TRAUMATIC SECURITY

> I feel that we have another war now – the economic situation and the unhealthy interpersonal relations, because people are over-traumatized. People are disappointed in society. Why am I telling you this? For example, if you happened to fall or trip during the war, at least ten people would run to help you. Today, you can see a man collapsing on a bus and not many would approach him. That's a consequence of the war. People suffer from PTSD, they are disappointed in people, society – in everything! – and they think 'I helped people in the war, I lost a part of my body, and I didn't get anything for it, and now I'm suffering. SO?'
> —Nurse from Sarajevo, who worked in the
> war hospital during the siege before she
> had a chance to leave high school

The quote above is more than a bit typical. Teenagers in Sarajevo (and elsewhere) grew up very fast in 1992, conscripted into the army, educated in basements, trying to go to clubs between sniper fire, cut off entirely if they lived in a neighbourhood like Grbavica or Dobrinja. The nurse quoted above was cut off for some time from Sarajevo proper, as she lived in the municipality of Ilidža, in Hrasnica. As she puts it, 'Sarajevo and Hrasnica were like two different states in the wartime. We almost couldn't go to the city, until later when they opened the tunnels.'

Three years without electricity, running water, basic food supplies, and living in apartments with windows that were boarded up, so neither sunlight nor sniper fire would enter, would traumatize any young person. Of course, in some ways, this was the least of the trauma, as most young people experienced much worse than deprivation. Officially, only boys over the age of eighteen were conscripted. However, we have met and interviewed many who suggested they were at least a bit younger. In any event, volunteers as young as fourteen joined the army; that is clear. Conscripts' mobilization should have involved eight to twelve weeks of intensive basic training (with further training once they were inside their units); some young soldiers told us they had little more than two weeks. And in any event, few families would not have had someone drafted into one of the warring armies and most families would suffer from the deaths, disappearances, torture, rape, and forced relocation that was visited across Bosnian society.

Interviews with medical workers evidence horrific conditions of practice, combined with an outstanding level of professionalism. Many in the medical high school or beginning their medical degrees at university volunteered – with little or no experience and unprepared for what lay ahead. Teenagers attended at surgeries, including amputations, conducted without recourse to anaesthesia. Gauze bandages in the more outlying hospitals were routinely used, then washed and reused. The veterans of this early 'medical training' unanimously report how little infection spread, but note the many hours spent trying to wash and rewash all forms of medical supplies after unendurable shifts. Many took pre-med classes in the basements of the hospitals or ambulatory facilities where they lived and worked, classes that were examined and later recognized as constituting a part of their future degrees.

However, inside the numerous stories of heroism and resistance and survival, there still emerges an uncomfortable truth. While the Sarajevan newspaper *Oslobođenje* continued to publish daily for 'as long as Sarajevo exists' (Kurspahic 1997), while Radio Zid was established and aired with a refusal to be used for any form of war propaganda, while neighbours helped neighbours and the little to be gleaned from grey market economies was often shared out, while young people risked (and often met with) death to carry on something like a normal life, an entire society was being schooled in the legacies of trauma.

What is most remarkable is that travelling across all of Bosnia, speaking to hundreds of people across 'ethnic', generational, gender, socioeconomic, and experiential divides, one common and unanticipated reflection recurs. Many people say that if it hadn't been for the gross level of atrocity that accompanied the conflict(s), things were actually better during the war. I would not say that this is a universally shared narrative (indeed, it is vastly more prevalent in Sarajevo for obvious reasons), but it comes up in the ethnography too often to ignore. People insist that the war was a time when people *had* to band together and help one another – the last dying breath of a lifetime before the divisive politics of consociation.

To be sure, there are numerous stories to support this claim. And while Sarajevo gives an un-representational aperture on this topic, it is not alone in testifying to the numerous Bosnians (and other citizens across the former Yugoslavia) who refused to be mobilized along ethnic lines (or, once mobilized, made extraordinary exceptions). There is no doubt that the level of inter-ethnic cooperation that occurred during the conflict(s) is often understated, as it disrupts a narrative convenient to the ethno-nationalist politicians and the international community alike.

However, one also cannot ignore the fact that we are looking at years of conflict that were marked by mass atrocity, genocide, and massacre; the systematic attack on civilian populations; and a contrived strategy of ethnic cleansing and political consolidation along ethno-religious lines. And we also know that the relative 'successes' of such a strategy were contingent on widespread participation in such efforts and a great level of denial on the part of non-participants. How could so many people, then, suggest that things were not only better before the war, but even, were it not for the killing and suffering, that they were better *during* the war?

This is part of a particular memory politics of nostalgia that runs rampant in Bosnia and Herzegovina at present. There is a nostalgia for the pre-war period, the freedom of travel afforded citizens of a non-aligned state, a freedom – let's say, security – bought at the price of being precariously neither East nor West during the Cold War. But what it was to be non-aligned and be courting too many allies is not often remembered. There is a nostalgia for the charisma of Tito, notwithstanding the many brutalities with which he could be credited. When university students and young adults (some of them war veterans) sing the old songs from those days at a venue like Kino Bosna in Sarajevo, it is far more an act of forgetting than an act of remembrance. What is remembered is the level of employment, the sense of community, shared ownership of apartment blocks and factories, although data might suggest that the former Yugoslavia was not exactly a 'people's paradise'. However, there is no doubt that the aftermath of the war brought abrupt and violent economic injustices and that the international community failed to realize the full impact of these rapid changes for a traumatized society being forced to imagine what social reconciliation might look like.

So what I want to suggest here, is that, for large swathes of the Bosnian population, the concept of justice and security that remains implicit in their day-to-day lived existences turns on the binary of order–affect – just as it does for the international community. However, the ethnography tells us an interesting twist in this story. From the top-down or external–internal perspective (i.e., from the ethnography conducted among members of the so-called international community), the concept of security suggests that affect was the cause of the conflict (s) and order the natural solution. For many Bosnians, the pre-war and even wartime period is portrayed as a time of order – *security* – that has been replaced by irrational, affective, and alienating times. For Bosnians, Weber got the chronology all wrong.

These are the times of traumatized security, the result of an ongoing temporal limbo, which keeps peoples' lives on hold and allows for a collective revisionist history. While there are officially at least three versions of the history of the conflict(s) – and, as I have suggested elsewhere, I think there are many more, they prove inconvenient to the collusion of ethno-nationalist politicians and the international community, who legitimize the enduring transition on the grounds of an intransient tripartite ethnic divide – what is shared is a politics of nostalgia that feeds the temporal void of the present. This politics of nostalgia presumes that a time of order was lost in the 1990s, giving way to the current sense of paralysis and stagnation, which is itself 'a temporality of danger' – and injustice. What it cannot allow for is a space for any real, emancipatory politics, since like its inversion (the past was affective, and the present is becoming orderly) it is based on a magical thinking enacted through what Kieran McEvoy has termed 'magical legalism' (2007: 421).

As argued above, the peace that was built was not orderly in its implementation, nor does it exhibit much order in its daily practice at present. 'Justice' as invoked by ordinary persons is what gets lost in translation. And likewise, history tells us that acts of genocide and mass persecution of all types tend to be orderly in their execution. What we see at present is the great mischief of a temporal binary, shared by a wide variety of actors, but whose sequencing remains contested. The order–affect binary is an unhelpful and overly facile rendering of the concepts of both justice/injustice and security in post-conflict Bosnia and Herzegovina. But it is the dissonance – not in the conceptualization of security as order versus affect but in the apportionment of which is cause and which is effect – that allows for the traumatized time of security that is Bosnia's enduring transition.

The 'enduring transition' that has marked BiH's twenty-plus years of post-conflict transition exhibits a wide chasm between a legally over-determined idea of justice imposed by the international community and the conceptualizations of socioeconomic justice, solidarity-building, and practices of the 'everyday' among a national community wrestling with the legacies of wartime atrocity. Unanticipated and underexamined complicities between an international community dedicated to the modus operandi of 'transitional justice', on the one hand, and the divisive in-fighting of ethno-nationalist politicians, on the other, have overshadowed the needs and efforts of the very people both parties claim to represent and serve. For many, what has been lost in these failing experiments at building a durable peace is a true invocation of justice itself.

CONFRONTING THE COSTS AND BENEFITS OF RESILIENCE-BASED POLICY

Let's return to the floods. Let's return to the generation that is either ready and prepared to bear arms again or to self-organize as a state. Either path is not a matter of 'misfortune' or solely the transgenerational transmission of trauma. This is a generation that has been schooled in the lexicon of inevitability, and they have either embraced that emotional vocabulary or rejected it with an impressive ferocity. At the time of the floods spoken about in the introduction, approximately 500 students from the University of Sarajevo organized to offer a rapid disaster response. They requested the loan of rafts from a tourist operation in Konjic, on the Neretva River; free shovels, spades, and wheelbarrows from OPI (a home improvement/gardening franchise); and free passage on buses to the north on Centrotrans. While the specific details cannot be verified, to be sure, the level of cooperation was much noted at the time (potentially lending to exaggeration), and there exist diaries that do substantiate the extraordinary level of grass-roots organization, from even the youngest parts of the society.

On the one hand, one can see the plenum movement, its aftermath (the Workers' University) and the 'local' reaction to the floods of 2014 as what is now lauded as the ascendency of 'resilience-based policy'. To be certain, I am in no doubt that there are lessons to be learnt from how BiH seems extraordinarily well equipped to deal with its 'enduring transition' through political improvisations that draw from its varied past as much as from its current frustrations. However, I also want to sound a note of caution.

I suppose that in a perfect world, 'everyday life' is 'neither conceived of as a problem nor romanticised as "resisting", but seen as providing a problem-solving resource of practices to be drawn upon' (Chandler 2014: 29). To the extent that that could prove true, much of the world has a great deal to learn from Bosnia and Herzegovina. However, one also has to be concerned about the possibility that 'resilience-based policy' tends to give political actors at the national, regional, and international levels a sort of 'get-out-of-jail-free card'. When one relies on the tenacity and creativity of 'local' evocations of justice, one has to be equally certain of two things: first, that such evocations of justice can sufficiently confront the temulent tides of political contrivances acting on other scales of engagement and, second, that those other, 'overseeing' actors will back up their endorsement of 'resilience' by structural and material means.

Certainly, in Bosnia and Herzegovina, a new-found celebration of civil society initiatives belies the abandonment of civil society immediately after the conflicts *and* the later distrust that national and international politicians have had for civil society when their resilience seems to go off script.

When we think back to the floods and the plenum movement (and their aftermaths), we bear witness to the absence of socioeconomic justice as a constituent part of a 'transitional justice' process. When we look to current calls for resilience-based policy to remedy this blind spot – in the absence of the necessary resources and only countenanced within terms of reference that do not critically confront the 'transitional justice' agenda – we are looking not solely at a caesura between disparate political epistemologies, but at ontological incommensurabilities about what 'justice' might mean and what it might look like. As Miller has aptly noted (but not specifically in the context of BiH), 'by leaving economic development, issues of resource distribution or inequality of power or wealth to separate courts or to executive control, transitional justice institutions implicitly tell society that development and conflict may be separated in fair fashion and that inequality itself is not to be prosecuted or amnestied' (2008: 268). Miller later adds: 'the same mistakes may easily be perpetuated, in a way that bespeaks not a conspiracy of interests but a coherence of blindness' (p. 272). It is the diagnosis of that blindness that needs to be addressed.

For my part, I would strongly argue that the blindness is symptomatic of an ontological incommensurability. (I would hasten to add that I think such incommensurabilities can be wildly productive and create the ground for new 'subjunctive politics', but that is outside the remit of this conclusion.) The competing notions of justice at play in the post-plenum moment of Bosnia and Herzegovina's 'enduring transition' stem from very distinct experiences and understandings of the conflicts and the transition that proceeded from them. As between the international community and 'local' actors on the ground, the parties are trying to apprehend – and *realize* – justice through apertures that, for the time being, seem not to be accommodated by the same camera. As Bubandt noted in the context of security concerns more generally, 'the imple-mentation of the statist idea of security [has] encountered local uni-verses containing ontological notions of safety and uncertainty that often accommodated and undermined the security project of the New Order rule in unexpected ways' (2005: 276). The current political dispensation of BiH offers empirical testimony to that observation.

The state of exception in Bosnia and Herzegovina is exceptional in many ways. Whereas anthropologists have elsewhere suggested that concerns about security can be understood in the need to ensure durable social reproduction (Holbraad and Pedersen 2013), the notion that such an idea could underwrite a security or transitional agenda in BiH is risible. Where the international community sees preceding 'durable social reproduction' as the cause of conflict, and local actors return to known social resources from socialist, pre-capitalist times, with an eye toward innovation and critique (in a way that terrifies the 'State Order' – national and international alike), the idea that human security could be 'defined as the absence both of threat and of sudden and hurtful disruptions in the pattern of everyday life' (Paris 2001: 89) becomes something of a nonsense. What people want is *change*. Indeed, the more important observation is that 'the politiciza-tion of security entails the constant manufacture of uncertainty' (Bubandt 2005: 280). In BiH, law's overdetermination of security and transition and its inability to relate to grassroots efforts to find a platform for emancipatory politics has been more than frustrating. Those unrecognized registers of justice both refuse the manufacture of uncertainty and look to unique capacities inside the society for political improvisation. From the occupation and reopening of factories to the entrenched refusal in some municipalities to privatize public resources, from the plenum movement and the immediate disaster response of civilians to the Worker's University and the Alternative Economic Platforms that preceded it, what outside observers can witness is not solely a reimagining of a *shared* world, but the assertion of a world, ontologically distinct in its everyday experience, that finds the manufacture of enduring uncertainty a folly for which it can no longer spare its time. Were outsiders to this apposite world of the enduring transition willing to take a leap of faith and offer the structural and material support necessary, perhaps these apposite evocations of justice might offer a model for the 'what if' – *subjunctive* – politics that so much of the world requires – not only Bosnia and Herzegovina.

Notes

1 This chapter is based on analysis of four years of fieldwork in Bosnia and Herzegovina undertaken for the European Research Council–funded project, 'Bosnian Bones, Spanish Ghosts: "Transitional Justice" and the Legal Shaping of Memory after Two Modern Conflicts'. The schedule for our Bosnia-based field research included twelve interconnected work packages as well as my own ethnography as principal investigator. This chapter in particular reflects (but is not limited to) life history work among four categories of persons, as well as some of the results of twenty-four focus groups that explored perceptions of foreigners and foreign intervention in BiH between 1995 and the present. These focus groups were organized in twelve of the eighteen field sites in which our team worked, where at each site we coordinated one group of laypersons and another of professionals involved with processes of 'transitional justice' (NGO workers, municipal workers, political activists) to address issues of human security concerns over the past twenty-plus years.

2 For the most articulate survey of the various theories about what 'internationalizes' a crime, see Schaack (2008).

3 On 22 December, the European Court of Human Rights, in the case of Sejdić and Finci versus the state of Bosnia and Herzegovina, ruled against BiH. Sejdić, a Roma Bosnian citizen, and Finci, a Jewish Bosnian citizen, cannot be elected to the House of Peoples nor hold one of the three places in the collective state presidency because they are not Serb, Croat, or Bosniak. The judgment noted that this, and the fact that a Serb residing in the Federation Entity or a Bosniak or Croat living in Republika Srpska would be in a similar position, was in violation of Article 14 of the European Convention on Human Rights. Further national elections were not to take place in BiH, pending a change to the constitution and the Election Act (2001). National elections were held less than a year later, in spite of the ruling and without any changes to the electoral system (ECHR application nos. 27996/06 and 34836/06).

4 For a consummate overview of the BiH legal system, see Jasenka Ferizović's working paper on the topic at: www.bosnianbonesspanishghosts.org, accessed 12 February 2012.
5 See Sivac-Bryant (2008) for discussion of educational reform in BiH.
6 Drvar currently sits in Canton 10, colloquially referred to as Livanski Canton. It is one of only two towns (the other being Olovo) in BiH that is currently petitioning to be moved into a neighbouring canton (Una-Sana) to alleviate some of its sense of social and political isolation (with thanks to Jim Marshall, personal communication).

References

Agamben, Giorgio. 2005. *State of Exception*. Chicago: University of Chicago Press.
Albrecht, Peter, Finn Stepputat, and Louise Andersen. 2010. 'Security Sector Reform, the European Way'. In Mark Sedra (ed.), *The Future of Security Sector Reform*. The International Center for International Governance Innovation, 74–87.
Arsenejević, D. 2010. *Forgotten Future: The Politics of Petry in Bosnia and Herzegovina*. Baden-Baden: Nomos.
2014. *Unbribable Bosnia and Herzegovina: The Fight for the Commons*. Baden-Baden: Nomos.
Bantekas, Illias, and Susan Nash. 2007. *International Criminal Law*. London: Routledge.
Barria, Lilian, and Roper, Steven. 2008. 'Judicial Capacity Building in Bosnia and Herzegovina: Understanding Legal Reform beyond the Completion Strategy of the ICTY'. *Human Rights Review* 9: 317–330.
Bieber, F., and D. Brentin. 2019. *Social Movements in the Balkans: Rebellion and Protest from Maribor to Taksim*. Abingdon: Routledge.
Bienefeld, Manfred. 1995. 'Assessing Current Development Trends: Reflections on Keith Griffin's "Global Prospects for Development and Human Society"'. *Canadian Journal of Development Studies* 16: 371–384.
Bose, Sumantra. 2002. *Bosnia after Dayton: Nationalist Partition and International Intervention*. London: Hurst & Company.
Bubandt, N. 2005. 'Vernacular Security: The Politics of Feeling Safe in Global, National and Local Worlds'. *Security Dialogue* 36(3): 275–296.
Campbell, Kirsten. 2004. 'The Trauma of Justice: Sexual Violence, Crimes against Humanity and the International Tribunal for the Former Yugoslavia'. *Social and Legal Studies* 13: 329–350.
2007. 'The Gender of Transitional Justice: Law, Sexual Violence and the International Criminal for the Former Yugoslavia'. *The International Journal of Transitional Justice* 1: 411–432.
Chandler, D. 2014. *Resilience: The Governance of Complexity*. Abington: Routledge.

Chehtman, Alejandro. 2011. 'Developing Bosnia and Herzegovina's Capacity to Process War Crimes: Critical Notes on a "Success Story"'. *Journal of International Criminal Justice* 9: 547–570.

Cryer, Robert, Friman, Hakan, Robinson, Darryl, and Wilmhurst, Elizabeth, 2010. *An Introduction to International Criminal Law and Procedure*, 2nd ed. Cambridge: Cambridge University Press.

Dabashi, H. 2015. *Can Non-Europeans Think?* London: Zed Books.

Douzinas, Costas. 2000. *The End of Human Rights: Critical Legal Thought at the Turn of the Century*. Oxford: Hart Publishing.

Drumbl, Mark. 2005. 'Collective Violence and Individual Punishment: The Criminality of Mass Atrocity'. *Northwestern University Law Review* 99: 539–610.

   2007. *Atrocity, Punishment, and International Law*. Cambridge: Cambridge University Press.

Greenhouse, C. 1996. *A Moment's Notice: Time Politics across Cultures*. Ithaca: Cornell University Press.

Gross, Oren., and Ni Aoláin, Fionnuala. 2006. *Law in Times of Crisis: Emergency Powers in Theory and Practice*. Cambridge: Cambridge University Press.

Hemon, Alexander. 2012. 'National Subjects'. *Guernica: A Magazine of Arts and Politics*. www.guernicamag.com/features/hemon_1_15_12/. Accessed 3 March 2012.

Hodzic, Refik. 2010. 'Living the Legacy of Mass Atrocities: Victims' Perspectives on War Crimes Trials'. *Journal of International Criminal Justice* 8: 113–136.

Holbraad, M., and M. Pedersen. 2013. *Times of Security: Ethnographies of Fear, Protest and Future*. Routledge.

Husanović, J. 2014a. 'Traumatic Knowledge in Action: Scrapbooking Plenum Events, Fermenting Revolt'. In D. Arsenejević (ed.), *Unbribable Bosnia and Herzegovina*. Baden-Baden: Nomos, 145–153.

   2014b. 'Resisting the Culture of Trauma in Bosnia and Herzegovina: Emancipatory Lessons for/in Cultural and Knowledge Production'. In D. Zarkov and M. Glasius (eds.), *Narratives of Justice in and out of the Courtroom – Former Yugoslavia and Beyond*. Springer International Publishing, 147–162.

   2015. 'Economies of Affect and Traumatic Knowledge: Lessons on Violence, Witnessing and Resistance in Bosnia and Herzegovina'. *Ethnicity Studies* 2: 19–35.

Knaus, G., and F. Martin. 2003. 'Travails of the European Raj'. *Journal of Democracy* 14: 60–74.

Kurspahic, Kemal. 1997. *As Long as Sarajevo Exists*. Chicago: Consortium Login Publishers.

Mani, R. 2008. 'Dilemmas of Expanding Transitional Justice, or Forging the Nexus between Transitional Justice and Development'. *The International Journal of Transitional Justice* 2: 253–265.

May, Larry. 2005. *Crimes against Humanity: A Normative Account.* Cambridge: Cambridge University Press.

McEvoy, Kieran. 2007. 'Towards a Thicker Understanding of Transitional Justice'. *Journal of Law and Society* 34(4): 411–440.

2008. 'Beyond Legalism: Towards a Thicker Understanding of Transitional Justice'. *Journal of Law and Society* 34: 411–440.

Miller, Z. 2008. 'Effects of Invisibility: In Search of the "Economic" in Transitional Justice'. *The International Journal of Transitional Justice* 2: 266–291.

Nettelfield, Lara. 2010. *Courting Democracy in Bosnia and Herzegovina: The Hague Tribunal's Impact in a Postwar State.* Cambridge: Cambridge University Press.

Paris, Roland. 2001. 'Human Security. Paradigm Shift or Hot Air'. *International Security* 26(2): 87–102.

Pickering, Paula. 2007. *Peacebuilding in the Balkans: The View from the Ground Floor.* Ithaca, NY: Cornell University Press.

Sarajlić, E. 2014. 'The Perils of Procedural Democracy: A Lesson from Bosnia.' www.opendemocracy.net/en/can-europe-make-it/perils-of-procedural-democracy-lesson-from-bosnia.

Schaack, Beth Van. 2008. 'The Internationalization of Crimes'. Working Papers. Paper 5. http://digitalcommons.lawscu.edu/working/5. Accessed 14 April 2012.

Shklar, J. 1990. *The Faces of Injustice.* New Haven: Yale University Press.

Sivac-Bryant, Sebina. 2008. 'Kozarac School: A Window on Transitional Justice for Returnees'. *The International Journal of Transitional Justice* 2: 106–115.

Tallgren, Immi. 2002. 'The Sensibility and Sense of International Criminal Law'. *European Journal of International Law* 13: 561–595.

PART THREE

EVERYDAY JUSTICE UNBOUND

CHAPTER SIX

TROUBLED CURRENTS AND THE CONTENTIOUS MORAL ORDERINGS OF DRAKES ESTERO

Kathleen M. Sullivan

INTRODUCTION

I explore the idea of 'everyday justice' by examining the ways in which one particular place, Drakes Estero in Point Reyes National Seashore, Marin county, California, USA, has been both justly and unjustly configured with regard to the presence or absence of a small (approximately thirty-one employees), family, owner-operated, wholesale and retail oyster production business. Uncompromising opposition over whether the company should stay or go characterized this conflict, despite a few people suggesting alternative ways of approaching, if not resolving, the conflict. Many more people argued that there was only an 'either' or an 'or': either the oyster company remained or it was demolished, either small-scale food production or wilderness preservation characterize contemporary conservation efforts, either justice would be done or injustice would prevail.

My goal is to refrain from adjudicating the issue of whether or not the US National Park Service should have issued the sought-after permits to the oyster company. The company has now been removed and was the last of several oyster companies located on the same spot in a usage that predated the national seashore. Not a few authors from antagonistic positions have mounted such efforts and still more efforts are forthcoming. What perhaps makes this conflict over Drakes Estero interesting is less the either/or conundrum, and more the way in which competing notions of justice and injustice in this conflict are anchored in competing notions of a coupled 'everyday' and 'place', which for all

135

of their differences are premised on a shared understanding of what Durkheim (1984: 91–96) calls negative or nonintegrative social solidarity. Whose everyday? Whose place? What moral assumptions anchor the different, yet equally heartfelt, concretely defended senses of justice and injustice? And in the larger frame, what forms of civics were enhanced or obviated in the social and legal processes of justice enveloping this conflict?

Following Sarat and Kearns (1999b), I take as my first starting point the idea that justice and injustice are moral notions, embedded in concrete historically and socially situated legal-civic orders. Occupants of different subject positions in any particular civic order are likely to define both justice and injustice differently, a point demonstrated by Hirsch (2010) and the chapters in Sarat and Kearns (1995a; 1999a), Clarke and Goodale (2010) and Brunnegger and Faulk (2016). Bearing in mind that not all subject positions make possible the same experiences, provide access to the same bundles of material and discursive resources, carry the same complex of shifting burdens, I explore the ways that justice and injustice intertwine, implicate and reconfigure each other.

A second starting point for my argument is an observation explored by both Marcus (1995) and Hirsch (2010), and that is a recognition that the mass character of many contemporary issues pertaining to justice complicates and renders problematic the many assumptions about fixed subject positions and face-to-face social relations that serve as the foundation of much of contemporary law. George Marcus (1995) argues that working notions of 'everyday' rest on unchallenged assumptions about the everyday as being anchored in concrete face-to-face social relations, and he further argues that legal representational practices are key to buttressing and reproducing these assumptions, even when these assumptions are simply a powerful illusion. I will return to the ramifications of this representational illusion illuminated by Marcus as I explore what the conflict over Drakes Estero might reveal beyond the either/or conundrum it posed, as I explore what the conflict might reveal about justice and injustice, and what it might reveal regarding contemporary civic engagement. My effort will return us to an observation made by Durkheim (1984) more than a century ago, about the way in which private property regimes militate against any form of integrative social solidarity.

I take as my third key starting point the observation that physical places often anchor claims of justice and claims of injustice in response to the ways in which a particular place is demarcated, entitled, governed, used, accessed, made available, or cordoned off. Place in California is thoroughly configured by courts and laws about property ownership, zoning, and entitlements. Legal meanings of place were centrally important to all sides in the conflict over Drakes Estero. I extend and apply Marcus's critique of the notion of the 'everyday' as a powerful illusion created through socio-legal relations, an illusion that at the same time reinforces these socio-legal relations in cases of torts and mass injury. Place is not Marcus's direct concern; his concern (as is Hirsch's concern) is for the ways in which assumptions about the everyday and face-to-face social relations operate even in socio-legal contexts far removed from the everyday and from face-to-face relations. Like the notion of the everyday, place is a socially made and powerfully convincing idea that often works hand-in-glove with notions about the everyday as being anchored in face-to-face social relations. I argue that Marcus's critique about the powerful illusions created by unquestioned assumptions about 'everyday' social relations can be extended to the notion of 'place' when place, like everyday, is deployed as an unexamined common-sense notion by people engaged in political and legal conflicts over landscapes and land uses. This critique helps illuminate the very truncated range of civics that could and would emerge in this conflict.

In what follows, I begin with a section describing the significant role of the courts and politically contested laws in legally constituting Drakes Estero. I then present a section analytically describing the ways in which the place and the conflict are represented in a still growing archive of official, popular, and scholarly media. In the section following this description of the archive, I delve deeper and closely examine five broadly brushed morally oriented narrative constellations found in the archive. Finally, I consider the implications of notions of 'everyday' and of 'place' for justice and injustice as evinced in this particular conflict.

Arguably, once the Point Reyes peninsula began to be reconceived as a park in the 1930s (Collins 2010: 250–251; Miller Johnson 2010a: 47; Stewart 2010a), and certainly since the late 1950s when actual planning for a national seashore began to take shape (Collins 2010: 236–276), Point Reyes peninsula has been uneasily situated in multiplying registers of materially influential places. These include county, state, and federal government offices; public hearings; mass public petitions; laws; and property transactions. At the same time, Point

Reyes peninsula has also been situated in less influential places, including local ranchers' operations, workers' lives, and the sovereign territories of the Coast Miwok and the Federated Indians of Graton Rancheria. What, I query, are the ramifications for claims of justice and injustice when 'everyday' and 'place' operate in so many different incommensurable registers?

Several other authors in this volume also find themselves grappling with similar social effects in relation to everyday operations of justice in their ethnographic field sites. For example, Chapter 7 examines the ways in which informal legal performatives contribute to the creation of lawful illusions, while Chapters 4 and 5 address the ways in which justice is defined differently by different groups of people engaging with each other in the context of overarching constellations of contemporary conflicts evincing tangled and unfinished histories.

LEGALIZING PLACE

Over the course of two years (2013 and 2014), the US federal courts ultimately decided what kinds of everyday activities would and would not continue at Drakes Estero. In November 2012, the forty-year terrestrial lease or Reservation of Use and Occupancy (ROU) and the Special Use Permit (SUP) obtaining between the federal government (US Department of Interior, National Park Service) and the Drakes Bay Oyster Company situated on the eastern shore of Schooner Bay in Drakes Estero (a large estuary with five bays located on the Point Reyes peninsula, and which drains into Drakes Bay) expired. On this terrestrial site, the oyster company had its nursery, processing, storage, and office facilities; worker housing; picnic tables; parking lot; and retail and wholesale shops. The owner-operated company applied for a ten-year SUP to continue operating once the original ROU expired, which the US National Park Service denied.[1] In December 2012, Kevin Lunny and his company filed for an injunction against the US Department of the Interior and its agency the National Park Service, and for a restraining order to temporarily keep his company open, while the court case was decided. In February 2013, the Superior Court determined that it lacked jurisdiction, opening the door for an appeal (Case No. 12-cv-06134 YGR Dkt89, 2-4-13). In turn, the Ninth Circuit Court of Appeals majority opinion found that the US Secretary of the Interior had discretionary power to make the decision regarding the expiration of the ROU and SUP, and the issuance of a new SUP, and had not violated any legal mandates in exercising their discretionary power (No. 13-15227 D.C. No. 4:12-cv-06134-YGR Opinion, Dkt70-1, 9-3-2013). Although Kevin Lunny's legal team tried, they were unable either to get an *en banc* hearing or to compel the US Supreme Court to hear the case. At that point, the parties were ordered to enter into settlement negotiations. This resulted in Drakes Bay Oyster Company having to vacate the property by the end of 2014 and the US National Park System finishing the clean-up that Lunny could not do (Case No. 12-cv-06134 YGR/DMR, Dkt157, 10-8-14). In January 2015, the US National Park Service began demolishing the remaining structures, removing equipment and shell stock, and documenting the process on the US National Park Service website.[2] These were not the only legal issues concerning the oyster farm, but the 2012 case effectively determined the end of Drakes Bay Oyster Company, the end of the other legal issues, and the future of Drakes Estero as a designated wilderness area.

Significantly, the Court of Appeal's decision concerned administrative practices, not the economic issues, nor the conservation issues, nor the social issues, nor even the scientific data issues that drove the heated controversy on the ground. The courts were in fact expressly concerned about everyday relationships between the judiciary and the agencies and departments of the executive branch.

Bearing in mind that as the oyster company required both a terrestrial site and an estuary grow-out site for its operations, a brief overview of the complex constellation of jurisdictions governing Drakes Estero and the ownership histories of the properties is in order. The Point Reyes National Seashore encompasses several different kinds of designated areas (zones), including a large designated wilderness area (Phillip Burton Wilderness Area), potential wilderness areas, park, beach, and pastoral areas. As one might expect based on the sheer size of the seashore and the property ownership histories within its boundaries, the jurisdictional lay of land is complicated, and its history has been fraught with conflicts, many relevant at least indirectly to the conflict over the issuing of a new SUP for Drakes Bay Oyster Company.

While Drakes Estero proper (the tidal water portion) was designated potential wilderness in 1976 as part of the Phillip Burton Wilderness Area (Public Law 94-544, 18 October 1976), with the removal of the oyster farm, Drakes Estero converted to designated wilderness. The land around much of the estuary is designated as pastoral, with local ranches, including the Lunny ranch, stretching down to the banks of the estuary. Like much land in Point Reyes National Seashore, the terrestrial site of the oyster company was privately owned in 1962 when Point Reyes National Seashore was established. Efforts to get Point Reyes National Seashore established in 1962 can be attributed to the work of local conservationists in Marin and the Bay Area beginning as early as the 1930s (Lage 2010a: I; Stewart 2010a: 231–236) as well as the work of politicians, US National Park Service directors, and county planners (Behr 2010: 113; Collins 2010: 236–276). The boundaries of the national seashore were drawn on the basis of 'watershed and "viewshed" boundaries' (Duddleson 2010: xvi), and on the basis of the peninsula's geology (Collins 2010: 239–254), which complicated management practices and costs (Behr 2010: 115; Duddleson 2010: vi–xviii). The federal money originally allocated to purchase the extensive private holdings within the boundaries ran out, and by 1969 it looked like much of remaining private property would go to real estate developers (Lage 2010b; Miller Johnson 2010b) and logging interests in the southern portions (Stewart 2010a: 262–265).

After the Point Reyes National Seashore was designated, the ranches within the national seashore boundaries occupied a precarious position (Stewart 2010a). The US National Park Service planners thought that the ranches could and should be allowed to stay, but also thought the ranches would disappear with attrition over time (Collins 2010: 257–260). Collins notes the oyster company as an interesting feature but not a contentious presence (p. 257), as does Gilliam (1962) writing for the Sierra Club, which strongly supported the conversion of the Point Reyes peninsula to public land. By 1969–1970, Stewart, a local rancher whose wife was a Marin conservationist, organized the property-owning ranchers (some of the ranches operated on privately held but leased land) to agree to a condemnation clause in the appropriations bill for funds to increase federal acreage in the national seashore, with the tacit understanding that the ranchers would get a fair price for their land and the right to continue their operations through long-term permits and leases (Stewart 2010a: 241–248, 265–267). The agreement to a condemnation clause made the appropriations bill possible (Stewart 2010b: 281–287). Many private holdings were then purchased by the federal government, including the oyster company's private terrestrial site in 1972. According to the US National Park Service (2007: 2), the government leased back the terrestrial site to then owner Charles Johnson, under a forty-year ROU.

Significantly, the ranches did not disappear and instead became part of a now established 'alternative food district', a smaller-scale production and consumption agricultural commodity chain that is not part of the agribusiness industrial complex that dominates California agriculture (Fairfax et al. 2012). Fairfax et al. note: 'The Sierra Club, never fully committed to the working landscape notion, led a successful effort in 1974 [sic] to designate portions of the Point, including most of the pastoral zone as wilderness or potential wilderness' (p. 95). However, as Fairfax et al. also point out, the Point Reyes National Seashore is located in Marin county, which has a strong sense of itself as having separate, clearly defined urban areas, working pastoral areas, and open-space parks, an equilibrium created through long-time countywide planning efforts (pp. 89–174). A founder of the Marin Agricultural Lands Trust (MALT) explained to me that MALT, an institutional fixture in Marin, is dedicated to preserving the ranch lands as working landscapes through the purchase of property rights adhering to the ranch lands (e.g., purchasing and holding the right to subdivide the lot), further preventing ranch land from becoming either urbanized or parkland. Fairfax et al. (2012: 93) point out that an upshot of this ongoing effort to keep ranching, parks and urban development in equilibrium has been the emergence of one of the wealthiest, best-educated counties in the United States and an ever more expensive quality of life in Marin county. That stratification, in both Fairfax et al.'s estimation (2012) and MALT's estimation (interview, Marin county, 2016), threatens the working family owned and operated ranches in Marin.

Kevin Lunny, whose family has leased and ranched the ranch land adjacent to Drakes Estero for two generations, purchased the Johnson Oyster Company from Johnson in 2004 or 2005 (depending on the source), changed the name to Drakes Bay Oyster Company, and began improving the business, which, according to several interviewees in 2016, had fallen into disrepair. The Johnson Oyster Company came encumbered with a number of environmental liabilities and the expiring ROU and the SUP, which, depending on how one aligns one's loyalties, the US National Park Service Regional Office either initially verbally promised to support for renewal or clearly indicated would not be renewed.[3]

The marine tidal estuary was equally a focus of controversy both in and out of the courts. The tidal estuary itself was publicly owned and controlled by the state of California before the Point Reyes National

Seashore was established. In 1965, California conveyed the tidal and submerged lands in the estuary to the United States, thus giving the US National Park Service control over the estuary, but California continued to issue bottom leases to the oyster company for grow-out racks, use of motor boats, and use of the sandbars for cultivation, permits that were contingent on the federal ROU and SUP.[4] In 1976, the marine tidal portions of Drakes Estero along with Estero de Limantour, which is part of the same bay–estuary complex, were included in the Phillip Burton Wilderness area as potential wilderness areas.[5] For the US National Park Service, the potential wilderness designation changed their legal and managerial approach to the estuary. The California bottom leases became a political focal point in the conflict over the oyster company because it was not clear, until a series of letters (including the letter referenced in note 4 above) were exchanged between government entities during the conflict, clarifying which government had final control over the continued operation of the oyster company situated as it was on both land and in tidal waters.

REPRESENTING PLACE

An extensive archive grew around the conflict over the oyster company, including official documents, Draft and Final Environmental Impact Statements, scientific reports, court documents, and a podcast from the Ninth Circuit courtroom posted by the Court. This archive also includes numerous blogs; guest op-eds and national, regional, and local news articles; videos; websites; journal articles; and books. A non-virtual archive also accumulated, including a collection of copies of George Russell's published political cartoons[6] that hung on the inside wall of the retail oyster building before it was torn down, and the numerous bright blue 'Save Our Shellfish', 'Save Our Drakes Bay Oyster Company', and the counter 'Save Our Seashore' signs that dotted fences and buildings in west Marin, some of which remain hanging and fading in the sun even as I write. Many shopkeepers' sidewalk chalkboards in the neighbouring Sonoma and Napa wine country counties blatantly advertised the availability of Drakes Bay Oyster Company oysters during the period when the company remained open by virtue of emergency injunctions after its forty-year terrestrial ROU expired. As the prolific archive suggests, this was an important issue for many people.

I draw my general understandings of the conflict from this extensive archive.[7] I first visited the oyster company in summer of 2014, and although some of the retail buildings and the picnic tables had been removed in a first round of US National Park Service demolitions, the sales, nursery, and processing facilities were still intact, and oyster sales were still in process. During the summer of 2016, I collected oral history interviews from people on mutually exclusive sides of the conflict, focusing on those who played a contributing role to the archive. I also revisited the old company site along Drakes Estero. All of the company buildings had been replaced by US National Park Service signage, restrooms, and fencing. While there, I overheard other visitors discussing the conflict, while pointing to bits and pieces of the built environment. Even so, mine is mainly an archival project.

As is any particular place, Drakes Estero is saturated by and constructed through concrete socio-historical relations. Drakes Estero is a palimpsest of legal, social, economic, mediated, biological, and physical relations. Any place, every place is emplaced and this contributes to the sense of the everyday as a dimension of place. Sarat and Kearns identify 'routine, habit, convention ... the domain of unalienated experience ... the domain of situated, bounded, local place and time ... the domain of lived experience' (1995b: 1, 2, 4, 8) and its practices as intrinsic to the notion of everyday. But very quickly, significant and complicated questions arise regarding Drakes Estero as a 'domain of lived experience' (1995b: 8). Whose everyday place was at stake in this conflict?

Although the oyster company enjoyed wide local support for its continued existence, one cannot simply sort all of the people of Marin into a pro–Drakes Bay Oyster Company category, because other Marin residents wanted Drakes Estero to take the legal course of conversion to designated wilderness. Likewise, the oyster company enjoyed support in nearby Sonoma and Napa Counties, but so too did the conversion to a marine wilderness. In a contrasting register, the 2012 content analysis for the Draft Environmental Impact Statement shows that 48,396 responses of a total of 52,473 responses expressed support for *not* issuing a new Special Use Permit to Drakes Bay Oyster Company. The majority of the responders to the survey used a web form, although a few opted to use a letter or a park form. Responses came from all fifty states and several United States territories, with 37.1 percent of the total survey responses coming from California. However and significantly, the spatial boundary, California, which could be read as demarcating nearness to Drakes Estero, is debatable given the size and diversity of California. This spatial demarcation was dictated by the spatial categories of the survey, which did not distinguish southern California responses from northern California responses, nor did the survey distinguish urban responses from rural responses – two place-based demarcations that are socially meaningful in California. New York weighed in with 6.6 percent of the responses, Florida with 4.6 percent of the responses, and thirty-four total responses came from other countries.[8] Nationally known figures Senator Dianne Feinstein, Sylvia Earle, Alice Waters, and Michael Pollan, who are located in the San Francisco Bay area, became aligned with one or another position. As is clear from this description of the numerous people taking a position on the future of Drakes Estero, the everyday place of Drakes Estero is not so easily situated.

MORALLY ANCHORING JUSTICE

In what follows, I briefly outline five broad, contrasting, morally oriented narrative or representational constellations into which many of the contributions to the popular and scholarly archive can be sorted. I call these representational constellations because no single narrative theme found in the archive works in isolation. Rather, several narrative themes are woven together by authors, and in that process, distinctive constellations representing distinct positions emerged. The archive predominantly represents Settler Society voices and concerns in local, regional, and national registers. However, before moving to those concerns, a necessary digression first highlights two constellations that cannot be ignored in a full accounting, but which more or less remained in the background.

The first representational constellation concerns the sovereign claims of First Peoples and is important because the US National Park Service and US federal government have variegated histories of relations with First Peoples. The Federated Indians of Graton Rancheria (formerly known as the Federated Coast Miwok, and includes Coast Miwok and Southern Pomo), whose traditional and cultural territories encompass both the terrestrial and sea components of Drakes Estero,[9] contributed three official letters addressed to the US National Park Service opposing the oyster company's practices and continuance.[10] The Graton Rancheria represents the history of its relations with Settler Society as a history of Settler Society obviating its ongoing original territorial claims on lands, freshwaters, and seas in the area, beginning in the late 1700s, and achieving a nadir in the US California Rancheria Act of 1958. In 2000, the US federal government, because of organized efforts by the Graton Rancheria, formally reinstated US federal recognition of Graton Rancheria, but without restoring Graton Rancheria's territorial lands and seas, except one privately held acre of the now parsed-out territories of the Coast Miwok and Southern Pomo.[11] Federated Indians of Graton Rancheria expressly do not represent themselves, nor their people and their territories, as having disappeared.

Nevertheless, many past and current Settler written histories about the Point Reyes National Seashore and its environs, including several narratives directly relevant to this conflict, portray the Coast Miwok as the original inhabitants of the Point Reyes peninsula, who were decimated by missionizing and military efforts, and who left a number of cultural and sacred sites behind, but not as a living First Peoples having still viable claims to the lands and seas of the Point Reyes peninsula (e.g., Gillium 1962; Sadin 2007: 11–17; Babalis 2011; Brennan 2015: 203–216). Accounts of the Coast Miwok also surface in the chronology on the Drakes Bay Oyster Company website.[12] The company's chronology discursively establishes a lengthy history of human occupation and resource use in the estuary, and situates the oyster company within this long history, a point derisively noted by one oral history interviewee who opposed the oyster company, and a point often reiterated as factual by supporters of the oyster company.

A second constellation concerns the Latinx immigrant company workers, who were made highly visible in many published images, but much less often given voice by being directly interviewed and quoted. Workers became an important symbol of potential injustices. Pictures of workers engaged in their jobs headed popular press articles, even when workers were not quoted in the text. The workers are featured on the Drakes Bay Oyster Company website, and in numerous court documents filed by the company where Kevin Lunny and the company expressed concern for the workers' futures, their children, and their company-provided housing should the company be closed. Taking a different tack, one that received much less overt press coverage, opponents of the issuing of a new SUP called into question the commitment of the oyster company to its workers. In my oral history interviews, depending on the person being interviewed, evidence for Lunny's support for his workers was offered, or counterevidence was offered regarding care for the workers. In practice, workers were often talked about rather than allowed to speak for themselves.

I turn now to the three dominant, morally oriented, representational constellations in the archive, and these are not discussed in any particular order. First, I will discuss the dominant constellation that revolves around the pastoral, ranching, or agricultural element of the landscape, sometimes called a 'working landscape notion' (Fairfax et al. 2012: 95). The second dominant constellation revolves around the idea of wilderness and is rooted in a long federal government history of carving out public lands to preserve undeveloped natural places, often at the expense of First Peoples. The third dominant constellation revolves around the idea of good science (and bad science) and its role in environmental social policy. When I asked about justice as I was interviewing, I almost always got passionately (and often loudly) expressed examples of the injustices of this conflict, and not a lot of talk about justice. The exceptions came from people who, often just as passionately, emphasized that law deemed the estuary to be a place of potential wilderness and a place from which the oyster company had to be justly removed because it was a non-conforming activity. Shklar (1990) argues that feelings and experiences of injustice in US culture are generally traceable to broken expectations and broken promises. Shklar's is an apt description for the sense of injustice evinced by all sides in this conflict, although exactly which promises were about to be or have been broken, and which expectations remain unmet and by whom, varies substantially from one subject position to another in this conflict. Shklar also argues that in the United States there is an inevitable link between a sense of injustice and a victimology wherein perpetrators come to see themselves as victims, but this link did not play out in the Drakes Estero conflict in the manner that she suggests the link between injustice and victimology usually plays out. To be sure, many victims have been named: the seals, the eel grass, the Lunnys, the US National Park Service staff, lovers of Drakes Bay Oyster Company oysters, the workers, the integrity and neutrality of science – the list is long. Images of victims were mobilized to change minds, and given that this is a common trope in mass media in the United States, its use should not surprise. Importantly, however, victims served as symbols marking the tips of much larger icebergs, tips of senses of place and deeply held convictions as to proper approaches to land use and proper procedures for deciding how to solve a pressing social problem. In the estimations of the people situated in the many different registers of this conflict, the outcome had both immediate irreversible material ramifications and far-reaching implications for other similar sites across the United States.

I observe that several narrative strategies were common to all of the following three morally oriented representational constellations, but these strategies were utilized with varying degrees of emphasis in the different constellations and by different voices. These include: (1) appealing to history and the use of historical narratives as evidence, for example, referring to the past to claim that this is what the park planners, politicians, and law-makers intended; (2) asserting a conservation-minded approach, that is, all sides portrayed themselves as being conservation and environmentally oriented, and each mobilized ample concrete evidence to support their claims; (3) appealing to the economic soundness of their position, with one side emphasizing jobs creation and small-scale food production as the proper economic usage of the resources of the estuary, and the other side emphasizing recreational usages, which are also commercial activities, as the proper use of the estuary resources; and (4) framing Drakes Estero as a legal place, including recitations of the laws that created and then shaped the Point Reyes National Seashore, along with careful interpretations of those laws to fit an argument either for continuing the oyster company's production or for removing the oyster company and turning potential wilderness into designated wilderness.

The first dominant morally oriented representational constellation is focused on preserving the working pastoral element in Point Reyes National Seashore.[13] Support for pastoral practices, working ranches, and farms is integral to Marin and to neighbouring Sonoma and Napa counties' senses of self, and is also integral to the region's alternative food production system on which Marin county economically depends (Fairfax et al. 2012). For many supporters of Drakes Bay Oyster Company, this conflict hinged on an understood promise that the federal government would keep pastoral operations in the Point Reyes National Seashore intact over time by continually renewing permits to the ranches after the government purchased the ranch lands in the 1970s. Ranching, including the Lunny ranch, extends to the banks of Drakes Estero. Supporters of Drakes Bay Oyster Company argued that this government promise extended to the oyster company. They pointed to the fact that the oyster company was already in place long before the national seashore was planned and was run by a rancher. Proponents of the oyster company expressed fears that the pastoral lands in the Point Reyes National Seashore had come under attack and that the oyster company was just the first domino. These arguments also stressed the economic contribution of the oyster company to the economy of rural west Marin, including the jobs created at the company, the company as oyster supplier to other companies and restaurants, and the overall contribution of the company to the agricultural economy of west Marin. Some of the strong opponents of the issuance of a new SUP for the oyster company also strongly supported the preservation and continuation of the working pastoral element of Point Reyes National Seashore but explicitly did not see that pastoral element as including the oyster company and oyster farming in Drakes Estero.

A second strand in this constellation was an expansive idea of outdoor recreation activities. Like the oyster companies on Tomales Bay to the east, the retail portion of Drakes Bay Oyster Company included a popular picnic area where people purchased oysters at the retail stand and stayed to picnic and barbeque with friends and strangers, take in a small educational oyster production tour and enjoy the estuary. The popularity of this picnicking practice in Marin and its unique sociality was one reason many regional people actively supported renewing the lease for Drakes Bay Oyster Company.

The third strand in the pastoral representational constellation revolved around the idea that small-scale food production is an environmentally sound form of conservation. This narrative theme situates the oyster farm and its owner concretely in Fairfax et al.'s 'alternative food district' (2012), not simply because ranching is a way of life, but because the entire alternative food system is a way of life. This strand expands on the first strand in this constellation to include not only production (ranching and farming) but also consumption practices, including individuals and restaurants emphasizing local food. This strand brought Hayes Street Grill in San Francisco, Tomales Bay Oyster Company, Michael Pollan, a nationally acclaimed author with appointments at UC Berkeley and Harvard University, and Alice Waters of Chez Panisse into the fray in support of Drakes Bay Oyster Company.

The second morally oriented representational constellation revolves around the creation of a national system of public wilderness areas, in which Drakes Estero figures significantly as a marine wilderness.[14] A widely circulated law review article authored by a group of Berkeley law students contextualizes the conversion of Drakes Estero to designated wilderness as significant addition to a pressured system of national parks (Nylen et al. 2012). Contributors to this constellation argued that the removal of the oyster farm would enhance the wilderness system and enhance the conservation, restoration, and preservation of biodiversity in Drakes Estero. Whereas representations in the pastoral constellation often featured workers and the oyster farm, this constellation often featured pictures without people, but included trash, seals, and scenic views. Opponents of the issuance of a new SUP for Drakes Bay Oyster Company insisted that wilderness is not supposed to be industrialized, and much discussion arose around the wording of the Wilderness Act of 1976, especially the meaning of the word 'untrammeled' found in the Wilderness Act. Proponents of the oyster company questioned how that was relevant now that a succession of oyster companies had been in there for decades, and opponents of the new SUP asserted that the estuary could be restored.

Another prominent moral strand in this constellation was that of legality and law. US National Park Service staff, along with the opponents of the new SUP, cast their arguments in terms of abiding by the law. In 1976, Drakes Estero was legally categorized as potential wilderness, and this strand emphasized that nonconforming activities (and this applied to oyster farming) were by law supposed to be removed, and that potential wilderness is supposed to be converted to designated wilderness. This legalistic strand also tended to emphasize having waited patiently for the ROU to expire, and having not pressed to have the oyster farm removed before the expiration of the ROU.

Another strand in this constellation invoked a much grander and more inclusive scale of interested stakeholders, while at the same time narrowing the range of outdoor recreation activities considered appropriate. Picnicking, hiking, and kayaking were accounted acceptable, but the raucous sociality of the crowded oyster farm picnic grounds was not considered appropriate, and neither was the radio-infused sociality of the workers at work. The representation of Point Reyes National Seashore and Drakes Estero as belonging to the American people was a centrepiece of this constellation. The boundary around who Drakes Estero belongs to, around who is included, dramatically shifts with appeals to the American people. This invocation is important because from its inception the US National Park System has relied on federal laws, national and regional political trade-offs, mobilization of national support, and the backing of Congress in order to cordon off and enlarge

149

national public recreation and conservation lands (Graf 1990; Leshy 2005). The 48,396 responses in support of removing the oyster farm discussed above echo the massive petition campaigns in 1969–1970 organized by the Sierra Club and (the original) Save Our Seashore group, which sent 350,000 signatures and perhaps as many as another 300,000 to Washington (Behr 2010; Duddleson 2010: xvii–xviii; Miller Johnson 2010a: 26–31, 76–77), without which there would be no Point Reyes National Seashore today. Consistently this representational constellation challenged the idea that community is situated solely in the local scale of west Marin county, or even Marin county as a whole. Sylvia Earle, highly acclaimed ocean conservationist, strongly supported this representational constellation.

One other strand mobilized in this constellation was that of questioning integrity and intentions, especially the continual questioning of who was supporting Lunny's legal effort. This was in turn countered by supporters of the oyster company, who emphasized that being targeted by the US government requires taking any help one can get, and who also emphasized local government control as outweighing distant government control. This strand of inquiry in this constellation carried over into the next morally oriented representational constellation where the accusations were even more sharply honed.

The third morally oriented representational constellation concerned science and revolved around specific scientific findings and, more generally, around the role of sound science in policy decision-making. Contrasts between good and bad science became a salient theme in this constellation, as did the theme of using substantive science and scientific methodology as a basis for adjudicating environmental conflicts, and the theme of holding the government accountable for its science. Conflicts over science came to a head during the US National Park Service's National Environmental Policy Act of 1969 process of producing a Draft Environmental Impact Statement for Drakes Estero, and over the scientific studies used in that draft. The range of science and science use issues continued to broaden, culminating in the public hearing before the House Committee on Natural Resources in April 2015.[15] All sides to the conflict expressed concern about the longer-term impact of the conflict on government accountability and scientific accountability (examples include US National Park Service 2007; Graeser 2013; Office of the Inspector General 2013; Ames 2015; Goodman 2016).

The morally oriented representational constellations are past-history oriented, particularly the First Peoples' sovereignty constellation, and the Settler Society pastoral and wilderness constellations, while also evincing future orientations. Settler Society future concerns include: (1) the future of small-scale ranching and local control over the immediate landscape and its uses; (2) the future of a nationally integrated system of wilderness conservation and preservation areas; and (3) the future role of science in environmental policy and planning. These constellations suggest that the everyday is not simply now, but also contains the seeds of the future every bit as much as it builds itself by using the past as a resource.

IMPLICATIONS OF EVERYDAY, IMPLICATIONS OF PLACE

As I write, the conflict over Drakes Estero continues despite the fact that the legal struggle has concluded, the oyster company buildings have been bulldozed, the production racks and stocks have been removed, and US National Park Service fencing and signage have been erected. Feelings continued to run high in the summer of 2016, as, for example, when one person passionately shouted at me that 'This will never be over!' Sentiments like this one are echoed throughout the archive, surfaced in other interviews, and were not, I emphasize, particular to one or another opposing side. I selected this particular conflict explicitly because it does not lend itself to a cleanly contoured narrative of resolution. Many ethnographers, who focus on spatial relations of power, refer to spaces that embrace multiple and even conflicting localities as being translocal. Although much of this work concerns immigrant communities (Smith 2005; Lowe 2009), Ganapathy (2013) shifts the topical focus and applies the notion of translocal to Settler Society and its reinvestment of First Peoples' lands with its own legalities and meanings, capturing the persistent, quotidian, uneasy way in which contrasting place-based practices both situate and are situated in the Arctic National Wildlife Refuge by Gwich'in Athabascan Peoples, Settler Society environmentalists, developers, planners, and governments. I suggest that the seemingly irresolvable nature of the Drakes Estero conflict, much like the general situation in the Arctic National Wildlife Refuge described by Ganapathy, is because Drakes Estero operates in multiple registers of situated-ness (everyday and place) that never come together; they are

151

incommensurate. In Drakes Estero, however, the dominant registers of difference belong to Settler Society, and Settler Society law cuts across these registers to leave its own mark.

Consider the issue of juxtaposed registers and scales. The task of grappling with justice and injustice in this conflict 'explodes the everyday as situated sense-making essence of social order' (Marcus 1995: 244), and the explosion of the everyday, that is, the explosion of the illusion of an agreed-upon and shared everyday, left only one place from which social order could proceed, and that was through the courts and lawsuits. Marcus observes that the realities of contemporary life in the United States challenge legal and social theoretical notions of the everyday 'as the moral, the pragmatic, the accessible, the commonsensical ... the last bastion of simple coherence and order' (p. 237). He argues that treating the everyday, in all of its normative weight, as primarily a site of immediacy and face-to-face relations makes it very difficult to account for 'processes that are not fixed temporally and spatially in situations – but rather exist in fragmented, discontinuous, and simultaneous space-time' (p. 245). His general observation in many ways describes the contested Drakes Estero, where there was no agreed-upon boundary around who was in and who was out, around whose face-to-face relations counted and whose did not, around here and there, near and far. The boundaries were instead instrumentally reconfigured in every register.

One supporter of the oyster company asserted to me that in his own analysis of the 48,396 responses against issuing a new Special Use Permit, he ascertained that a great number of people were simply checking the box and hitting send, demonstrating to him very little engagement with the issue. But for people who argue Drakes Estero belongs to the American people, the boundary around belonging is not Marin county, not California (the smallest designated area on the survey), but encompasses quite literally the whole country. This expansive territorialized boundary has served as a very powerful argument in the establishment of the public system of National Parks, National Monuments, and Wilderness Areas (including the US Fish and Wildlife Service–administered Arctic National Wildlife Refuge), even as that boundary is not as inclusive as it implies. Greenhouse (1998) critically examines not the everyday per se, but the common site of the everyday, the 'local'. She observes that Anglo-American law largely frames the conventions of scale that treat the local and by extension the 'community', as socially and morally coherent geographic units, a discursive construction that can, in turn, be deployed to achieve and justify instrumental ends. Establishing a register of belonging for all Americans was crucial in garnering federal funds to purchase numerous tracts of privately owned land on the Point Reyes peninsula and convert them to the contiguous public land that comprises the Point Reyes National Seashore today, which of course later led to the expiring ROU and this very conflict. It was equally important to the supporters of the oyster company to mobilize an everyday grounded in local and regional support for their locally grown and distributed product, and to mobilize the sentiments that support working agricultural landscapes in the region.

Tsing suggests that as proliferating scales of place come up against each other, the processes produce creative frictions (2005). One product of that friction in this case is exactly this imaginary and elusive illusion of an 'everyday place' that induces enough passion to keep the morally oriented representational constellations active, to keep people vociferously engaged. But in this case, that illusion and friction also worked to inhibit or prevent the creation of avenues for exploring shared governance (as opposed to court-driven) solutions to landscape, seascape, sea and land use conflicts. Several people commented in my 2016 interviews that the real questions are still pending in spite of the volumes of public records and public interchanges circulating around the oyster farm and Drakes Estero. When I asked what specific questions those might be, one environmentalist and opponent of the issuance of a new SUP answered that there needs to be a discussion about the role of wilderness today, and a supporter of the oyster company answered that there needs to be a much deeper discussion about the role of accountability and transparency regarding science in public policy (both points are echoed in the archive).

Consider the way law leaves its mark as it cuts across the juxtaposed but never commensurate registers of 'everyday' and 'place.' The different registers of everyday and place in this context are evinced in the irreconcilable morally oriented representational constellations, even as each constellation also mobilizes an illusion of a coherent, common sense everyday place as its own starting point and end point. The turn to the courts signalled the last avenue open for bringing these disparate, multiple everydays to heel and forcing them into orderly social behaviour. The irony is that the courts' legal decisions did not concern the issues that were so important to people on the ground, including the proponents of wilderness, who arguably won with the outcome of the courts' decisions, and who took the 1976 potential wilderness *legal* designation to be situated on the highest moral ground because it is the law. 'Change the law', an environmentalist told me, if you do not like what it does. He then pointed out that that was exactly what Senator Feinstein had tried and only partially accomplished with her contested rider on the 2009 appropriations bill, which authorized but did not require the US Secretary of the Interior to grant the company its permits (Public Law 111-88-October 30, 2009, Sec 124, 123Stat2932). The courts, even as they lined up these multiple registers and brought them into order, did not concern themselves with potential wilderness designations, food production regimes, recreation, conservation, or cultural social issues. The courts instead concerned themselves with administrative policy and the judiciary's limits on interfering with the operations of agency discretion. The courts concerned themselves with their own ecology of everyday and, not surprisingly, because the legal system in representing society does not concern itself with individual interests but 'does apply to the particular case submitted to it the general and traditional rules of the law' (Durkheim 1984 90). However, law's mark does not quite end here, and a brief return to Durkheim's aim to connect different legal forms with different kinds of social solidarity is relevant.

Consider now the juxtaposition of morally oriented and never commensurate registers of 'everyday' and 'place' in the larger frame. In focusing on its own ecology of the everyday, the US courts upheld the right of the landlord, in this case the US Department of the Interior acting for the American people, who properly follows legal protocols, to decide for itself how it wishes to manage its property (to lease or not to lease, and to whom). Viewed through this lens, the picture shifts again.

Concerned to understand social solidarity, Durkheim observes that in a social system like the one currently operating in California and the United States, 'real' rights concern relationships between people and things; private property law links people to things, not people to people (1984: 91–92). Durkheim asserts:

> The solidarity that arises from this integration is wholly negative. It does not cause individual wills to move toward common ends, but only causes things to gravitate around those individual wills in an orderly fashion.... Such a solidarity thus does not shape from the elements drawn together an entity capable of acting in unison. It contributes nothing to the unity of the social body ... the law of property is its most excellent exemplar.
> (p. 92)

The decision of the US courts reinforced and protected the US private property rights regime. The everyday face-to-face relations fostered by the courts' decisions were those of private property, those of the relationship of the self to its own(ed) things. This was a court where only the narrowest of social relations were a priority. This was not a court where fostering the possibility of working through everyday shared governance problems could emerge. This was a court that could reinforce only what Durkheim calls negative social integration and that could in the end only militate against the emergence of even rudimentary socially integrative solidarity.

This conflict largely played out as a conflict within Settler Society over Settler Society's self-claimed public lands in which the Settler Society government is representing the American people (problematic as that assertion may be in actuality) through both its executive branch and its courts. In the Afterword to this volume, Greenhouse emphasizes the importance of unpacking the nuanced and fraught relationships obtaining between law and the state, and between law and neoliberal ideologies. The particular case of Drakes Estero, set in California with its uniquely and highly litigious climate, pushes Greenhouse's observation farther, urging us to tease out the imbrications of law and an economic system that is deeply dependent on and thoroughly configured by a private property rights regime. This conflict over Drakes Estero exemplifies the way that law entangled with place in the context of a privileging of private property rights, can recognize only a narrow moral orientation and a narrow range of governance practices, mainly those pertaining to and supporting the relationships between owners and their things.

Watt (2002; 2012), Babalis (2011), and Goodman (2016) each suggest, in light of the conflict over Drakes Estero, alternative ways in which civic processes that determine land uses, and determine whose social values matter, might be improved. Their substantive suggestions – for example, rethinking the idea and definition of wilderness, turning to natural history, improving government accountability for its science – have merit and indeed echo longings expressed by interviewees in 2016. However, their suggestions do not address the way in which the 'everyday', that spectre of coherence, is actually fragmented and situated in multiple different everydays, all enveloped by an overriding economic and legal context where the longer-term and deeper civic implications of the primacy of private property rights remains unexamined. The US courts were effective in protecting the overarching

American property rights regime and in cutting through layers of conflicting notions about place, local-ness, the everyday, and bringing these conflicts into a forced, if never fully complete, resolution. The courts were not at all effective at creating a space where people could and even had to come together and find some form of shared understanding and appreciation for each other's positions, a space to creatively brainstorm a shared future, a space for an alternative to the civics of the owning self. There is little or no impetus to seek a means for practicing a more equitable, respectful shared civics when a litigious private property rights regime posits the only 'everyday' that counts.

Notes

1 Letter of 29 November 2012 from US Secretary of the Interior to the Director of the US National Park Service instructing that the permit for operations be allowed to expire, thereby ending Drakes Bay Oyster Company's lease with the federal government.www.nps.gov/pore/getinvolved/upload/PORE_Nov-29-2012-Secretary-s-Memo.pdf, accessed 18 November 2016.

2 www.nps.gov/pore/learn/management/planning_drakesestero_restoration.htm, accessed 9 September 2016.

3 See page 3 of letter referenced in note 1.

4 Letter from the California Resources Agency, Department of Fish and Game, Office of General Counsel to Assembly member Jared Huffman, 25 March 2008, www.nps.gov/pore/learn/management/upload/planning_dboc_sup_deis_references_cdfg_2008_080325.pdf, accessed 18 November 2016. This letter also distinguishes between public fisheries, which California continues to control, and aquaculture products, which are private property. Hence, Drakes Estero is included in the California Marine Protected Areas Network as a California State Marine Conservation Area, as well as being part of the Phillip Burton Wilderness Area.

5 www.wilderness.net/NWPS/wildView?WID=455&tab=General, accessed 11 November 2016. Public Law 94-544, 18 October 1976.

6 For examples, see http://savedrakesbay.com/core/editorial-cartoons/, accessed 16 November 2016.

7 I bracket materials generated roughly between 2002 and 2016 as primary sources. I draw on earlier materials in this archive to outline the historical foundations of the current conflict. Fairfax et al. (2012) discuss oystering as a piece of the Marin agricultural landscape, especially in Tomales Bay, but do not comment on Drakes Estero, and thus I use their text as a secondary source.

8 Preliminary Content Analysis Report, 2-26-12, Dco. ID 43390, DEIS DBOC SUP www.nps.gov/pore/learn/management/upload/planning_dboc_sup_deis_public_comments_content_analysis_report_preliminary_120226.pdf, accessed 1 March 2019.

9 https://gratonrancheria.com/, accessed July 25, 2019.

10 Letters from the Federated Indians of Graton Rancheria to: (1) Don Neubacher, Superintendent, Point Reyes National Seashore, 21 May 2007; (2) Jon Jarvis, Regional Director, National Park Service: Pacific West, 28 March 2008; and (3) Ken Salazar, Department of the Interior, 22 November 2012. All three public letters object to Drakes Bay Oyster Company's activities in Drakes Estero.
11 www.gratonrancheria.com/culture/, accessed 15 June 2016.
12 www.drakesbayoyster.com/history/, accessed 16 August 2016.
13 For a range of examples, see www.drakesbayoyster.com/history/, accessed 16 August 2016; https://oysterzone.wordpress.com, accessed 18 November 2016; Farm to Consumer Legal Defense Fund, www.farmtoconsumer.org/blog/2014/09/08/why-we-must-save-the-drakes-bay-oyster-farm/, accessed 17 November 2016; savedrakesbay.com/core/, accessed 17 November 2016; Alliance for Local Sustainable Agriculture, http://cares.ucdavis.edu/resource/alliance-local-sustainable-agriculture-alsa, accessed 1 March 2019; Watt 2002; Riles and Bush 2009; Hein 2013.
14 For example, savepointreyeswilderness.org; National Parks Conservation Association, www.npca.org/search?q=Drakes+Estero, accessed 18 November 2016; Environmental Action Committee of West Marin, http://eac marin.org/drakes-estero-wilderness/, accessed 17 November 2016; Protect Our Shoreline News, http://protectourshorelinenews.blogspot.com/2013_09_01_archive.html, accessed 17 November 2016; Trainer 2013.
15 http://naturalresources.house.gov/newsroom/documentsingle.aspx?DocumentID=398459, accessed 16 November 2016.

References

Ames, Michael. 2015. 'The Oyster Shell Game'. *Newsweek*, 18 January 2015. www.newsweek.com/2015/01/30/oyster-shell-game-300225.html, accessed 18 November 2016.

Babalis, Timothy. 2011. 'Restoring the Past: Environmental History and Oysters at Point Reyes National Seashore'. *The George Wright Forum* 28(2): 199–215.

Behr, Peter. 2010 [1993]. 'Oral History Interview with Ann Lage'. In *Saving Point Reyes National Seashore, 1969–1970: An Oral History of Citizen Action in Conservation: Oral History Transcript/1993*. Berkeley, CA: Bancroft Library Regional Oral History Office and Nabu Press.

Brennan, Summer. 2015. *The Oyster War: The True Story of a Small Farm, Big Politics, and the Future of Wilderness in America*. Berkeley, CA: Counterpoint Press.

Brunnegger, Sandra, and Karen Faulk (eds.). 2016. *A Sense of Justice: Legal Knowledge and Lived Experience in Latin America*. Redwood City, CA: Stanford University Press.

Clarke, Kamari Maxine, and Mark Goodale (eds.). 2010. *Mirrors of Justice: Law and Power in the Post–Cold War Era*. Cambridge: Cambridge University Press.

Collins, George L. 2010 [1980]. 'Oral History Interview with Ann Lage'. In *The Art and Politics of Park Planning and Preservations, 1920–1979: Oral History Transcript/and Related Material, 1978–1980*. Berkeley, CA: Bancroft Library Regional Oral History Office and Nabu Press.

Duddleston, William J. 2010 [1993]. 'Oral History Interview with Ann Lage'. In *Saving Point Reyes National Seashore, 1969–1970 An Oral History of Citizen Action in Conservation: Oral History Transcript/1993*. Berkeley, CA: Bancroft Library Regional Oral History Office and Nabu Press.

Durkheim, Emile. 1984. *Division of Labor in Society*, W. D. Halls, trans. New York: Free Press, Simon and Schuster.

Fairfax, Sally K., Louise Nelson Dyble, Greig Tor Guthy, Lauren Gwin, Monica Moore, and Jennifer Sokolove. 2012. *California Cuisine and Just Food*, foreword by M. Nestle. Cambridge, MA: MIT Press.

Ganapathy, Sandhya, 2013. 'Imagining Alaska: Local and Translocal Engagements with Place'. *American Anthropologist* 115(1): 96–111.

Gilliam, Harold. 1962. *Island in Time: The Point Reyes Peninsula*. New York: Sierra Club, Scribner.

Goodale, Mark, and Kamari Maxine Clarke. 2010. 'Introduction: Understanding the Multiplicity of Justice'. In Kamari Maxine Clarke and Mark Goodale (eds.), *Mirrors of Justice: Law and Power in the Post–Cold War Era*. Cambridge: Cambridge University Press, 1–27.

Goodman, Cory S. 2016. 'The President's Unfinished Promise: The Federal Government Still Lacks a Meaningful Scientific Integrity Policy'. *Huffington Post*, 26 February 2016. www.huffingtonpost.com/corey-s-goodman/scientific-integrity-policy_b_9024578.html, accessed 17 November 2016.

Graeser, Julie. 2013. 'The Role of (Junk) Science in Wilderness Management: Lessons Learned in the Wake of Drakes Bay Oyster Company'. *Hastings West-Northwest Journal of Environmental Law, Policy* 19: 307–333.

Graf, William L. 1990. *Wilderness Preservation and the Sagebrush Rebellions*. Lanham, MD: Rowman and Littlefield.

Greenhouse, Carol J. 1998. 'Figuring the Future: Issues of Time, Power, and Agency in Ethnographic Problems of Scale'. In Bryant Garth and Austin Sarat (eds.), *Justice and Power in Sociolegal Studies*. Evanston, IL: Northwestern University Press, American Bar Association, 108–135.

Hart, John. 2012. *An Island in Time: 50 Years of Point Reyes National Seashore*. Mill Valley, CA: Pickleweed Press.

Hein, Jayne Foyle. 2013. 'Of Mollusks and Men: The Wilderness Act and Drakes Bay Oyster Company'. *The Berkeley Blog*, 4 January 2013, http://blogs.berkeley.edu/2013/01/04/of-mollusks-and-men-the-wilderness-act-and-drakes-bay-oyster-company/, accessed 18 November 2016.

Hirsch, Susan F. 2010. 'The Victim Deserving of Global Justice: Power, Caution, and Recovering Individuals'. In Kamari Maxine Clarke and

Mark Goodale (eds.), *Mirrors of Justice: Law and Power in the Post–Cold War Era*. Cambridge: Cambridge University Press, 149–190.

Lage, Ann. 2010a [1993]. 'Introduction'. In *Saving Point Reyes National Seashore, 1969–1970: An Oral History of Citizen Action in Conservation: Oral History Transcript/1993*. Berkeley, CA: Bancroft Library Regional Oral History Office and Nabu Press.

Lage, Ann, ed., 2010b. *Saving Point Reyes National Seashore, 1969–1970: An Oral History of Citizen Action in Conservation: Oral History Transcript/ 1993*. Berkeley, CA: Bancroft Library Regional Oral History Office and Nabu Press.

Leshy, John D. 2005. 'Contemporary Politics of Wilderness Preservation'. *Journal of Land Resources and Environmental Law* 25(1): 1–13.

Lowe, Setha. 2009. 'Claiming Space for an Engaged Anthropology: Spatial Inequality and Social Exclusion'. *America Anthropologist* 113(3): 389–407.

Marcus, George E. 1995. 'Mass Toxic Torts and the End of Everyday Life'. In Austin Sarat and Thomas R. Kearns (eds.), *Law in Everyday Life*. Ann Arbor: University of Michigan Press, 237–274.

Miller Johnson, Katy. 2010a [1993]. 'Oral History Interview with Ann Lage'. In *Saving Point Reyes National Seashore, 1969–1970: An Oral History of Citizen Action in Conservation: Oral History Transcript/1993*. Berkeley, CA: Bancroft Library Regional Oral History Office and Nabu Press.

2010b [1993]. 'A "Katy-gram": Fact Sheet on Point Reyes for Congressmen 1969'. Reprinted in *Saving Point Reyes National Seashore, 1969–1970: An Oral History of Citizen Action in Conservation: Oral History Transcript/ 1993*. Berkeley, CA: Bancroft Library Regional Oral History Office and Nabu Press, unnumbered page between 67 and 68.

Nylen, Nell Green, Elizabeth Long, Mary Loum, Heather Welles, Dan Carlin, Brynn Cook, and Sage Adams. 2012. 'Will the Wilderness Act be Diluted in Drakes Estero?' *Ecological Law Currents* 39: 46–99.

Office of the Inspector General. 2013. *Investigative Report of Drakes Bay Oyster Company Environmental Impact Statement*. Office of the Inspector General, US Department for the Interior. 7 February.

Riles, Ellie, and Lisa Bush. 2009. *The Changing Role of Agriculture in Point Reyes National Seashore*. Berkeley: University of California Cooperative Extension.

Sadin, Paul. 2007. *Managing a Land in Motion: An Administrative History of Point Reyes National Seashore*. US National Park Service.

Sarat, Austin, and Thomas R. Kearns (eds.). 1995a. *Law in Everyday Life*. Ann Arbor: University of Michigan Press.

Sarat, Austin, and Thomas R. Kearns. 1995b. 'Law and Everyday Life: Editorial Introduction'. In Austin Sarat and Thomas R. Kearns (eds.), *Law in Everyday Life*. Ann Arbor: University of Michigan Press, 1–20.

(eds.). 1999a. *Justice and Injustice in Law and Legal Theory*. Ann Arbor: University of Michigan Press.

Sarat, Austin, and Thomas R. Kearns. 1999b. 'Legal Justice and Injustice: Toward a Situated Perspective'. In Austin Sarat and Thomas R. Kearns (eds.), *Justice and Injustice in Law and Legal Theory*. Ann Arbor: University of Michigan Press, 1–18.

Shklar, Judith N. 1990. *The Faces of Injustice*. New Haven, CT: Yale University Press.

Smith, Michael Peter. 2005. 'Power in Place/Places of Power: Contextualizing Transnational Research'. *City & Society* 17(1): 5–34.

Stewart, Boyd. 2010a [1993]. 'Oral History Interview with Ann Lage'. In *Saving Point Reyes National Seashore, 1969–1970: An Oral History of Citizen Action in Conservation: Oral History Transcript/1993*. Berkeley, CA: Bancroft Library Regional Oral History Office and Nabu Press.

2010b [1993]. 'Boyd Stewart Testimony – 1970'. In *Saving Point Reyes National Seashore, 1969–1970: An Oral History of Citizen Action in Conservation: Oral History Transcript/1993*. Berkeley, CA: Bancroft Library Regional Oral History Office and Nabu Press, 281–287.

Trainer, Amy. 2013. 'It's Time for Drakes Estero to Run Wild'. *Latest News Earth Island Journal, Earth Island Institute*, 16 May. www.earthisland.org/journal/index.php/oeuvre/Amy-Trainer/, accessed 17 November 2016.

Tsing, Anna Lowenhaupt. 2005. *Friction: An Ethnography of Global Connection*. Princeton, NJ: Princeton University Press.

US National Park Service. 2007. 'Clarification of Law, Policy, and Science on Drakes Estero'. Public Letter, 18 September,

Watt, Laura. 2002. 'The Trouble with Preservation, or, Getting Back to the Wrong Term for Wilderness Protection: A Case Study at Point Reyes National Seashore'. *APCG Yearbook* 64: 55–72.

Watt, Laura. 2012. 'Realizing the Potential'. *West Marin Citizen* 6(11): 6 September.

CHAPTER SEVEN

EVERYDAY JUSTICE AT THE COURTHOUSE?

Governing Lay Participation in Argentina's Criminal Trials

Santiago Abel Amietta

INTRODUCTION

The first trial I observed as part of my ethnographic study on the introduction of lay participants in Argentine criminal justice commenced on a sizzling December morning, with the temperature higher than 30°C. The embezzlement trial was due to begin 9 AM in the criminal courthouse of a mid-sized city in the Province of Córdoba. The courthouse was in a relatively new purpose-built venue inaugurated in 1998, and the air-conditioned hearing room contrasted with the humidity and blistering heat outdoors. Nevertheless, as the hearing went on, the chilled air felt increasingly less comfortable. About an hour and a half after the start of the hearing, after the declarations of the first few witnesses, a recess was ordered. A middle-aged juror, wearing a blouse, linen pants, and sandals, interrupted my conversation with the trial prosecutor to reproach him about the room temperature:

> 'It is freezing in there. Why do you have the air conditioning so high? We will all die,' she said.
> 'You say that, my lady', the prosecutor replied, 'because you don't have to wear this suit and a tie.'
> 'Then tomorrow I'll come in a suit and tie,' she said, rushing to the cafeteria for a hot coffee.

The juror later told me that she disliked the patronizing tone of the prosecutor, but the episode remained largely anecdotal for the protagonists. For me, instead, it seemed to be a strong cue to what I was looking for in my immersion in the life and workings of Córdoba's criminal courthouses. That curiosity lay at the outset with the novel, ultimately commonsensical ways of making justice that ordinary people were supposed to bring – according to scholars, activists, and popular wisdom alike – to the realm of professionalized, rule-bound, technical knowledge–based decision-making processes of legal professionals. The weight of a customary, unwritten rule in the official's answer pointed to a more complex intertwinement of norms, formalities, and common sense in the power-laden encounters between laypersons and jurists.

Research on law and the *everyday* has tended to assume the 'negative constitution' between these two realms, pitting the space of official state legal institutions inexorably against the antipodal *everyday* (Valverde 2003a; see Chapter 6 in this volume). Discussions around law and justice, in their turn, have examined the interaction and tensions between the two notions. Jacques Derrida (1992) famously claimed that the language and mechanisms of state law appear insufficient as a vehicle to convey and satisfy the desire for true justice.[1] This tension has been a staple of studies of the operation of lay juries interested in the notion of justice. They have argued that commonplace notions of justice clash with the limited possibilities of state systems of justice administration (Maynard and Manzo 1993; Finkel 2001; see also Chapter 1 of this volume).

This chapter dialogues with these bodies of literature and proposes a related but different path in its contribution to theory-making efforts around *everyday justice*. It does not resort to the binary of formal–informal as epitomic of ontologically discrete realms. Instead, it suggests juxtaposing the formal and the informal within judicial proceedings as heuristic devices to turn the very boundaries between the everyday and the institutional into part of the empirical examination. Inspired by Mariana Valverde's discussions of *jurisdiction* and *scales of governance* as tools for socio-legal theory-making (Valverde 2014; 2015), my main conceptual claim in this chapter is that it may be more useful to investigate these boundaries as an effect of the power-laden attempts at governing the very formal/informal, legal/extra-legal divides in discrete contexts.

This approach implies an expanded gaze at the authorities that put these governance attempts into action. The above vignette serves as a reminder not only of the magnitude of legal professionals' need for posturing and appearances that convey formality and detachment, or of the fact that those solidified mores and practices are not necessarily isomorphic to general written rules. It also draws our attention to the multiple spatialities and temporalities that make up judicial authority – well beyond those that conventionally embody this authority at the courthouse, namely, judicial proceedings and decisions. These usually mark the epistemological limits of legal research, thus demoting the multiple other ways in which judicial authority and justice-seeking practices are performed around judicial procedures to the rank of *means* (Barrera 2011). Many authorities regulate the dimensions of the incorporation of laypersons into decision-making, but they have not necessarily been granted such authority by statutory bodies of rules. This chapter examines the workings of some of these authorities and their role in defining the contours of *participation*.

These two points converge in the chapter's exploration of everyday interactions and practices at Argentine criminal courthouses as they accommodate lay participants for the first time in history. Relying on a governance perspective (Foucault 1978; 1984; 1991), I look at the workings of entities that have become entitled to govern the role of laypersons within judicial proceedings. I claim that this includes the authorization to introduce informalities within what is seen as a succession of formal, rule-bound bureaucratic steps. The chapter argues that the very boundaries of what is conceived as 'everyday' – associated in this context with the candid, spontaneous, and assumedly extra-legal nature of jurors' behaviour and conduct – emerge at least in part as *effects* of such governing activity. While jurors' breaches of formalities are readily framed and attributed to their condition as outsiders, the stretching of legal rules in legal proceedings by legal professionals remains normalized and largely invisible. Jurors' ambiguous status and alterity is thus constituted and reinforced through courthouse practices' own *everyday*, as the result of the work of myriad authorities, mostly invisible to the law-centred gaze of legal studies.

The analysis is based on fieldwork conducted between October 2012 and April 2013 in four locations in Córdoba, including interviews with judicial officials, lawyers, and individuals who served as jurors; close reading of documents (including case files and decisions, laws, draft laws, and transcripts of constitutional and legislative debates); and observation of courthouse routines and proceedings with and without lay participants. Further interviews and archival research were conducted in Buenos Aires and La Plata.

LAY PARTICIPATION, LAW, AND THE EVERYDAY

Until about three decades ago, the history of lay participation in state justice systems in Argentina had largely been one of promise and absence. Jury trials had been included in all the institutionalization attempts during the transition to formal postcolonial independence since the beginning of the nineteenth century. The first National Constitution (1853–1860) mentioned them in three different clauses (Cavallero and Hendler 1988). Until the 1980s, however, the actual implementation of lay participation was rarely addressed in spheres of authorized legal discourse in Argentina, despite its remaining untouched in the constitutional text (Hendler 2008). During this period, only one legislative project was presented to the National Congress to establish criminal jury trials in 1873 (Bergoglio 2011: 834), and the Supreme Court ruled on (and rejected) only three petitions of defendants claiming their constitutional right to be judged by peers in 1911, 1932, and 1947.[2] With the return of constitutional rule following the last dictatorship (1976–1983), a general process of legal and judicial reforms ensued and the visibility of the notion of lay participation increased. The first system, a mixed tribunal of three professional judges and two laypersons, was introduced in 1991 in the Province of Córdoba. In 2004, the same province enacted a new system, currently in force. This is a mixed tribunal in which eight laypersons –plus four substitutes – are summoned to take part in the decision of a single case (the most serious murders and cases of public corruption), sitting with three judges and deciding the verdict by majority.[3]

The creative work of activists and reformers advocating for lay participation in criminal justice in Argentina, of which Córdoba's experiment was the first success, was characterized by the multiple, overlapping, and contradictory political rationales underlying their programs (Amietta 2016). Some of these reformers put lay participation forward as a tool for the democratization of the judiciary and a step toward the full democratization of state governance (Bergoglio 2010). Others brought to the fore the need for a judiciary with a stronger public image, and lay participation as a way to infuse its decisions with legitimacy and its officials with trust (Bergoglio 2011). Even the ubiquitous demand for security in the face of violent urban crime, pervasive in Argentine and Latin American political and media talk (Kessler 2009), found a space within the political rationales put forward as the participation of lay persons in the decisions of criminal trials was discussed and implemented in the Province of Córdoba (Bergoglio and Amietta 2012; Amietta 2014).

These overlapping and even contradictory political logics evidence the heterogeneity of 'participation' as a governmental rationale, as much as the strength of its legitimizing force. They also alert us to the intrinsically contingent nature of the outcomes of reform programs (Amietta 2016). But one more pervasive discursive thread traversed the politically diverse pro-jury advocacy of the last few decades in Argentina: lay participation has been consistently put forward as a way to empower society against the discrete realm of the state, which activists see epitomized in what they depict as overly bureaucratized, elitist, and out-of-touch judicial officials. This put the romance of *everyday justice* in the limelight of this process of reforms, embodied in tropes like 'common sense' and in the thrust for empowering the 'wisdom of the streets' vis-à-vis the overly technical views of legal professionals. The imaginary of lay participation as a channel to bring the commonsensical forms and substance of everyday justice to the realm of institutionalized decision-making is of course neither new nor exclusive to the Argentine discussion. Such references abound in jury discourse elsewhere: *You must consider all the evidence in the light of reason, experience, and common sense* is, with little variation, an ode to everyday justice brought to court usually found in jury instructions in many US states' court systems, and bears testimony to common law's 'dream of a common knowledge' (Valverde 2003b).

Socio-legal studies of law and the everyday, however, since their emergence in the 1980s in the work of a group of American law and society scholars, have largely sidestepped mechanisms of lay participation in official judicial procedures as locales for inquiry. Characterized by an interest in de-centring 'the law', scholars have searched instead for ordinary people's deployment of legal practices and meanings outside and beyond the workings of official legal institutions (Williams 1993; Greenhouse et al. 1994; Ewick and Silbey 1998). When the loci have been sites of formal decision-making (Yngvesson 1989; Merry 1990) or other state agencies (Sarat 1990), the focus has remained on the receiving, disempowered end of the implied law–society divide – common citizens and their meaning-making processes in encounters with such institutions. In this body of work, the jury appears reified as a constitutive part, if not an epitome, of the formal legal system, sometimes explicitly so (Marcus 1993; Sarat and Kearns 1993; Silbey 2005).

The negative constitution of the everyday against the law situates the jurors at the other extreme of the continuum, essentially delinked from times, spaces, and practices of the everyday while they serve at the courthouse.

From the empirical vantage point of the recent incorporation of lay participation to a historically professionalized criminal justice system, this chapter proposes a possible avenue to bridge this gap in our debates on law, justice, and the everyday. The ethnographic account that follows suggests an understanding of the incorporation of laypersons into the decision of criminal trials as a dynamic assemblage co-produced by formal and informal practices, spatiotemporal conditionings, and different meanings attached to participation and judicial authority by multiple authorized entities. Resorting to the formal–informal binary as a heuristic device, the discussion turns the divide between 'everyday' and institutionalized justice into part of the empirical question, intending ultimately to problematize the nature of the boundaries we draw between them. In this line, I argue that the very dichotomy may be more usefully studied – and perhaps ultimately collapse – if looked at in situated local contexts from a governance perspective.

GOVERNING PARTICIPATION AT THE COURTHOUSE: JURORS AND THE EVERYDAY OF JUSTICE

This brief account of the incorporation of laypersons into the network of places, practices, persons, and things that make up the hybrid of Córdoba's criminal justice begins when they are not yet there. A file has arrived at one of the twenty-one criminal courts of the province from the office of a prosecutor, who has collected enough evidence to consider the file 'ripe' enough (Latour 2010) to move to its final trial stage. Allied with supporting staff, documents, testimonies, police officers, legal doctrines, and judicial precedents, the prosecutor has come out with a 'legal qualification' for the crime investigated. This means it has been provisionally subsumed within one of the categories listed in the Criminal Law Code as crimes (*delitos*). And according to that qualification – for instance, a particularly hideous homicide or the bribery of a public official – it turns out to be mandatory for the trial to be judged by a mixed tribunal.

For the member of the court staff in charge of the case this entails the need to organize a trial with jurors.[4] They shall, once a date for the trial is set, form a panel of eight laypersons – plus four substitutes, should any of them need to be replaced during the procedure – to sit with the three permanently appointed professional judges of the court. The formation of the panel is materialized in an *incidente* – a smaller file within the case file, with a similar pastel-coloured cardboard cover entitled '*Incidente de constitución de jurado popular*' (incident of jury constitution) or a similar expression. The unintendedness and unexpectedness that the term *incidente* conveys in ordinary talk accurately summarizes court-house bureaucrats' perceptions of this occasion: an undesired complication, an additional inconvenience building on what is perceived as an already tough set of daily routines. These routines, in their view, have been crafted over years mirroring the ahistorical formal mandates of the law and the professional experience of courthouse dwellers. Jurors, from the moment of this merely embryonic presence, unsettle and produce a breach in a sense of normality in judicial activity. This is more complex than the charges of unwillingness to share the 'power to judge' that many pro-jury advocates ascribe to judicial personnel and officials.

But let us take a closer look at the process of formation of the panel of lay decision makers, as a first illustration of the effect of their incorporation on the balance of the court's everyday proceedings. The constitution of the panel is the object of a detailed regulation in the law. The trial court should request the list of jurors for the corresponding judicial district and organize a hearing to which the trial prosecutor and parties shall be summoned.[5] In that hearing, according to the law, a list of twenty-four candidates to the final integration of the mixed tribunal shall be drawn up, thus turning the possibilities of participation entirely a matter of chance.[6] My observations and interactions at court offices showed a different picture as to the way in which this group of candidates is drafted. Curious about the technological devices deployed to draft them, I probed into this with assistant clerks. The question was rather pointless to most of them, as the fortuitous draft actually does not happen. Among assistant clerks I questioned, only two claimed to do it randomly. They mentioned technologies that the rest of the courthouse personnel ignored, and that I did not have the chance to see at work. One of them said he uses 'a little software' and another mentioned a 'lottery spinner'. Several others admitted that no ballot is done and described a range of tactics for the selection, laying bare a fascinating, multifarious procedure with different expressions in different courts. Among these were an assistant clerk who claimed that he estimates the age of female jurors according to their ID numbers in order to summon young ones (likely a one-off case) and another one who does not pick jurors with no land line telephone as these are often harder to contact. The most consistent rationale seemed to be favouring jurors with the best prospects of turning up, making proximity of their address and previous attendance in other trials the most popular criteria.[7]

Once the twenty-four initial candidates are selected, they are summoned for a hearing where the final panel of eight jurors and four substitutes is to be formed. The law is straightforward: the first twelve jurors originally drafted 'in the chronological order of the ballot' shall form the panel. Subsequent ones shall cover the positions of those who did not attend, had an excuse worthy of consideration, or were disqualified.[8] Besides issues that could affect their impartiality (such as a previous relationship with a party in the trial or having publicly expressed their opinion on the case), the law only accepts as excuses health issues of the juror or a dependent relative, or proof of the service causing them a 'severe financial damage'.[9] The very informality of the initial twenty-four selection turns this into rather a set of negotiations between those who actually attend – often not the twenty-four summoned – and the court clerks in charge, who act as the final adjudicating authority. An experienced assistant clerk mentioned 'people who have come before in good vibes' as her favourite choices, turning the selection criterion into a *qualified* one: not only is previous service desired, but a certain form of previous service. 'Young women with little children', on the other hand, are persons she is lenient with if they do not want to serve. In contrast, people who fear they may lose their jobs do not get away with it if she is in charge: she claims to have talked over the phone with a number of employers to make their legal obligations clear. All in all, she told me, 'after a while you get to know the people', and the selection becomes more straightforward. After having specific issues adjudicated through conversations with prospective jurors, the clerks go into the court offices (while candidates wait, normally in the hearing room) and come back to inform those who have been chosen.[10]

That the ballot is not random gives judicial bureaucrats tools to regulate participation. It also authorizes them to evaluate jurors' performances and to do so according to their particular understandings of what meaningful participation and justice-making should mean and entail. Hence the point is not to denounce cunning plots of these state officials to curtail participation by hand-picking jurors at their convenience. These practices are not intended to be unmasked here as deviant – their normalization and the openness with which they were shared with me would make such labelling problematic. The aim is to shed light on the powerful authorizing tool that comes with the possibility of defining how, where, and why everyday informalities can be introduced within a process presented as a series of depersonalized bureaucratic procedures.

Far from the splendour of the *juris dictio*, the *saying the law* from the positivistic understanding of law with which judicial officials identify themselves, and equally distant from the macro-sociological imagination of reformers and activists, assistant clerks hold a crucial form of jurisdiction whose workings remain invisible to the limelight of authorized studies of the law. The practice for the jurors' draw is these clerks' translation (Callon 1986; Latour 1987; 2005) of a careful regulation produced in different jurisdictional loci, with different political aims and temporalities in mind, directed to different audiences and foregrounding some concerns while underplaying others. In legislatures and offices of pro-jury NGOs such processes were crafted as detailed procedures legible as the official way to achieve random and democratic participation in the administration of justice. In the anonymity of the courts' offices, where the *everyday* also takes place, they are reinterpreted with the purported choice of jurors that have already proved or are presumed to be diligent (because they live nearby, have no problems with their employers, or seem more willing to make the effort). *Participation*, the *people*, and the *everyday* they are supposed to bring to the courthouse become *qualitatively different* epistemological objects (or, rather, reveal their epistemological heterogeneity) as they are targeted by different governmental gazes (Valverde 2005: 431). The ontological distinction between institutional and everyday ways of making justice and the traits we associate with each of them are thus also problematized.

The 'mundane practices of collusion and evasion' (Mathew 2008; see also Li 2011) enacted in forming the panel of jurors are, however, not the end of the story of translations and detours. One of the assistant clerks who described to me in detail the 'apocryphal' procedure also handed me a copy of the file. It contained the minutes of a hearing that did not take place and described the result of a ballot which did not exist, listing officials who were not there. Crucially, their signatures will be in the original version of the file, making possible the work of imputation and assignment that is critical to law's form of assignation (Latour 2010: 276–277). As the act leaves the closed sphere of the courthouse offices and is re-crafted in its public form ready to circulate as the official version, its performance recovers the isomorphism with the letter of the law. The official story is challenged in the discretion of everyday courthouse offices' mundane practices and talks, and simultaneously remains unchallenged in any public way. This is relevant for my argument in this chapter, as performing and recording the official story of the law in the most visible and perennial storage medium (i.e., the file) is one of the ways in which clerks and court bureaucrats contribute to stabilizing the implied divide between the candid and spontaneous lay participants and the imaginary of the rule-bound operation of legal institutions.

The incorporation of jurors does not simply bring the extra-legal spontaneity and candidness of the everyday into the otherwise legal rule-bound courthouse. It finds them, instead, involved with and affecting the enmeshment of formal and informal practices. However, moments of unobserved formalities on the side of jurors are governed and rendered visible in a very different way. Let me turn to my ethnographic notes to illustrate this point. The setting is a mixed tribunal trial in a court of Córdoba's capital city; five defendants are accused of murdering a moneylender. After a week of hearings, the last witness was the experienced police detective in charge of the investigation. The interrogation laid bare patent deficiencies in the detection work and featured harsh comments from the judges about the consequences of the seasoned officer's poor performance for the trial. The outcome, foreseeable from the very first day of hearings, was entirely clear by the end of this declaration: the defendants would be acquitted due to insurmountable doubts. Before the final allegations of the prosecutor and defence lawyers, a short recess was called. As is usually the case in recesses, the prosecutor, lawyers, and audience (consisting in this case only of myself and an assistant from the prosecutor's office) were asked to leave the hearing room. In the corridor, the tense ambiance of other breaks during the now virtually concluded trial had dissipated. Smiles abounded and talks had shifted to weekend plans until one of the jurors appeared. On his way to the toilet, he somewhat effusively congratulated the defence lawyers:

'Well done, Doctors, congratulations', he said, clapping the back of the youngest.

The defence lawyer rapidly reacted: 'No, no, you can't say that, please.'

A moment of awkward silence followed; and the lawyer turned to me (the only stranger, though dressed up as a lawyer) to state: 'They don't know. They have no idea. They should be told about this kind of thing.'[11]

The misconduct of the juror seemed a minor one, and it would certainly not have further consequences. It fitted the relaxed, 'work-done' ambiance of the corridor and the tone of the last moments of the hearing. The reaction it engendered and the conversation on the topic that followed seemed to contrast with the undisputed, normalized stretching of legal rules throughout the jurors' selection process described before. What was unsettling in the view of the legal professionals involved was the jurors' lack of information as to *which* formalities are to be strictly respected, or at least strictly performed. One of these, as I myself learnt at that moment, is that decision makers do not publicly anticipate a verdict (even the most obvious one), as it is central to the performance of objectivity and detachment that characterizes law's operation, even (and perhaps especially) outside the hearing room in a more relaxed time and space.[12] The juror's presence in this space and time was due to his consideration as an outsider – otherwise he would have been allowed to use the court's private toilet and bypass any contact with the 'public' of the hearing. His conduct, while rendering the naturalized workings of the rule visible, added to this standing as an outsider in the eyes of legal professionals who pointed out the deviation. Moreover, it created space for further interactions that accentuate jurors' alterity vis-à-vis legal professionals and their modes of conduct. The heightened sense of otherness of jurors, in turn, also upholds their identification with a commonsensical view alien to the rules of legal procedures (Amietta 2016).

This obscures the fact, evident from my fieldwork, that in the courthouse jurors tend to presume the strictly formal nature of the proceedings they take part in and to perform accordingly. During a trial, for example, a clerk found it slightly amusing that a juror very quietly approached him to ask for permission to go to the toilet. The day before, incidentally, a judge had left the hearing room for more than fifteen minutes in the middle of a witness testimony without any explanation. Just as with the bespoke selection process, the advent of jurors generates new opportunities to stretch, or subvert, the legal regulations for those who hold the authority to do so. Norma, a juror who served in the trial of a police officer who killed a teenager with a supposedly non-lethal weapon, told me that the forensic doctor and the expert in ballistics had visited the jurors as they waited in a private room before a day's hearing. The forensic doctor, she recounted, had testified at the hearing only about certain 'specific' issues such as how the body was when he saw it. But later, in their private meeting, he was able to explain to them in detail how such a death could have occurred. The ballistics expert, besides giving further details about the conditions of operation of the weapon and technicalities like the distance of the shot, had a rubber bullet gun like the murder weapon with him. He took advantage of his visit to provide a practical demonstration of how it is operated. Norma, generally happy with the expanded explanation, found this a bit discomforting and politely asked him to point the weapon in a different direction.[13]

In the public stages of proceedings, it is also possible to see this kind of tactical less-than-legal manoeuvres being used, and going similarly unchallenged. In the second day of hearings of the moneylender murder trial mentioned above, the only eyewitness (a young, foreign, female domestic worker) was presenting a version of the facts different from her original testimony at the police station. Amid a growing impatience, intensified by her difficulty in understanding Spanish, the presiding judge reminded her of the risk of being charged with perjury by ordering her to be taken to the *alcaidía* – a small police dependency functioning in the basement of the courthouse where prisoners wait for their trials. A couple of hours later, after other witnesses had testified, she was brought back. Her testimony continued, this time with the Consul General of her country acting as a translator. The practice (certainly not a part of the proceedings described in the Criminal Procedure Code) struck me, and I tried to get more information about it. Assistant clerks of the court informed me that it is a relatively common practice, particularly with that presiding judge, as witnesses sometimes need to 'be scared a bit'. Accounts of different members of the staff were contradictory as to whether she had actually been taken to the *alcaidía* or just stayed in background offices of the court with police personnel – who, I was told, know how to advise people in these situations.[14]

The point of these vignettes is, once more, not to denounce these practices as illegal. The sheer contrast with the law's procedure (and with the rights-based discourse that judicial officials would entertain in our own conversations, often to express their angst about vengeful jurors) seemed to go unnoticed. The importance of principles such as the oral public trial or the possibility of counter-examination of witnesses for the proper exercise of the right to defend oneself (markers of their own, law-backed, institutional way of making justice) is temporarily underplayed in a way that seems to go unnoticed by judicial clerks and officials. The courthouse has its own *everyday*, and disregard for the knowledge produced therein by those who devise legal procedures is accepted by judicial bureaucrats as a natural consequence of the division of state powers, but also deployed as a justification for diversions. The limited practical possibilities and the local tactics they engender are, however, not delinked from particular governmental rationales and epistemological claims as to the meaning of otherwise abstract objects, such as *justice* or *participation*. I suggest looking at these everyday petty knowledge practices as more than simple markers of gaps between the written law and its operation. Instead, they pivot between the macro-politics of reformers, the principles of rational law, and the need for getting things done on the ground.

The fact that legal decision-making processes 'evoke the modes of operation of a professional and depersonalised bureaucracy' as they construct and develop particular forms of knowledge is a well-known finding of legal and institutional anthropology (Barrera 2011: 62). Also well established is that such professional and depersonalized operation embodied in formal proceedings is actually enmeshed with informal practices that blur the legal–illegal divide (Koğacıoğlu 2003; Navaro-Yashin 2007). Drawing on the particular juncture of the incorporation of laypersons into a historically professional judicial system, I have contributed to these discussions in several ways. We have seen that (1) these practices contribute to authorizing agents to govern and to define the shape and meanings of participation in the everyday workings of the criminal justice system, (2) the very boundaries of what is seen as 'everyday' (inasmuch as characteristic of the candid, spontaneous, and assumedly extra-legal nature of jurors' behaviour and conduct) emerge at least in part as an *effect* of that governing activity and of the authorization to introduce and normalize those informalities into legal procedures, and (3) the breaches of formalities by jurors – who show great concern for respecting the ritualistic nature of legal proceedings – are readily signalled and attributed to their condition as outsiders, while the legal proceedings' own mix of formality and informality remains normalized and largely invisible.

CONCLUDING REMARKS: THE EVERYDAY, ROMANCE, AND BOUNDARIES

Part of the seduction of the everyday may come from what George Marcus described as its occupying, equally in social theory and legal discourse, 'the space of the moral, the pragmatic, the accessible, and the commonsensical bastion of simple coherence and order', thus offering 'an elusive escape from abstraction' (Marcus 1993: 237–238). My own arrival at lay participation in criminal justice as a research interest, after being trained as a lawyer, was out of this sort of curiosity. This conveniently coupled with the temptation – widespread among scholars of law and everyday life – of standing on the side of those at the receiving end of power, especially when it comes from a technology with the ideological firepower of modern state law and in a context of historical professional monopoly over judicial decision-making.

My fieldwork, however, proved to me that the everyday is not as accessible, concrete, unequivocally authentic and easily identifiable with *the people*'s interests, desires, and practices as we would like it to be. It is also an effect mediated by the work of numerous experts (detached by their very expertise, just as we are, from the realm of the everyday) who put it forward as a magic bullet for certain social problems to be solved – in the particular locale of this study, through the introduction of laypersons to criminal justice. The multiplicity of authorities entitled to give *participation* content and practical expression in the courthouses (like clerks who summon and accommodate the jurors into the physical and metaphorical spaces of the formal justice) are also required to make knowledge claims they would not have done had lay participation not been introduced into their jurisdictional realm. Every regulatory power is, hence, an epistemological power as well (Valverde 2009), and the divide between spaces, times, and practices of the 'everyday' and those of institutionalised justice-making mechanisms is also the effect of the workings of these powers.

Much of the socio-legal work on law and everyday life has tended to endorse a clear-cut distinction of the everyday as a realm opposed to formal institutions. As this location at the antipodes of state power accounts to a great extent for the romance of the everyday (Abu-Lughod 1990), the warning is against setting epistemological boundaries between these categories, and treating them as attached to ontological realms devoid of contextually specific content (Valverde 2003a). The locale of my study provided insights into how frail these boundaries can turn out to be. Looking more closely at the encounters of laypersons with judicial proceedings – and especially at the manifestations of authority that surround the judicial decision, often considered the only researchable outcome of such proceedings – in the search for contrasting ways of understanding justice gave me the unexpected opportunity to document law's own contradictions. *Formal* and *informal* worked as heuristic devices in this chapter to highlight the fact that they occur in stabilized and undistinguished ways during court proceedings, bearing no signs of differentiated statuses. This serves as a reminder of law's plural and multi-scalar operation that, at times, resembles its self-presentation as a set of rationalized general rules but, at many other times, has much of the convenience, pragmatism, common sense, and simplicity often attributed to the everyday. On the other extreme of the continuum, those identified by authorized legal discourse as bearers of the everyday do not necessarily behave accordingly: unaware of the nuances, jurors tend to make unremitting efforts to stick to formalities during proceedings; but when they slip, their faults are pointed out. I have argued that, much in the form of a self-fulfilling prophecy, this singles jurors out as outsiders, reinforces their alterity, and ultimately feeds their identification with the *everyday*, as well as legal professionals' self-perceptions – and capital – as guardians of the law and its unique rule-bound justice-making procedures.

Law and justice, it has been argued, exist in an irresolvable aporetic relation in which the former cannot aspire to achieve or materialize the latter (Derrida 1992). This, however, means neither that they are irreconcilably opposed, nor that justice simply represents a higher ideal form that, pitted against law, mirrors the philosophical binary ideal versus real (Valverde 1999: 657–659). The contribution of this chapter to the theory-making efforts on justice remains modest and pragmatic, in that it looks at power asymmetries and their effects on the ground as opposed to universal ethical or political stances. Law and justice exist, here and now, in a dialogical relation at any point in which one engages in a certain action that one deems just and through which they lay a claim to know a certain other to a certain extent – namely, a judicial decision (Valverde 1999). The actualization of justice by means of law contributes to justify law's own force, not only as exercised through 'enforcement' over the body of defendants (Derrida 1992:

6–7), but also in the minutiae of everyday encounters among those called to seek justice.

Proponents of the incorporation of lay participation in Argentine criminal trials, from across the political spectrum, coincided in their putting forward the potential of lay participation to bridge the gap between commonsensical understandings of justice and the truth-seeking processes of the criminal justice system. Looking at the inter-action of lay jurors and legal professionals on the ground unveiled a much more complex picture in which authorities claiming expertise in different places and times co-produce legible versions of the story of this institutional innovation. Their tales and actions contribute to the network that regulates the existence and experience of lay participation and, I claimed, help produce certain conceptions of the everyday and its justices. This dynamic machinery of knowledge *in the making* (Callon 1986; Latour 2005) also contains us scholars of 'law and society', a fact that even those leaning toward critical examinations of the law sometimes fail to recognize – although we rarely fail to claim allegiance to reflexivity. My own understandings of participation and everyday justice are also part of such assemblages of knowledge claims, of the blind spots they may be creating, and of their power effects, just as the networks we look at are not only externally given but are affected by us and in turn make us possible.

Notes

1 'Law [*droit*] is not justice. Law is the element of calculation, and it is just that there be law, but justice is incalculable, it requires us to calculate with the incalculable; and aporetic experiences are the experiences, as improbable as they are necessary, of justice, that is to say of moments in which the decision between just and unjust is never insured by a rule' (Derrida 1992: 16).

2 *Don Vicente Loviera* v. *Don Eduardo T. Mulhall* – Injurias y Calumnias, sobre competencia (Fallos 1911, 115–192); *Ministerio Fiscal* v. *Director Diario La Fronda* – por desacato (Fallos 1933, 165–258); and *David Tieffemberg* – Competencia penal, delitos en particular, desacato (Fallos 1947, 208–225).

3 The workings of this system provided the bulk of the data produced during my fieldwork. The provinces of Neuquén (2011) and Buenos Aires (2013) have now followed Córdoba and implemented lay participation systems in line with the classic English jury. Chubut, Chaco, Mendoza, Río Negro, and San Juan have also passed jury trials legislation but have not implemented it yet. Legislative projects wait to be discussed in the legislatures of several other provinces and in the National Congress.

4 Such is the mechanism for the division of labor in Córdoba's criminal courthouses: each file is handled by a single member of the staff who deals with it from its arrival to its end. It is common to hear someone asking 'whose' case file this is.
5 The general list of one juror per 1,500 voters is balloted yearly from the voter registry by the Electoral Court. As voting is mandatory in Argentina, the registry contains the names of every person over the age of eighteen.
6 Law 9182, Articles 17 and 18.
7 Repetition of jurors is not permitted by the law. The regulation indicates that once jurors are drafted for a trial, their names should be given to the administrative office in charge of them to be excluded until every person on the list has been drafted (Law 9182, Article 22). The marks next to the names of jurors on the list that circulates through the courts are used for exactly the opposite aim. A tangible consequence is the repetition of jurors, some of them having been summoned for up to six cases. The explanation for this visible side of the process, when administrative officers in charge are asked, is that the law failed to set a reasonable ratio of jurors to voters, the current one being insufficient.
8 Law 9182, Article 22.
9 Law 9182, Article 19.
10 Field notes, November 2012; February and March 2013.
11 Field notes, February 2013.
12 For a comparison of the objectivity of scientists – who show themselves enthusiastic about their objects of study without complexes – and that of law's experts – for whom detachment is essential to retain a sense of objectivity – see Latour 2010 (especially ch. 5). Departing from opposed epistemological underpinnings, Pierre Bourdieu interestingly raises a similar argument in his celebrated critical account of the production and use of legal knowledge, in which he describes the jurists as reinforcing the autonomy of the legal field (especially from the realm of economic activity), not only as a matter of deployment of intellectual capital in the form of expert knowledge, but also as a question of posture – even physical posture (Bourdieu 1987; see also Bourdieu 2003).
13 Interview with juror, Case 47.
14 Field notes, February 2013.

References

Abu-Lughod, Lila. 1990. 'The Romance of Resistance: Tracing Transformations of Power through Bedouin Women'. *American Ethnologist* 17(1): 41–55.
Amietta, Santiago A. 2014. 'Devising the Juror: The Power and Knowledge of Participation in the Introduction of Laypersons in Criminal Trials in Argentina'. Paper presented at the annual meeting of the Law and Society Association, Minneapolis, MN, May 29–June 1.

2016. 'Governing Lay Participation: Power, Knowledge and Legal Consciousness in the Making of Argentina's Juror'. PhD diss., University of Manchester.

Barrera, Leticia. 2011. 'Más allá de los fines del derecho: expedientes, burocracia y conocimiento legal' [Beyond law's ends: files, bureaucracy and legal knowledge]. Íconos. Revista de Ciencias Sociales 41: 57–72.

Bergoglio, María I. 2010. Subiendo al estrado: La Experiencia cordobesa de juicio por jurados [Taking the stand: Córdoba's experience of trial with jurors]. Córdoba: Ed. Advocatus.

2011. 'Metropolitan and Town Juries: The Influence of Social Context on Lay Participation'. Chicago-Kent Law Review 86: 831–853.

Bergoglio, María I., and Santiago A. Amietta. 2012. 'Reclamo social de castigo y participación lega en juicios penales: lecciones desde la experiencia cordobesa'. Revista de Derecho Penal 1(3): 49–60.

Bourdieu, Pierre. 1987. 'The Force of Law: Toward a Sociology of the Juridical Field'. Hastings Law Journal 38: 805–853.

2003. 'Los juristas, guardianes de la hipocresía colectiva' (trans. J. R. Capella). Jueces para la Democracia 47: 3–5.

Callon, Michel. 1986. 'Some Elements of a Sociology of Translation: Domestication of the Scallops and the Fishermen of St Brieuc Bay'. In John Law (ed.), Power, Action and Belief: A New Sociology of Knowledge. London: Routledge, 196–233

Calzado, Mercedes C., and Sebastián Van Den Dooren. 2009. '¿Leyes Blumberg? Reclamos sociales de seguridad y reformas penales' [Blumberg laws? Social claims for security and penal reforms]. Delito y sociedad: revista de ciencias sociales 27: 97–113.

Cavallero, Ricardo, and Edmundo Hendler. 1988. Justicia y participación – El Juicio por jurados en materia penal [Justice and Participation – The Criminal Jury Trial]. Buenos Aires: Ed. Universidad.

Clark, John, Marcus T. Boccaccini, Beth Caillouet, and William F. Chaplin. 2007. 'Five Factor Model Personality Traits, Jury Selection, and Case Outcomes in Criminal and Civil Cases'. Criminal Justice and Behavior 34: 641–660.

Cole, Simon A., and Rachel Dioso-Villa. 2006. 'CSI and Its Effects: Media, Juries, and the Burden of Proof'. New England Law Review 41: 435–469.

Conley, John M., and William M. O'Barr. 1990. Rules versus Relationships: The Ethnography of Legal Discourse. Chicago: University of Chicago Press.

Cruikshank, Barbara. 1999. The Will to Empower. Ithaca, NY: Cornell University Press.

Derrida, Jacques. 1992. 'Force of Law: The "Mystical Foundation of Authority"'. In Drucilla Cornell, Michel Rosenfeld, and David Gray Carlson (eds.), Deconstruction and the Possibility of Justice. New York: Routledge, 3–67.

Diamond, Shari S., and Mary R. Rose. 2005. 'Real Juries'. *Annual Review of Law and Social Science* 1: 255–284.

Dzur, Albert W. 2012. *Punishment, Participatory Democracy, and the Jury.* New York: Oxford University Press.

Ewick, Patricia, and Susan S. Silbey. 1998. *The Common Place of Law: Stories from Everyday Life.* Chicago: University of Chicago Press.

Ferrer, Carlos, and Celia A. Grundy. 2005. *El Nuevo juicio penal con Jurados en la provincia de Córdoba [The New Criminal Trial with Jurors in the Province of Córdoba].* Córdoba: Ed. Mediterránea.

Finkel, Norman J. 2001. *Commonsense Justice: Jurors' Notions of the Law.* Cambridge, MA: Harvard University Press.

Fleury-Steiner, Benjamin. 2002. 'Narratives of the Death Sentence: Toward a Theory of Legal Narrativity'. *Law & Society Review* 36: 549–576.

2003. 'Before or against the Law? Citizens' Legal Beliefs and Experiences as Death Penalty Jurors'. *Studies in Law, Politics, & Society* 27: 115–137.

Foucault, Michel. 1978. *The History of Sexuality, Volume 1: An Introduction,* trans. R. Hurley. New York: Pantheon Books.

1984. 'Polemics, Politics, and Problematizations'. In Paul Rabinow (ed.), *The Foucault Reader.* New York: Pantheon, 381–390.

1991. 'Governmentality'. In Grabham Burchell, Collin Gordon, and Peter Miller (eds.), *The Foucault Effect: Studies on Governmentality.* Chicago: University of Chicago Press, 87–104.

Gastil, John, Burkhalter, Stephanie, and Black, Laura W. 2007. 'Do Juries Deliberate? A Study of Deliberation, Individual Difference, and Group Member Satisfaction at a Municipal Courthouse'. *Small Group Research* 38: 337–359.

Gastil, John, Pierre E. Dees, Philip J. Weiser, and Cindy Simmons. 2010. *The Jury and Democracy: How Juror Deliberation Promotes Civic Engagement and Political Participation.* New York: Oxford University Press.

Gould, Jon, and Scott Barclay. 2012. 'Mind the Gap: The Place of Gap Studies in Sociolegal Scholarship'. *Annual Review of Law and Social Science* 8: 323–335.

Greenhouse, Carol, Barbara Yngvesson, and David Engel. 1994. *Law and Community in Three American Towns.* Ithaca, NY: Cornell University Press.

Guagnini, Lucas. 2005. *Blumberg. En el nombre del hijo [Blumberg. In the name of the son].* Buenos Aires: Sudamericana.

Hans, Valerie P. 2003. 'Introduction: Lay Participation in Legal Decision Making'. *Law & Policy* 25: 83–92.

2008. 'Jury Systems around the World'. *Annual Review of Law and Social Sciences* 4: 275–297.

Hendler, Edmundo. 2008. 'Lay Participation in Argentina: Old History, Recent Experience'. *Southwestern Journal of Law and Trade in the Americas* 15(1): 2–24.

Jimeno-Bulnes, Mar. 2011. 'Jury Selection and Jury Trial in Spain: Between Theory and Practice'. *Chicago-Kent Law Review* 86: 585–611.

Kalven, Harry, and Hans Zeisel. 1993 [1966]. *The American Jury Special edition*. New York: Gryphon Editions, the Legal Classics Library.

Kessler, G. 2009. *El Sentimiento de inseguridad. Sociología del temor al delito* [*The feeling of insecurity. Sociology of fear of crime*]. Buenos Aires: Siglo Veintiuno.

Koğacioğlu, Dicle. 2003. 'Law in Context: Citizenship and Reproduction of Inequality in an Istanbul Courthouse'. PhD. diss., State University of New York at Stony Brook.

Kutnjak Ivković, Sanja. 2007. 'Exploring Lay Participation in Legal Decision-making: Lessons from Mixed Tribunals'. *Cornell International Law Journal* 40: 429–453.

Latour, Bruno. 1987. *Science in Action: How to Follow Scientists and Engineers through Society*. Cambridge, MA: Harvard University Press.

　2005. *Reassembling the Social: An Introduction to Actor-Network-Theory*. New York: Oxford University Press.

　2010. *The Making of Law: An Ethnography of the Conseil d'Etat*, trans. Marina Brilman and Alain Pottage. Cambridge: Polity Press.

Li, Tania. 2011. 'Compromising Power: Development, Culture, and Rule in Indonesia'. *Cultural Anthropology* 14(3): 295–322.

Machura, Stefan. 2011. 'Silent Lay Judges – Why Their Influence in the Community Falls Short of Expectations'. *Chicago-Kent Law Review* 86: 769–788.

Marcus, George E. 1993. 'Mass Toxic Torts and the End of Everyday Life'. In Austin Sarat and Thomas Kearns (eds.), *Law in Everyday Life*. Ann Arbor: University of Michigan Press, 237–274.

Mathew, Andrew. 2008. 'State Making, Knowledge and Ignorance: Translation and Concealment in Mexican Forestry Institutions'. *American Anthropologist* 110(4): 484–494.

Maynard, Douglas W., and John Manzo. 1993. 'On the Sociology of Justice: Theoretical Notes from an Actual Jury Deliberation'. *Sociological Theory* 11(2): 171–193.

Merry, Sally E. 1990. *Getting Justice and Getting Even: Legal Consciousness among Working-Class Americans*. Chicago: University of Chicago Press.

Navaro-Yashin, Yael. 2007. 'Make-Believe Papers, Legal Forms and the Counterfeit: Affective Interactions between Documents and People in Britain and Cyprus'. *Anthropological Theory* 7(1): 79–98.

Pratt, John. 2007. *Penal Populism*. London: Routledge.

Rose, Nikolas. 1999. *Powers of Freedom: Reframing Political Thought*. Cambridge: Cambridge University Press.

Rose, Nikolas, and Peter Miller. 1992. 'Political Power beyond the State: Problematics of Government'. *British Journal of Sociology* 43(2): 173–205.

Sarat, Austin. 1990. 'Law Is All Over: Power, Resistance and the Legal Consciousness of the Welfare Poor'. *Yale Journal of Law & the Humanities* 2: 343–379.

1995. 'Violence, Representation and Responsibility in Capital Trials: The View from the Jury'. *Indiana Law Journal* 70: 1103–1135.

Sarat, Austin, and Thomas Kearns. 1993. 'Beyond the Great Divide: Forms of Legal Scholarship and Everyday Life'. In Austin Sarat and Thomas Kearns, (eds.), *Law in Everyday Life*. Ann Arbor: University of Michigan Press, 21–61.

Silbey, Susan S. 2005. 'After Legal Consciousness'. *Annual Review of Law & Social Sciences* 1: 323–368.

Valverde, Mariana 1999. 'Derrida's Justice and Foucault's Freedom: Ethics, History and Social Movements'. *Law and Social Inquiry* 24(3): 655–676.

2003a. '"Which Side Are You On?" Uses of the Everyday in Socio-legal Scholarship'. *Political and Legal Anthropology Review* 26(1): 86–98.

2003b. *Law's Dream of a Common Knowledge*. Princeton, NJ: Princeton University Press.

2005. 'Authorizing the Production of Urban Moral Order: Appellate Courts and Their Knowledge Games'. *Law & Society Review* 36(2): 419–455.

2009. 'Jurisdiction and Scale: Using Law's Technicalities as Theoretical Resources'. *Social & Legal Studies* 18(2): 139–157.

2011. 'Questions of Security: A Framework for Research'. *Theoretical Criminology* 15(1): 3–22.

2014. 'Studying the Governance of Crime and Security: Space, Time and Jurisdiction'. *Criminology and Criminal Justice* 14(4): 379–391.

2015. *Chronotopes of Law: Jurisdiction, Scale and Governance*. New York: Routledge.

Vidmar, Neil, and Valerie P. Hans. 2007. *American Juries: The Verdict*. New York: Prometheus Books.

Vilanova, Lucas. 2004. *Juicio por jurados y construcción de ciudadanía: relaciones entre procedimiento y democratización* [Jury trial and construction of citizenship: relationships between procedures and democratization]. *Actas del V Congreso Nacional de Sociología Jurídica*, 463–473. La Pampa, November.

Williams, Patricia J. 1993. 'Law and Everyday Life'. In Austin Sarat and Thomas Kearns (eds.), *Law in Everyday Life*. Ann Arbor: University of Michigan Press, 171–190.

Yngvesson, Barbara. 1989. 'Inventing Law in Local Settings: Rethinking Popular Legal Culture'. *Yale Law Journal* 98: 1689–1709.

CHAPTER EIGHT

EVER IN THE MAKING

Actors and Injustice in a Papua New Guinea
Village Court

Eve Houghton

We are sitting on a bandstand in Bialla, one of the regional districts of
West New Britain Province (WNB), Papua New Guinea (PNG). Back
resting on the chipped white wood, Rosie sits beside me swatting the
flies around her ankles with a cloth she always carries. Rain is falling,
hitting the corrugated iron roof of the bandstand hard, filling the air
with a sound like static. Nearby, a mother rocks her baby furiously as it
screams over the proceedings. This is Bialla's village court.

The five magistrates present in Bialla's village court today would
have been formally appointed by a government minister. However, as
magistrates are required to represent the 'traditional population group-
ings of the area' (Village Courts Act 1989: 4.17(2)), and be 'persons
whom the people respect and feel confident about, that is, who know
the customs of the area well' (Village Court Secretariat 1975, cited
Goddard 2009: 53), the government minister's decision is likely to
have been informed by the input of more local officials and reliant on
acceptance by the local population as much as any kind of official
recognition by government agencies.

The authority of the magistrates is made apparent today when they
come together on the bandstand and, unshaken by the noise of rain and
teary babies, sit in court for hours working through case after case.
Debt. Adultery. Theft. The usual. Eventually, there is one dispute that
breaks the familiar pattern: that of Angelo and Lou. The court clerk
moves to the front of the bandstand, a trusted green notebook in his
hand, and hollers their names over the wet field that surrounds us. Two
men make their way through the rain and stand before the magistrates,

ready to begin. As always one of the magistrates asks for their summonses. Angelo moves forward to hand his over, but Lou hesitates, and explains he has no summons to give.

'*Yu bin givim no summons?*' The magistrate asks, surprised.[1]

It is soon established that although Lou's summons had been sent out, it had been trusted to a man on Lou's oil palm block to pass on, and it had never made it to him.[2] On hearing this the magistrates instantly agree that the case cannot proceed until Lou has received his summons, and the two men are promptly dismissed. Despite having seen many cases turned away in the past due to one party's absence or the case being classed as outside village court jurisdiction, for some reason my head is instantly awash with unanswered questions about Lou and Angelo. If Lou never received his summons, then how did he know to turn up to village court that day? Acknowledging that he obviously knew he was required for the case, what was a summons needed for? Why not just copy Angelo's summons and give it to Lou to save finding the mysterious man on the oil palm block?

Unsatisfied with my own interpretation of events, I direct these questions to Rosie, who is still fly swatting next to me. She seems confused by the nature of my queries, and to each she manages to answer with a variant on the response, 'He doesn't have his summons with him. He doesn't have a case. He can come back when he does.' It seems to me that the session had been set back by a week or perhaps more for a piece of paper that would play little to no part in the case at all once both parties have turned up on the same day.[3] To the magistrates and Rosie, however, it is obvious that Lou needs to be issued with that summons for the case to exist at all, and yet through our discussion the summons is never described as necessary in order to fulfil government-instituted court procedures. It is needed instead to '*mekim case*'.[4]

So, what can a single, unconcluded case from a village court in Bialla tell us about conceptions of justice and its intersection with the everyday lives of those living there?

This chapter considers how certain everyday interactions between what I will be referring to as 'court-making actors' (such as chairs, flags, and documents) are utilized as a means for the village court to emerge as a flexible place, with the ability to oversee a wide range of disputes as defined by local residents. The summonses, along with a number of other court-making actors that I will be describing in this chapter, come together in such a way as to materialize a disputant's 'sense of injustice' in the form of both a case and a venue in which to discuss it (Shklar 1990: 35). Disputants' senses of injustice inform the emergence of their cases in the village court and the presence of court-making actors in this process. As the abrupt rejection of Lou and Angelo's dispute helps to illustrate, the summonses distributed to each disputant have a certain significance in the definition of how an injustice appears in court. There is therefore cause to consider how a summons features as a component of a dispute's definition in its entirety. As I argue in this chapter, creating and maintaining relationships is highly valued among Melanesians. This relationality, which is well documented as influencing many aspects of life and practice in the region, extends seamlessly into disputes and informs the purpose of the courts and definition of justice. At its heart, this means disputes are shaped by the need to appropriately reconcile a relationship, rather than seeking to address the rights of any individual involved. As I will explain later, one result of this relationality is that looking to a single case in a single dispute forum such as the village court is too narrow for a full investigation of what justice could mean or be in Bialla. Instead, by looking at the significance of a village court summons, and other examples like it, I am able to explore how dispute forums emerge as products of disputants' conceptions and experiences of injustice. They are tools capable of identifying certain relationships that are threatened by disputes and providing disputants the means to begin to repair them.

Although this narrative of relationality is now synonymous with the region at large, that's not to say each city, town, and village within the region cannot demonstrate striking differences in how this informs everyday (and not so everyday) events and interactions. With this in mind, my chapter begins with an introduction to Bialla. Following this, I introduce my approach to relational justice and how that has informed my emphasis on everyday objects as actors within the context of courtrooms. The main body of this chapter then goes on to examine how a court summons acts as a vital component of the existence of a court case. Here, I describe how a summons is required to 'live' as an actor that connects and define other actors in such a way that they are able to access justice through the village court. This section is followed by an expansion on this idea where I question how other ostensibly everyday objects (e.g., a chair, a flag) are of vital importance not only to the existence of individual cases but to the existence of the village court in its entirety. Finally, I use the unmaking of the village court as further evidence for the importance of these court-making actors, and their necessity in facilitating local paths to justice through their combined articulation of authority – an authority that is just as vitally disbanded following the court sessions' end.

Before I get to all that, let me first introduce you to Bialla, its village court, and the conceptual importance of relationality.

INTRODUCING BIALLA'S VILLAGE COURT: 'THERE ARE MANY LIKE IT, BUT THIS ONE IS MINE'

Located four hours west of Kimbe (WNB's provincial capital), Bialla town is a place where many people come together to shop and spend their time. Thanks partly to the growing economy of the region, Bialla has attracted many people from all over PNG, and over the course of forty years the social landscape has changed dramatically.[5] Although much of the population still identify as Nakanai, a group that gain their name from the nearby mountain range, the local population (and diversity within that) has seen a dramatic increase. Workers have moved from all over PNG to join the local oil palm company's ever-growing workforce.[6] The growth of Bialla's high street is a direct consequence of this as more businesses have moved into the area to cater to the needs of the growing number of potential customers living there. The town plays host to numerous stores (selling mostly dried and tinned goods), a small health centre, a post office, a market, and a bank. It is also close to a number of sizable schools. As for the bandstand that plays host to the village court, this is located on a large field not two minutes' walk from the high street.

Officially recognized and defined by the Village Courts Act (1973), there are now hundreds of village courts in various locations all over PNG. These courts were originally established (on paper) on the cusp of independence in 1973, in an effort to give a more local means of state-sanctioned legal access than the district or national courts (PNG's other official courts) were able to provide. A sister court to these other venues, the village court is in a position to pass cases up to the district and national courts when considered to be out of its own jurisdiction. These courts can take place anywhere, even relocating to suit the needs of the local population, although in Bialla the bandstand is by far the most common location where sessions were held. In theory the village court here holds sessions twice a week, although in practice it is more like once a week – weather, magistrates, and registered disputes permitting. This is only true of Bialla, as in some other regions of the country, such as Milne Bay, village court sessions are much more of a rarity and have far more operational logistics to overcome (see Demian 2014). The length of a court sessions depends entirely on how many cases are registered, meaning some days the court would be held for twenty minutes and others it would go on for hours.

(RELATIONAL) JUSTICE

I should begin by making clear that justice is not something that can be realized in the isolated context of a village court. As such, justice cannot readily be observed or defined there. In order to understand conceptions of justice in Bialla one needs to take into account the large number of other dispute forums available in the region. This is because over the course of my research I have come to find that a single dispute (as they appear in dispute forums) is made up of multiple 'fragments'. A dispute can emerge in many ways as different fragments are addressed. It can therefore also involve a large number of people, who use different forums over time to address certain concerns that have been unmet in other dispute hearings. These different fragments are generated by the numerous relationships that are engaged in a dispute, each needing to be tended to, often in different ways that cannot be done within a single court hearing.

The reason that so many relationships are commonly involved in a single dispute is because 'creating, realizing and maintaining relationships' is the thing that Melanesians most value (Robbins 2010: 175). They therefore often sit at the heart of disputes, whatever the content of the dispute may be. Situated in Melanesia, it may come as little surprise to many when I suggest that the significance of relationality that has been observed in so many aspects of life in the region carries through into disputes and the forums in which they are addressed.[7] As Robbins has suggested in his attempt to define a 'Melanesian model of justice' (2010: 174), it is often the rights of relationships, rather than the claims of any individual, that are addressed during disputes. That being the case, looking to a single case in a single dispute forum such as the village court becomes too narrow for a full investigation of what justice could mean or be in Bialla. Instead, by looking at the significance of a village court summons, and other examples like it, I am able to explore how dispute forums emerge as products of disputants' conceptions and experiences of injustice. They are tools capable of identifying certain relationships that are threatened by disputes and providing disputants the means to begin to repair them (see also Chapter 3).

A full discussion of the many fragments of a dispute and the relationships that inform it (and in turn I believe would go on to inform the realization of justice in the region) is somewhat beyond the scope of this chapter. However, by focusing on how experiences of injustice (often informed by expectations of a relationship) are communicated in dispute forums, I am able to introduce the idea that interactions between certain actors – particularly, everyday objects –determine the material manifestation of the village court. I submit that certain everyday interactions (such as between a person and a chair, or receipt of a document) are influential in shaping the way that conceptions of injustice are defined and addressed in Bialla.

THE LIFE OF A SUMMONS: BEING AND DOING IN THE VILLAGE COURT

In order to recognize the role that the summonses play in dispute forums in Bialla, it is first important to acknowledge that to not be 'living' does not automatically mean not to have 'life' as an actor (Ingold 2013). By considering what I will be referring to as the 'life' of a summons – from the day a single case is associated with it, to the day it ceases to exist – we are able to see how it is engaged in the framing of an injustice, the creation of a case, and the materialization of the village court at large. At the heart of this premise lies the idea that certain documents in Bialla not only represent more than the words written upon them, but are capable of *doing* more. Up to a point a human/nonhuman divide serves a practical purpose. A document has no say in what is written, and, more than that, the paper it is written on not only has no opinion on the matter, but lacks the capacity to care about it. It is, after all, a piece of paper. However, what a discussion of injustice in Bialla highlights is that, when it comes to understanding the impact of village courts in specific communities, an assumption of the significance of some actors, at the expense of others, ultimately constrains any efforts to fully recognize what really takes place in the village court-making process. Indeed, many previously overlooked nonhuman actors in the court may in fact be more 'reliable' reflections of its use than human counterparts (Latour 1993: 23).

Although disputes can often seem like 'out-of-the-ordinary events' (Colson 1995: 65), for those of us seeking to better understand the intersection between justice and the everyday, dispute forums provide a valuable resource as they often require people to make explicit the previously tacit ideals, beliefs, and expectations that have informed the sense of injustice in question. I therefore begin my discussion with a detailed description of how a dispute may arise within the court, and how I have come to identify the significance of certain everyday interactions that take place between the court-making actors involved.

Before anyone attends a village court, the creation of the case begins when a complainant explains their understanding of a dispute to a village court officer. This explanation is entered as a pending case in the village court register, and then two summonses are created. The first two spaces on the summons forms are for the names of the parties involved, after which the complainant is required to explain their dispute to the court officer, who writes it down almost word for word (space permitting). The statement is then copied onto a second summons, and both copies are marked with an official village court secretariat stamp. The summonses also provide both parties with a court date. At this point it is fair to say that the life of a summons has begun.

Distinguishable now from the number of other identical forms with which these summonses were originally grouped, these two documents have become representative embodiments of a particular dispute, and as such will facilitate the continuation of the process that began when the complainant entered the village courts office. Of course, a sense of injustice was already felt by the complainant before the summonses were ever created, and it is this that motivated the complainant to go to register it with a villager court officer to begin with. So to say that these summonses embody a dispute means it is through the existence of the summonses, and the steps they go through during their life, that other actors are forced to consider the dispute in a new way and act in accordance with that understanding.

It is in the creation of the summonses that we are able to identify a previously intangible sense of injustice gain a material shape that will go on to inform not only the other actors involved, but the entire venue in which it will be discussed. This emergence of the significance of summonses in a dispute and the definition of disputants that they identify is what Galanter would describe as a 'reformulation' that may ultimately restrict the scope of a dispute through a condensing of time and space, or through the specification of individuals (1981: 10). Beyond causing the complainant to think about their dispute in regard to this legal reformulation, these village court summonses initiate a process – a process that ultimately results in the creation of a 'case' – a vital part of what the village courts are often thought of as there to oversee. Said another way, a case is what the village courts are thought to *do*. Cases, as they exist in the village courts, do not take place in any of the other mediation forums that also play a big role in conflict resolution in the region. They are a unique part of the village court process and can take place only if the summonses successfully connect with a number of required actors.

On completion both summonses are carefully folded and placed into envelopes. The next step is for one copy to be delivered to the respondent whose name appears on the summons itself. The other stays in the complainant's possession. This step is important because it is where the respondent is created. By requiring the complainant to name a single recipient who will be called to attend court, these forms see the complainant's sense of injustice acquire a fixed focus of responsibility. Returning to Robbins's (2010) emphasis on 'relational justice', what the summons facilitates here is not the identification of individuals, but instead the isolation of a single relationship involved in the dispute. It temporarily suspends this piece of the dispute from the multiple other relationships and expectations that may also be involved, and that similarly may require redress. In the village court, the identification of a respondent may require a single person to represent the actions and interests of far more extensive relationships than themselves.

It is usually the job of the complainant to pass the summons on to the correct second party, but in many instances it was made clear the delivery had been made by a third party, perhaps a court official or the police, so the rules of delivery are by no means set in stone. I mention this in order to highlight that it is not *who* delivers the summons that creates a connection between the complainant, the respondent, and the village court. Rather, it is through the identification of an individual as the respondent by a third party, combined with their required interaction with the summons, that they become the respondent themselves. It is therefore not purely knowledge of the information written on the summons that helps to make the complainant's sense of injustice explicit in a form that can be dealt with in the village court. Instead, it is through a summons' physical interaction with the correct respondent that allows for the creation of a case to continue. It is through this 'nexus of acts' (Munn 1992: 9) that the summons undergoes prior to

189

being received by the respondent that we can identify the importance of this stage in the case-making process.

If we consider how the summons is valued differently depending on the actors it connects with, we see how the case is shaped by the complainant's original idea of what the injustice is, but goes on to be formed by the acceptance actors have of that frame. It is through a growing recognition of the injustice, as defined by the complainant, that leads actors to ensure the summons finds the correct respondent. On receiving their summons, of course, the respondent remains the same person that ever they were. What the summons can be seen to do is make them part of a bigger network involving numerous evaluative actors who redefine them for the purposes of the case. The respondent then simultaneously exists as an autonomous individual and, to use an idea presented by Munn, finds themselves temporarily constrained 'within more encompassing relations' (1992: 18). Throughout this the summons remains the same, and yet it contributes to the creation of the respondent and provokes their next interaction with the dispute – attendance at court. The result of this interaction materializes when both parties are called up in court and are able to present their summonses to the magistrates, who proceed to read them out.

What Lou and Angelo's case presents us with is an example of what happens when this case-making process is left incomplete. The fact that the magistrates cannot consider overseeing the dispute in this instance demonstrates the extent to which the completion of the summons' journey is necessary, not only for a hearing to take place, but for a case to exist at all within the village court setting. The path of the summons brings together actors who are each defined in regard to a single sense of injustice. They appear not as individuals so much as representatives of a relationship that is under threat. The reason this is significant is because in Bialla disputes often involve numerous people who may all relate to a dispute in a different way. Disputes involving marriages provide a good example of this, as it was often not the married couple who would appear in court to discuss a case of adultery or abuse, but their parents, who instead saw the dispute as one related to bride-price and the obligations between families, not individuals.[8]

Depending on who initiates the dispute hearing, by framing a conflict on the summons different people (and the relationships they embody) will be called on to respond, and the case itself will take a very different shape than if the same dispute were brought forward by someone else involved. This also means a single dispute can be raised in numerous ways in the court (or any of Bialla's other dispute forums) over time as different fragments of the dispute are addressed. This immediately means that for those of us seeking to gain a grasp on conceptions of justice, we cannot merely look for resolutions to guide us and is perhaps why injustice is a useful place to start. It is worth keeping in mind that one ruling in court by no means settles a broader sense of injustice experienced in different ways by larger family, clan, or kinship groups.

Returning now to the summonses, through their interaction with different actors what these documents do is set the parameters of the dispute in a way that can be addressed within this specific dispute forum. This brings a case into existence in a way that is not only embodied through the summons' own existence, but through the responses of other actors who also contribute to the forming of the case and the construction of the village court as a whole. Through their interaction with each summons, different actors are forced to react or undergo redefinition to fit the frame of a dispute. For example, it is only on receiving a summons that both parties will be able to share in the materialization of the case, and Lou will become a respondent with full access to the village court. Handing over both summonses finalizes the transition of the original dispute into a fully formed case, and, having passed them over, the magistrates become a vocalization of everything the summonses have done up to that point.

If the case is seen through to the end (and this is by no means guaranteed) the summonses cease to contribute to the events that follow. They vanish at the end of the court session to such an extent that I never caught on to who removed them or where they ended up. The case itself may have results that continue long after the conclusion of the court hearing, but once a ruling is made the dispute itself does not continue to exist in the same way that it did before the court hearing. Even on those occasions when court rulings go unmet and the disputants return to village court months or years later, the disputes are unrecognizable from the original appearance on the summons. The sense of injustice changes over time and therefore so too must the summonses and the village court itself. The continued active existence of those original summonses would therefore serve only to undermine what the village court worked to mediate. For this reason, it is important that their lives are concluded. The end of the summonses' lives illustrates the temporary nature of each village court case, and the place that comes to constitute the village court itself. Later in this chapter

I will be exploring this significance further through the change that the court undergoes on the very rare occasion when a summons not merely disappears but is publicly ripped to pieces.

For now, it is worth noting that in the case of Angelo and Lou of course we do not see the successful completion of the summonses' path, and as such the documents' lives must be extended for as long as they continue to be necessary in their capacity as case-making actors. In Angelo and Lou's case this means the one summons that was presented in court is returned to Angelo. It will uphold its role as a case-making actor until it is brought to court again alongside the summons intended for Lou. By extending the life of these actors we are shown the important role that they fulfil in village court disputes and the creation of cases. Not only that, but we see once again the significance of these specific summonses being used to facilitate the hearing of Lou and Angelo's case that no other summons could duplicate. They have not changed physically from their existence as documents, and yet they remain seriously distinguishable from any other summonses in their role as actors in this dispute.

Although distinctive in the way they frame the dispute and help to create the respondent, the court summonses are not the only actors that can be seen to have a significant role to play in the use of Bialla's village court. For that reason, I now turn my attention to a number of other court-making actors, and consider how interactions between said actors contribute to the materialization of the village court, as well as inform the framing of disputes overseen there.

MAGISTRATES, FLAGS, AND CHAIRS: THE FURNISHINGS OF INJUSTICE

By considering the influential roles of different entities such as the court summonses alongside one another, an increasingly elaborate network of actors that act in a combination that creates the village court in Bialla begins to emerge. As the summonses are only one example from a number of actors all interacting to make the village court, it is worth considering the contribution a selection of these other actors makes to the village court's creation each week. It is by looking at the everyday interactions between these actors (such as a person sitting on a chair) that one can begin to identify how the village court is engaged as an authority to explicate those senses of injustice that are played out as disputes. Here I will consider how court-making actors differ from one another, and yet ultimately come together as a united material expression of what the village court is, and facilitate all that the village court does. I do not intend to go into vast detail of every actor involved in what I hope I have made clear is a lengthy and complex process that starts the moment a summons is created. Instead, I want to focus my discussion on how authority is embodied through the interactions between chairs, flags, and magistrates.

Setting up the village court was always a lengthy procedure, and quite a performance for those gathered around waiting for their cases to be seen. Nothing could happen before an appropriate number of magistrates had confirmed their attendance, at which point the bandstand was physically transformed into the courtroom.[9] This was identifiable when each week a table and chairs were carefully carried out from the nearby offices. Having positioned this furniture in the middle of the bandstand the table would be hung with WNB's provincial flag, held in place by items that could be gathered from the local vicinity. One week it would be a large stone, and the next week an unopened can of soda, or a magistrate's mobile phone. If ever the flag was dislodged, or slipped from the table, proceedings would continue but a magistrate would always ensure it was repositioned. Although not explicitly referenced during hearings, I never saw the village court commence without it.

A noted feature of a number of PNG's other village courts (see Goddard 2005: 55; Demian 2015), the hanging of the flag is a particularly useful event to consider as it can be approached in a number of ways. PNG's national flag has already been recognized for its part in nation-making, and as a symbol that denotes local connections with the state (Strathern and Stewart 2000; Foster 2002; Goddard 2009). An interesting aspect of this approach is that it allows for an examination of how communities living in different areas across PNG are able to create and maintain relationships with an often absent state, and harness some of the authority associated with it. I mention this as a means to highlight the fact that all the actors I will be considering (including the summonses) are capable of doing, and *being*, more than one thing. It is entirely possible that the flag in Bialla is simultaneously creating the court as a local authority, and playing out much broader conceptions of state influence. However, to stretch Munn's concept, within the context of the bandstand the flag acts and receives definition through the 'encompassing relations' that the situation provides, not reducing the flags potential to do more, but certainly overshadowing it (1992: 18). Therefore, in order to gain insight into disputes and the village court, this broader potential of the flag as a symbol of the state is not what colours my examination of its presence in Bialla. I return instead to my consideration of the flag as a court-making actor.

Present in every village court session I attended in WNB, the consistent presence of the flag allows me to clarify how I have identified what constitutes court-making actors in Bialla's village court. By comparing the role that the provincial flag plays with the can of soda, phone, or rock used to hold the flag in place, we can see that some 'things' (Henare et al. 2007) contribute to what the village court physically is and, as a result of their court-making capacity, influence what the village court is able to do. In contrast to this, other 'things' may be required in court to fulfil certain roles, such as weighing down a flag, but do not act in the court-making network in the same way. Without the can of drink, the village court would still take place. Without the flag, there may be no court to begin with.

Unlike the national flag examined elsewhere and which hangs in the town's district court, it is the blue provincial flag of WNB that adorned the village court in Bialla. It is details such as this that encourage us to reassess an approach that would suppose flags only promote local authority through a connection to the state at large. Far from demonstrating a connection to the state, the flag in Bialla's village court asserts its position as a relatively local authority, allowing the magistrates and all those who utilize the village court 'to bring into play a marker of power and claim their own special relationship to it, so that they effectively localized its power' (Strathern and Stewart 2000: 42). The affective capacity of the flag identified by Strathern and Stewart lies in an understanding that it already exists as a 'marker of power', made active when it interacts with other actors at the bandstand. As a result, it contributes to the authority of this localized dispute forum. What this means for the village court, and for the flag as an actor in its own right, is that once laid out on the bandstand that place is made into one of authority. From that moment on, everything else that interacts with it becomes accepting of the fact that they are interacting with a dispute forum. Not only that, but through the flag's legitimation of this local authority there becomes an unspoken pressure on everyone involved in a case to settle it amicably in order to maintain future access to this village court in this way – isolated from, but simultaneously referencing, state influence. The implication is that only trusted and familiar magistrates are qualified to truly understand and oversee disputes there.

These concerns about unwanted state influence were made most explicit during instances when cases escalated to the point of yelling during a hearing. In order to calm disputants down, the magistrates would refer to the positives of having the power to solve the problem locally, exclaiming things such as 'Pawa i stap wantaim yumi yet!' (We still have the power here!) to remind disputants of this. The implication is that overseeing disputes locally is a good thing, and if the village court system was deemed to be inefficient in this role, then cases would lead to more state-imposed interest and presence in the region. In this way, the provincial flag's presence in Bialla's village court not only contributes to the creation of the space as a formal court setting, but simultaneously demonstrates an emphasis on local power, and a certain pride in that demonstrated by the magistrates and other court officials.

What we see here is not a disregard for legislation or the power of the state. If that were the case, it is more likely the flag would be abandoned altogether, and so too would the stamps, uniforms, and other formalities seen in the village court. Instead, we see a clear acceptance and even harnessing of state power and influence in Bialla, but within reason, and all made use of in an effort to provide the village court with the authority required to resolve disputes. This is the case to the extent that, in some instances, the flag being the best example, the state becomes a presence that is referenced as something to unite against, which in turn defines the capacity and role of the village court.

Where we saw the summonses work together to contribute to the creation of a case, the flag and procession with which furniture is carried to the bandstand is a more physical representation of the court's existence, and the materialization of the authority it embodies. Confirmation of the magistrates' attendance is physically presented through the chairs that are carried to the bandstand, demonstrating once again the court's reliance on these material signs in order to be made present. Although unremarkable when taken by themselves, much as we have seen with the life of summonses, these actions and objects interact to define important aspects of the village court and reveal how it seeks to interpret and address injustice.

THE STORY OF A CHAIR

During a long and bumpy car journey one day, another researcher working in WNB told me a story about their experience of conducting local interviews. On arrival in PNG she had established connections with the women of a certain village, who all agreed to be interviewed. Following the conclusion of her first interview the researcher had simply walked over to the next house and asked the woman living there if she was ready for her interview as well. She was told by that woman, and all the women of the village, that she would need to return the next day to continue her interviews. She did so, and the next afternoon after she had finished her second interview she once again attempted to move straight on to another house in order to continue. Again she was told that she would need to return the following day. This continued until one afternoon she finally realized that every day she was welcomed into the home of her interviewee and graciously offered a seat on a plastic chair. She came to realize that the same chair was being moved from house to house in preparation for her interviews. It was only when she started refusing the chair that the frequency of her interviews began to increase.

The reason I mention this now is because this is the story that always came to my mind when I watched the magistrates set up the village court. Through consideration of the chair, and the meaning it was imbued with in the village, we see not only the interviewees' expectations of what would make my researcher friend comfortable, but that the chair itself comes to embody and express a multitude of expectations, social networks, and elements of regard present in the village that ultimately influenced the researcher's findings. Through her own interaction with the same object (particularly when she began to refuse it) she was able to redefine the way in which her experience of the village played out thereafter. It is stories such as this that remind us of the importance of identifying how multiple entities contribute to events beyond the input of subjective persons.

Perhaps the reason I was so frequently reminded of this story was because each week in Bialla I sat and watched a small table and four chairs as they were carried, rain or shine, across the field to the bandstand from one of the nearby offices. Much like the experience of my researcher friend, during my first few visits to Bialla's village court I unwittingly managed to cause chaos as an additional chair was sought out for me. A seemingly frustrating task, so much so that to this day I remain convinced that there are only six chairs in the entirety of Bialla. I should say that I am making a distinction here between 'places to sit' and 'a chair'. Bialla is well endowed with 'places to sit' – makeshift wooden benches are commonly seen in peoples' homes, and otherwise there is usually a stoop or the shade of a tree that provides respite from the hot sun and tired feet. A chair, however, is much less common. Used in schools and businesses, it was rare for someone to make use of chair unless it was a special occasion, and as a result their appearance on the bandstand not only signified the event about to take place, but endowed those who sat upon them with a certain authority over proceedings. This authority was so tangible to me that for the first few weeks of my village court visits I was actively uncomfortable seated alongside the magistrates. Eventually my stubborn requests to watch proceedings from the floor like everyone else were accepted, and everything got slightly easier after that.

I was not the only one who experienced seating difficulties at court. On occasions when there were more magistrates than chairs, a sort of elaborate dance would commence. Any magistrate who did have a chair would periodically relinquish it to whomever was left standing, so that by the end of each day every magistrate would have been sitting for an equal duration. If the care that went into carrying the chairs out each week was not enough to make me recognize their significance in court procedures, the careful balance created among the magistrates' interactions with them most certainly did. Much like the provincial flag, these chairs contributed to the creation of a certain place. A place which had authority, and simultaneously both shared that authority with and received it from other actors within it (Ingold 2009). This perhaps becomes most evident when we consider the magistrates themselves and the rulings they make within the court environment that is created.

When the village court is not in session the magistrates are still recognized in regard to their roles within it. They may be called on to mediate disputes outside the court, or turned to as an authority in moral matters on a regular basis. They are also commonly referred to by their title when fulfilling these duties, or on occasion by those they pass in the street wishing them well. So what changes when the magistrates meet at the bandstand? As in the case of the summonses, we see a reformulation occur when the magistrates come together as actors in the court. Confirmation of how many magistrates will be in attendance on any given day is a key part of whether the village court can be made that day at all. Their attendance triggers the movements and roles of the other actors that physically create the courtroom, and once they arrive they unite in their role to bring about the existence of cases by acting as recipients of the summonses.

The magistrates' unified role in the court solidifies most strikingly as they work to maintain, and even perform, their equality in the village court. The chairs help us to identify their shared authority, as the time each magistrate spends seated and standing must be balanced in order to maintain and convey equivalence between them. The magistrates interact with the chairs in a way that facilitates the sharing of their power, as well as responsibility, combining to create the physical make-up and contribute to how the overall proceedings take place in the village court. The existence of the magistrates and their role in the village court make the chairs active in the court's creation, while simultaneously the chairs act in a way that allows the magistrates to work as one during court sessions and distinguish themselves from everyone else present. The interaction between these actors can be seen to help to define the roles of one another, and facilitate the fulfilment of those roles as well.

This realization has significant ramifications in a discussion of how justice intersects with the everyday. Of course, these entities, both chairs and magistrates alike, exist prior to and removed from the context of the village court, but in their mutual interaction with one another, and the court-making process, they become relevant actors defined by the interactions they have with one another and other actors also engaged in this process. The chairs in themselves are not able to create the village court on the bandstand, but, much as we have seen with the summonses, through interaction with a number of other court-making actors the chairs are able to contribute to the material realization of Bialla's village court, and their absence is able to undermine that. In this way, a chair does not merely work as a symbol of the authority of the magistrate who sits on it, but instead acts as one contributor to the authority held in the village court. Ultimately, the way these actors influence their appearances as features of the village court also impacts how the court is used and experienced by disputants. They shape part of the experience of seeking justice, and inform how injustices are framed. What we see happening between the chairs and the magistrates is one example of how humans and nonhumans can both be treated as actors, engaging with and influencing one another. In the case of the village court this engagement results in the temporary creation of a place in which disputes can be overseen by calling on an intangible authority, but made both visible and possible through the relationships played out by local actors.

A VILLAGE COURT NO MORE

Conceptions of injustice and the forums that can deal with them are mutually explicated and materially realized through the interactions that take place between court-making actors. But this lasts only as long as the dispute at hand. The court, and the injustice, emerge only temporarily in time and space. With no permanent material form, or fixed reliance on legal parameters, the court has the capacity to shift and change each time it materializes. This fluidity of the court allows it to adapt to ever-changing senses of injustice in each iteration of its physical existence – by which I mean each time the village court (or any dispute forum) goes beyond internal conception or legal documentation to find material purchase in the world as relevant court-making actors (as conceived by the magistrates and disputants alike), such as chairs, are successfully brought together or removed in different ways as a means to define the physical existence of a dispute forum – even if that requires the unmaking of the village court in order for a more appropriate forum to take its place. In order to introduce how court-making actors can be seen to facilitate the realization of other forums besides the village court, I want to return to my example of the court summons and consider the impact of its physical destruction.

We were four cases into a village court session when the court officer called a new set of disputing parties up to the bandstand for their case to be seen. Both parties arrived before the magistrates, diligently handed over their summonses, and stood awaiting instruction. The magistrates read through the case as it had been described on both summonses. At this point the magistrates would usually ask the complainant to describe the case to them, but on this occasion neither party was given the opportunity to speak. Instead, one of the magistrates told the disputants that the village court would not hear this case. As this announcement was made, another of the magistrate took hold of both summonses and ripped them dramatically right down the centre. He stood holding the torn pages aloft for a moment before returning them to the table and himself to his seat. Following this, the magistrates all stood and announced that the court was closed. The reason this event was so striking is because summonses usually disappeared without a mention at the end of a case. It also stands apart from other disputes that the magistrates were unwilling to oversee and refer up to one of the other official courts available in the region. This is not common, but does happen in cases are that are deemed to be beyond the village court's remit, such as murder or cases involving oil palm companies.[10] What the ripping of the summonses signalled to the onlookers is that the dispute in question required another means of oversight that sat outside any of these recognized forums and familiar procedures. The ripping of the summonses was not a sign of resolution, but a trigger of events that would see the village court transform into another forum entirely.

Still slightly confused about the abrupt end of proceedings, I sat and watched as the magistrates relinquished their chairs, and a number of court officers helped to carry them back into the nearby office buildings along with the flag, table, and court notebook. One of the magistrates announced that they were getting ready to take care of this dispute as a mediation. On hearing this I looked once more around the bandstand. It had changed quite a lot in the short time since the village court had closed. Not only were the flag and chairs removed, but an evident change in atmosphere had occurred too. The bandstand stood vacant of all village court paraphernalia save for the magistrates themselves, who now, far from sitting in the centre at a table, took up residence in spots across the floor and on the bannisters around the edge of the stage. Some had donned caps and sat drinking canned drinks or chewing *buai* (betel nut) – a habit that called for them to regularly spit red saliva from the edge of the bandstand and into the grass below. The disputing parties from the case that had just been dismissed also showed none of the signs of formality usually required during village court sessions. They kept their bags with them and sat where they would have been standing if the court session had taken place. Every so often a child would wander up onto the bandstand to get the attention of one of the respondents. In village court circumstances all of this behaviour would have been strictly forbidden and in some cases even punishable. In this new forum that had emerged, these actions were not even mentioned.

Rather than discussing exactly how this mediation attempts to cater to disputes, I would like to consider how this forum relies on the unmaking of the active qualities of court-making actors in order to address aspects of injustices that are deemed unsuitable for the village court setting. A great importance is placed on the transition from one place (in this case the village court) to another before a dispute can be discussed. The bandstand is materially and conceptually altered to the point of becoming another place. If we look once again at how the summons was so important to the materialization of the village court in the previous section, here I will explore how its role as court-making actor is intentionally interrupted. This must occur in order for the village court to be unmade and a new forum – crucially, with different capabilities – to emerge in its stead.

As I have previously discussed, when a case is successfully concluded in the village court, the summonses that worked toward its creation cease to exist, or, in keeping with the terms previously used, their lives end. As the summonses are usually removed invisibly by the magistrates, seeing them torn up becomes quite a striking act. This is the first physical event that works to divide a mediation from the village court that preceded it. The reason the destruction of the summons is necessary to this transition is because every step that was required for this dispute to be seen as a case in the village court had been completed. The case, and the court itself, had already come into existence. As the content of the dispute was then recognized by the magistrates to be beyond the scope of the village court (in this instance, it was regarding a broken promise and a large debt), something had to be done to stop the case from progressing. The extent of the influence of court-making actors becomes apparent here, as the magistrates are unable to undo the creation of the case themselves once they have received both summonses. All they can do is trigger the events required to create a new, more appropriate place in which to discuss the dispute. Through their destruction of the summonses the magistrates manage to alter the forum that had been established by court-making actors. It is for this reason that, rather than simply putting the summonses aside, the magistrates publicly destroy them. With them goes any influence they had over proceedings and the village court's existence as a whole.

The reason the summonses' destruction is so striking and identifiable as part of an unmaking process is because this act takes place within a larger actor-network. Removal of one court-making actor in this public manner begins a process by which the village court's temporary materialization is ended. At which point, rather than the bandstand returning to a vacant space, it allows for a new forum to form in its absence. Put simply, within the village court context that they have helped to make, the summonses are no longer able to work in isolation from the larger actor-network. Therefore, in order for a mediation to take place, the other court-making actors must continue what the destruction of the summonses began. This unmaking may begin with the summonses' destruction, but it is continued by the removal of other significant actors that worked to stabilize the village court, such as the chairs and provincial flag.

In order to distance further events from those of the village court, those court-making actors that remain on the bandstand must also undergo some transformation. In order to distance the magistrates from their official capacity, for example, they change their positions, language, and behaviour. It is quite striking to see the straight-backed magistrates rise from their chairs, bow to indicate the closing of a court session, and take up positions slouched on the ground, mouths red with *buai* within minutes. Held in direct and immediate comparison to one another, the new roles of what had been court-making actors are able to divide the two dispute forums extremely effectively.

Ultimately, many elements remain the same between the village court and the mediation forum that follows (e.g., the disputants, the bandstand, the day, and the dispute itself), and yet enough changes occur that allow disputes to relate to the place in which they are dealt with very differently. Removing the law as the dominant and presumed static frame of reference in disputes, and instead looking at how actors interact in a way that provides different avenues of dispute resolution, allows us to consider how conceptions of injustice are responded to in these venues, and the consequences this actor-interactivity has on the way these conceptions are ultimately addressed. This approach may open a means of future investigation into what justice may mean to those using the village courts and other dispute forums available in PNG.

CONCLUSION

I have suggested there is no single actor or event that can be considered ultimately responsible for the making, unmaking, or use of dispute forums in Bialla. Identifying the contribution made by these actors is important because their existence means we cannot take it for granted that the village court (for example) is a permanent and fixed entity. Instead, it is the combined efforts of these actors each week that lead to the court's creation and introduces us to how the village court gains the capacity to address senses of injustice.

Summonses, a flag, chairs, and magistrates so far have all been identified as court-making actors. Each exists in one form removed from the court setting, and yet when successfully united they work together to allow for the village court to take place and disputes to be overseen. This, of course, cannot guarantee the completion of a case. Certainly, a much larger discussion would be required in order to begin to understand how the outcomes of these dispute forums contribute in any way to local experiences of justice. This is especially the case when one considers ideas of relational justice (Robbins 2010) and broader aspects of moral orders (Robbins 2004) and community expectations that can be so influential in the region (Houghton 2014). Instead, these actors merely create the place and frame within which a case can begin and the significance of injustice can be identified.

Having identified the importance of these actor-networks to the village court's very existence, perhaps what remains most striking is the fact that the village court-making process currently remains invisible in the eyes of the government and other legislative bodies. This is due to the fact that so far no one has thought to report the significance of actors such as summonses, chairs, and flags to these authorities, and they are not necessarily the first place you would look to learn more about conflict resolution at courts around the country. As a result, how village courts like that in Bialla are able to oversee disputes in the way that they do, and those cases resolved in the mediation forum that emerges in the village court's absences, remain entirely undocumented, unreported, and unseen. Ultimately, opinions on the uses of the village courts and events that take place in them throughout PNG are most commonly based on information taken from the reports by village court officers and deemed complete. These reports require cases to be categorized and disputes to be summarized in ways that adhere to fields that appear on preconceived forms. Refocusing our approach to the village courts' existence allows for better recognition of what makes a sense of injustice into a case and allows us to observe how that case contributes to more extensive networks of dispute forums as a whole. By doing so, it becomes apparent that the village court in Bialla may not be doing what is being reported on any of the current legislative forms provided to magistrates. Instead, they may be doing more.

Notes

1 'You were not given a summons?'
2 A block is a unit of land given over to the growth of oil palm – a prolific regional crop.
3 Cases are often delayed when one party is absent from court.
4 'Make the case.'
5 This by no means applies only to Bialla. WNB has seen dramatic social and infrastructural changes take place more broadly for a wide number of

reasons since independence. Research conducted by Ann Chowning during the 1980s and 1990s acknowledges how Christianity (1990) and alcohol (1982) have influenced a range of communities in West New Britain. In more recent years, anthropologists such as Andrew Lattas (2001) have explored the changes resulting from capitalism and PNG's growing cash economy.

6 Between the census taken in 2000 and in 2011, the population of WNB rose from 184,508 to 264,264. Despite the steady overall increase in population in the country, the dramatic increase in population in WNB is centred heavily around the provincial capital (Kimbe) and nearby Hoskins and Bialla. For this reason, I am confident that this increase can be tied specifically to the growth of certain industries in those regions.

7 See Strathern (2005) and Robbins (2010) for further discussion of the significance of a relational approach to anthropology in Melanesia.

8 It is worth considering this subject within the broader context of discussions regarding relationality in Melanesia and specifically the identification of self first as the product of relationships (a *dividual* – see Strathern 1988) rather than as an individual.

9 That the village court requires an odd number of magistrates of three or more is one of the original parameters established in the Village Courts Act in 1974. This was strictly adhered to in every session I attended in WNB.

10 There are a number of laws that describe the remit of the village court, for example, the village courts are not supposed to deal with disputes concerning amounts of money over 5,000 kina. However, I have not referred to them here as I found these remits to be flexible to the magistrates, depending on the situation. For example, if a murder is linked to sorcery, some magistrates may feel entitled to oversee the case as one concerning custom, not murder, therefore placing the matter back within the court's remit.

References

Colson, E. 1995. 'The Contentiousness of Disputes'. In P. Caplan (ed.), *Understanding Disputes: The Politics of Argument*. Oxford: Berghahn, 65–82.

Demian, Melissa. 2014. 'Overcoming Operational Constraints in Papua New Guinea's Remote Rural Village Courts: A Case Study: Legal Innovation Part 3'. *In Brief*, 2014/52. Canberra: Australian National University.

2015. 'Theatre of Grievance: Affective Performance as Evidence in Suau Village Courts'. Paper presented at the State of the Pacific Conference, Australian National University, Canberra, September 7–9.

Foster, Robert. 2002. *Materializing the Nation*. Bloomington: Indiana University Press.

Galanter, Marc. 1981. 'Justice in Many Rooms: Court, Private Ordering and Indigenous Law'. *The Journal of Legal Pluralism and Unofficial Law* 13(19): 1–47.

Goddard, Michael. 2005. *Unseen City: Anthropological Perspectives on Port Moresby, Papua New Guinea.* Canberra: Pandanus.

2009. *Substantial Justice: An Anthropology of Village Courts in Papua New Guinea.* New York: Berghahn.

Henare, Amiria, Martin Holbraad, and Sari Wastell (eds.). 2007. *Thinking through Things: Theorising Artefacts in Ethnographic Perspective.* New York: Routledge.

Houghton, Eve. 2014. 'The Role of Community in an Alternative Mediation Forum in West New Britain Province, Papua New Guinea: Legal Innovation Part 2'. *In Brief*, 2014/46. Canberra: Australian National University.

Independent State of Papua New Guinea. 1973. *The Village Courts Act.*

1989. *The Village Courts Act.* Available at www.paclii.org/cgi-bin/sinodisp/pg/legis/consol_act/vca1989172/vca1989172.html?stem=&synonyms=&query=village%20courts%20act, accessed 23 September 2016.

Ingold, Tim. 2009. 'Against Space: Place, Movement, Knowledge'. In P. W. Kirby (ed.), *Boundless Worlds: An Anthropological Approach to Movement.* Oxford: Berghahn, 29–44.

2013. *Making: Anthropology, Archaeology, Art and Architecture.* New York: Routledge.

Latour, Bruno. 1993. *We Have Never Been Modern*, trans. Catherine Porter. Cambridge, MA: Harvard University Press.

Lattas, A. 2001. 'The Underground Life of Capitalism: Space, Persons, and Money in Bali (West New Britain)'. In A. Rumsey and J. F. Weiner (eds.), *Emplaced Myth: Space, Narrative, and Knowledge in Aboriginal Australia and Papua New Guinea.* Honolulu: University of Hawai'i Press, 161–188.

Munn, Nancy D. 1992. *The Fame of Gawa: A Symbolic Study of Value Transformation in a Massim Society.* Durham, NC: Duke University Press.

Robbins, Joel. 2004. *Becoming Sinners: Christianity and Moral Torment in a Papua New Guinean Society.* Los Angeles: University of California Press.

2010. 'Recognition, Reciprocity, and Justice: Melanesian Reflections on the Rights of Relationships'. In K. M. Clarke and M. Goodale (eds.), *Mirrors of Justice: Law and Power in the Post–Cold War Era.* New York: Cambridge University Press, 171–190.

Shklar, Judith N. 1990. *The Faces of Injustice.* New Haven, CT: Yale University Press.

Strathern, Andrew J., and Pamela J. Stewart. 2000. '"Mi les long yupela usim flag bilong mi": Symbols and Identity in Papua New Guinea'. *Pacific Studies* 23(1–2): 21–49.

Strathern, Marilyn. 1988. *The Gender of the Gift: Problems with Women and Problems with Society in Melanesia.* London: University of California Press.

2005. *Kinship, Law and the Unexpected: Relatives Are Always a Surprise.* Cambridge: Cambridge University Press.

AFTERWORD

Carol J. Greenhouse

This volume claims *justice* for sociolegal studies in distinctive ways at once theoretical and methodological. For readers accustomed to thinking of justice as the universal endpoint of good law, there will have been many surprises in these pages. Primary among these is the ethnographic inquiry into justice as an empirical question in the first place, not to speak of one located in the comings and goings of everyday life. Indeed, after a century of relativity as a core principle of cultural analysis in the social sciences, the topic of justice might seem to pose a limiting condition to just such a project. The expectation that justice is by definition "something almost transcendental and universal" (Hinton 2010: 1), convergent in some ultimate way, pushes expectation toward abstraction, away from the everyday – toward questions framed around *ideas* of justice, rather than what those ideas might be about, where they have been encountered or rehearsed, and how they might be realized in daily life. This book challenges all such expectations through ethnographic studies that find the visible plausibility of justice in everyday life, as knowledge that people have and hone, feeling its weight, in lives they share with others. In this afterword, I reflect on some of the complexities and merits of that challenge.

The volume's call for corrective measures in the form of an exploration of "justice beyond law," emphasizing "everyday justice," might seem to be counterintuitive (both quoted phrases are from Chapter 1). But, as the very diversity of the chapters shows, ethnography – the primary research method and mode of writing associated with sociocultural anthropology – is particularly well attuned for exploration of the "justicescapes" (Chapter 1) in which people form their own sense of justice, injustice, and indifference from their everyday relations. The differences internal to the volume are central to its aims and implications, showing justice to be not the preserve of judges alone, as endpoints to their deliberations to be reconciled, but as a property of anyone's thinking – or, as in this volume, impulses, expressions, episodic before and after the fact, inconsistent, proliferating, condensing. The contributors follow justice through myriad forms of rehearsal, expression, and materialization in the social contexts of their research sites. These sites range from informal to formal, improvisational to ritualized; this diversity – that is, the connection between diversity and everyday justice – is in itself significant in relation to the book's themes.

Moreover, the ethnographies that form the basis of these chapters demonstrate that it is in their own observed relations that people formulate their self-understandings as objects of others' purposes and, equally, as subjects – actors in their own milieus – as they test their own relevance to the world around them in light of unfinished pasts and possible futures. In this way, the authors in this collection draw social relations, real times, and actual places squarely into view as infrastructures of justice. In these accounts, in other words, justice emerges as an alert sensibility to one's own place in a circuitry of power.

But even more than their demonstration of people's awareness of the sources and methods of their own social conditions, these ethnographic accounts of everyday justice point to *justice* as an active principle of consciousness. By this I mean that justice speaks in a *now* that is already revised (literally, re-viewed) as a new beginning – a form of freedom grounded in the social, and requiring its own form of politics for its fulfilment (see Arendt 2018). It is something like this grounding that rescues justice from the false predicates Brunnegger notes in her introduction to this volume. Everyday justice in these pages emerges as a faculty of ethical judgment both personal and communal. This is what makes it available to ethnography – as each of this volume's contributors demonstrates. Read together, the chapters challenge the conventional assumption that justice and injustice are complementary, in some zero-sum relation. On the contrary, the volume nourishes the thought that justice and injustice are not each other's opposite, as if more of one would mean less of the other. In these pages, justice is not cabined as a corrective to injustice in the world we inhabit in the here and now; rather, it refers to an affirmative refashioning of the world we live in, in some more subjunctive but still realistic temporality. In this sense, too, the diversity of situation and aspiration is integral to the theme.

To the extent that an anthropology of justice might seem to be counterintuitive or even contradictory as a comment on this world, some part of that sceptical response might be a consequence of a long intellectual genealogy in social studies of law that presupposes justice to be either the source or result of law – an ultimate critical judgment (a judgment of law's judgments, so to speak) of its pragmatic consequences or even its legitimating proximity to what might be supposed to be transcendent or even divine judgment, as some ultimate social design. This genealogy is not anthropology's alone. That anthropology was engaged with law from its earliest years as a late or post-Enlightenment discipline is evidence not only of the theoretical stakes of the discipline to be found in law but also of anthropology's debts and contributions to adjacent disciplines of sociology, philosophy, history, religion, and law itself. Indeed, the social sciences engaged with law share a long horizon with anthropology along a conceptual fold where the idea of justice invites empirical inquiry as a question of how ultimate ideals are deliberated in cultural terms, materialized in legal judgment, and lived. That image of a smooth circular flow of law through society and culture (i.e., social relations and ways of thinking) is no longer a model that sociolegal scholars defend; however, the persistent legalism of justice shows its enduring traces in the presumptions of its abstraction, its emergence in linear time, its coherence, and its foundational relevance to social norms and actions. These elements may reflect the key terms of a judicialization of justice, but they do not capture the features of the ethnographic studies collected in this volume.

The ethnographies contained in this volume also mark a difference from anthropological traditions with law. Anthropology's longest research traditions with respect to justice focus on access to law and dispute processes, approached ethnographically and comparatively (Nader 1965; Moore 1969; Collier 1975; see also Nader 1980; Rosen 2000). From Durkheim onward, the idea of justice has drawn anthropologists' attention to other worlds, ethnographically to the diverse legal cultures in the world around us, and in a more visionary or critical vein, to other world futures (Greenhouse 1986; 2015). As contributors to a recent forum on emergent issues in the anthropology of law suggest, anthropological studies of law have tended to focus on law's institutions and techniques, professional cultures, and forms of knowledge – showing the discursive dominance of judicial paradigms even where law is theorized more broadly as a "moral register" (Goodale, in Kesselring et al. 2017). The scholars in that forum argue for fresh starting points that would break the habit they ascribe to legal anthropologists – that is, their privileging of legal institutions, legal actors, and the law itself as self-evidently dominant in social life. Overestimating law's dominance tends to occlude the "depoliticizing effect of legal frameworks on social wrongs and political collectives" (Babul, in Kesserling et al. 2017). This volume's contributors encourage instead an understanding of everyday justice as the beginning of politics, not its endpoint or (even less so) its Other.

In some respects, justice has been – and remains – an implicit subjunctive mood for anthropology. That subjunctive mood has tended to be cabined in the ethnographer's critical voice – often an ironic voice – rather than as a warrant for a research focus on justice such as exemplified by this volume's contributions. This volume can be read as a series of interventions in the larger project of rethinking law as an ethnographic and theoretical object, in the spirit of current debates that call for a critical suspension of the distinction between law's "makers" and "consumers" (Kesselring, in Kesselring et al. 2017) and, more generally, putting law in its place – hence Brunnegger's theoretical and methodological openness to "justice beyond law" (Chapter 1).

THE STATE AS SOCIAL FACT

The presumed dominance of law in relation to justice reflects law's conventional association with the state, and its putative centrality to the state's hegemonic expression and efficacy. Once law's dominance is called into question, its deceptive place in relation to justice can be seen more clearly. In other words, some part of the apparent elusiveness of justice is actually the elusiveness of the state. The "slippery" quality of the state (Abrams 1988) rests in part on a classic definition of the state as an entity that can be understood in terms of its "formation, structure, functions, laws, and relations with other similar entities" – "a macropolitical perspective, which tends to produce a relatively abstract representation from above" (Fassin 2015: preface). From that standpoint, normative thinking is easily conflated with legal thinking – as if the subjective interiority of the social is the result of the a priori effectiveness of some external legal entity. This dilemma is a source of long-standing debate in relation to legal pluralism – is law everywhere? Are all norms in some way legal?

The spurious interchangeability of personal conscience and external norms tends to be reinforced by a construction of justice as the morality of state power – a proposition that rehearses specific expectations of law as involving a legitimate monopoly of authority. Such a proposition owes more to states' practices of self-legitimation than to actual justice-seeking or justice-making – or, as in this book, justice-recognizing. Thus, an anthropology of justice offers an opportunity to reset expectations, particularly in relation to the taken-for-granted monism of state legitimation and its articulation through law. Rejecting the conventional definition of states, Didier Fassin proposes another "theory of the state ... constructed empirically ... The state, we believe, is what its agents do under the multiple influences of the policies they implement, the habits they develop, the initiatives they take, and the responses they get from their publics" (2015: preface). Seen this way, out from under the conventional structural-functional account of states as entities, the ethnographic availability of justice emerges more clearly as integral to the status of the state as a social fact. The issue undergirding the explorations of everyday justice in this book is not that justice is unknowable as a practical matter, but that it cannot be known primarily by interrogating what states or law do. Identity, agency, and attachments of many kinds emerge as the predicates of justice-seeking.

In that spirit, this volume asks us to think more curiously – which is to say, more ethnographically – about justice. *Justice*, in these pages, offers no ready distinction between singular and plural – much as wisdom, love, and courage (among other qualities) resist the arithmetic of singularities and sets. Anthropology has a long tradition of representing justice as the essential spirit of cultural legalism (Pirie 2013; Pirie and Scheele 2014); however, this book – while clearly indebted to that ethnological tradition – leads us in other directions. Working from field sites in the times and spaces of the everyday, the contributors have examined settings in which justice is key to actors' understandings of their own milieus – milieus in which the evidence of justice appears to them diversely as motivation, materiality, registers of expertise, networked agency and personal self-expression, literacy and legibility, among other potentialities.

Justice, in these accounts, is neither the means nor end of the legal process, but a name for the very possibility of a non-zero-sum relation. We see this in the discussions of legal processes (including the

customary and quasi-legal processes and assertions of rights consciousness) in this book in Chapters 2, 4, 6, and 8. In this sense, as noted by
Amietta in his discussion of Argentine criminal trials (Chapter 7), the
relationship between the state and the "everyday" cannot be "antipodal," given the embeddedness of social knowledge in legal processes
and the mutually recursive effects of lay and legal knowledge (such as in
jury deliberations). In short, justice – as treated by this volume's
contributors – is an analytic path for inquiry, not a bounded categorical
object of inquiry in search of definition. Indeed, one characteristic in
common across the contributions is their attention to the dynamic and
improvisatory aspects of the situations they explore.

JUSTICE ON THE GROUND: TRANSITIONAL JUSTICE, HUMANITARIANISM, AND HUMAN RIGHTS

Appreciating these points leads productively to a consideration of the
book's contributions to other emergent studies of law in anthropology,
as the collection offers significant engagement with critical and ethnographic concerns beyond justice per se. Primary among these are
ethnographic studies of transitional justice, humanitarianism, and
human rights. Anthropologists in these relatively new fields share these
contributors' priority on the critical importance of temporality, place,
and personal relations as conditions of justice – and as a corrective to
more teleological and state-centred accounts in anthropology and
sociolegal studies (see Fassin 2012).

Recent critical studies of transitional justice by anthropologists
(including Chapters 4 and 5 in this volume) and other sociolegal
scholars offer meaningful points of comparison with the primary critical
and ethnographic concerns of this volume's authors – particularly in
resisting the dualism of universal rights and local practice, as if the
"local" were a structural "level" or a lacuna where tradition abides
(Shaw and Waldorf 2010: 4, 6). Recent ethnographers of truth and
reconciliation processes, like this volume's contributors, are alert to the
importance of real time and actual social relations as critical stand-
points against the implicit teleology of transition, and integral to that
teleology, the self-valorizing claims of national states and their self-
legitimation work through TRCs. For Kimberly Theidon, to take one
major example, the ethnographic project around the TRC in Peru
involved many modalities of "justice talk" (Theidon 2012: 12) in
speech, but also in the language of the body and in memories, in the

tribunal but also well away from its platforms and protocols (see also Wilson 2001; Dwyer 2015; Vera-Lugo 2017). The critical through-line in the present collection is the dynamic interlegality (tacking across multiple normative idioms) and cross-temporality (moving back and forth across times) of justice. As noted above, another through-line is improvisation, given the inevitable incompleteness of justice, its uncontainability in any single institution or act, and, accordingly, the futility of a functionalist account. An outcome may be just, but justice is not an outcome.

Ethnographic studies of humanitarianism illuminate further key aspects of this volume's contributions. For Didier Fassin, humanitarianism has emerged as a feature of contemporary global governance, introducing characteristic forms of reasoning about humanitarian imperatives to war and peace, killing and saving – as such "fugaciously and illusorily bridg[ing] the contradictions of our world, and mak[ing] the intolerableness of its injustices somewhat bearable" (2012: preface). "Humanitarian reason" requires victims and strong states, and in practice sustains a steep asymmetry, a sharp unilateralism, between those who deliver humanitarian aid and those who receive it without prospect of "returning the gift." Indeed, in this process, humanitarian assistance inserts government into the very notion of *being human* (Feldman and Ticktin 2010: introduction), in this way precluding a relation of equals. The anthropology of everyday justice, as presented in this volume, similarly attends to the ways people bridge the contradictions of status and value (in their own experience or as they observe it), at least provisionally, but the contradictions remain. In the contexts discussed in this book, legal institutions are as likely to produce instability as stability, injustice as much as justice, depending on how they intervene (if they do) in people's efforts to assert a relation of equality (or even more fundamentally, of humanity – as in Chapter 3).

On this point, it is worth noticing that with the important exception of Kathiravelu's Chapter 3 on migrant laborers in Singapore, each of the chapters involves fellow citizens in their home states – a lateral relation of "empirical citizenship" (Greenhouse 2012: envoi). Kathiravelu suggests that the humane logic of citizenship is not limited to fellow citizens in the technical sense. Across nationalities – whether in shared or unshared space – empirical citizenship (the sense of belonging to each other through the state, but not because of the state) entails justice implications not open to other relations, as when contests pit individuals against each other for control of governmental, economic, or other powers. Given the proliferation of transnational institutions and international investment agreements in recent decades, the conditions of solidarity and exclusion are highly mixed. As anthropologist Marc Abélès observes, politics today is subject to a "dual displacement" involving the altered interests and idioms of both national governments and resistance movements in the context of globalization. In his prescient analysis, "[t]he present moment can be characterized by the emergence of a new political stage" defined by the "confrontations" between the "national powers" that govern global capitalism (such as the World Trade Organization) and the counter-globalization mobilizations arrayed against them, resulting in new "intranational antagonisms" over supranational governance (2010: 88). This volume's ethnographic accounts of tensions over various scenarios at the intersection of local and supranational frames (e.g., over wages, authority, and the government's service to citizens) might be one indication of such cross-currents.

From that standpoint, one important contribution of an anthropology of justice is its suspension of conventional scalar distinctions constructed on the basis of jurisdiction (Valverde 2009; see also Chapter 7 in this volume); indeed, it makes jurisdiction secondary, if it is relevant at all. In these accounts, the primary location of justice is intersubjective – questions of possible justice being inseparable from questions of possible relationships (see Kesselring 2016: 74–75). One implication of an ethnographic focus on justice, then, is its calling into question of top-down formulations of legal consciousness and, more broadly, rights consciousness as an effect of "legalization" (Kesselring 2016: 84). As Erica Weiss observes, "the bureaucratic encounter is not a one-way mirror" (2016: 21). The "vernacularization" of human rights (Merry 2006) is horizontal as well as vertical, bottom-up as well as top-down. Consequently, the relevance of rights to the actuality of everyday justice involves far more than awareness of rights and the means of access to legal arenas. As the chapters in this volume suggest, rights consciousness is first of all social consciousness, and its arenas of realization are potentially anywhere people gather, or find a public wall for their poster or spray-painted message (see Chapter 2).

JUSTICE AND CONTEMPORARY LIFE

These observations bring us to the question of how and why the possibility of an anthropology of everyday justice arises now, and with such timely fruitfulness. The unsettlement of paradigms and categories discussed in the preceding sections is less a sign of paradigmatic change in the discipline(s) than of specific challenges in contemporary circumstances. For purposes of discussion, I point to three elements of the contemporary "justicescape" that have developed since sociolegal studies has matured as a scholarly field. Abélès (2010) charts one of these elements in his analysis of contemporary politics as opening a divide between the means and ends of global governance, on the one hand, and the counter-globalization activists, on the other. The relatively borderless world of global capitalism churns with political and legal tensions along the horizon where it confronts the very different relevance of territory in nations' enforcement of citizens' rights and human rights (or not, as the case may be) (Aman and Greenhouse 2017: ch. 7).

Relatedly, a widening democracy deficit has been pervasively integral to the mainstreaming of neoliberalism as a policy principle for public and private sector management around the world, hollowing out the political spaces in which publics might conjoin. In the absence of such state-sanctioned space, anthropologists find widely divergent proxies in local communities (compare, e.g., the bureaucratization of quasi-judicial hearings studied by Ellison 2018 and the violence of neighbourhood self-policing analysed by Goldstein 2004). But even where the public's participation is part of a state process, this does not mean that the process is automatically or necessarily inclusive in a substantive way. For example, in a recent article on indigenous claims hearings in New Zealand, anthropologist Fiona McCormick notes their silencing effect on indigenous participants, given their exclusion from the agenda-setting process. She finds that the hearings are driven by a neoliberal logic that normalizes dispossession, reinforcing the asymmetries of the parties (McCormick 2016: 229).

Finally, to the extent that pervasive privatization has pressed personal and corporate identities into the rubric of personhood, neoliberal legality fosters a moral discourse common to both – if incompletely for now – in ways that (at least in the United States) shift the justiciable valence of *identity* from its personal and community associations to corporate associations and antagonisms (Greenhouse 2018). Given the extent to which government functions have been privatized around the world, perhaps most people in the world today encounter their own state government only or mainly through the services of state contractees in the private sector. As a result, today, a significant dimension of

citizenship and non-citizen residence is their status as third-party beneficiaries of public/private service contracts. This is yet another reason
why an anthropology of everyday justice must look beyond law and the
state to find visible signs of justice.

The justice that emerges ethnographically from this book's chapters
suggests that there is counter-movement to each of these situations in
the authors' research sites, making the project timely in an empirical
sense. It is also timely in a reflexive sense, as the project of reclaiming
justice through ethnography foregrounds critical issues of theory and
method involving states, citizens, the moral economies of public life,
and both the temporalities and substance of political agency. In these
chapters, in short, justice emerges as a register of social experience
actively committed to the future. The political possibility that Hannah
Arendt finds in the relation between action (conceived as beginning
anew) and freedom is an insight friendly to ethnography, since ethnography, too, begins in actual people's sense of purpose and possibility. Importantly, Arendt is more concerned with the possibility of
everyday miracles than she is with the terms of their fulfilment: "[I]f
it is true that action and beginning are essentially the same, it follows
that a capacity for performing miracles must likewise be within the
range of human faculties" (Arendt 2018: 239). Her idea returns us to
Chapter 1, Sandra Brunnegger's introduction, affirming ethnography's
relevance to the prospect of bringing futures into the present, where
everyday justice marks the difference between thinkable and unthink-
able miracles.

References

Abélès, Marc. 2010. *The Politics of Survival*. Trans. Julie Kleinman. Durham,
    NC: Duke University Press.
Abrams, Philip. 1988. 'Notes on the Difficulty of Studying the State, 1977'.
    Journal of Historical Sociology 1(1): 58–89.
Aman, Alfred C., and Carol J. Greenhouse. 2017. *Transnational Law: Cases
    and Problems in an Interconnected World*. Durham, NC: Carolina Aca-
    demic Press.
Arendt, Hannah. 2018. 'Freedom and Politics, a Lecture'. In Jerome Kohn
    (ed.), *Arendt, Thinking without a Bannister: Essays in Understanding
    1953–1975*. New York: Schocken Books, 220–244.
Collier, Jane. 1975. 'Legal Processes'. *Annual Review of Anthropology* 4(1):
    121–144.
Dwyer, Leslie. 2015. 'Reimagining Transitional Justice in Bali'. Allegra Lab,
    22 January. (Electronic document: allegralaboratory.net)

Ellison, Susan. 2018. *Domesticating Democracy: The Politics of Conflict Resolution in Bolivia*. Durham, NC: Duke University Press.

Fassin, Didier. 2012. *Humanitarian Reason: A Moral History of the Present*. Trans. Rachel Gomme. Berkeley: University of California Press.

(2015. *At the Heart of the State: The Moral World of Institutions*. Trans. Patrick Brown and Didier Fassin. London: Pluto Press.

Feldman, Ilana, and Miriam Ticktin. 2010. 'Introduction: Government and Humanity'. In Feldman and Ticktin (eds.), *In the Name of Humanity: The Government of Threat and Care*. Durham, NC: Duke University Press, 1–26.

Goldstein, Daniel. 2004. *The Spectacular City: Violence and Performance in Urban Bolivia*. Durham, NC: Duke University Press.

Greenhouse, Carol J. 1986. *Praying for Justice: Faith, Order and Community in an American Town*. Ithaca, NY: Cornell University Press.

2012. *The Paradox of Relevance: Ethnography and Citizenship in the United States*. Philadelphia: University of Pennsylvania Press.

2015. 'Durkheim in the United States: 1900'. In Olivier Jouanjan and Élisabeth Zoller (eds.), *'Le Moment 1900': Critique sociale et critique sociologique du droit en Europe et aux États-Unis*. Paris: Éditions Panthéon Assas, 35–51.

2018. 'Citizens United/Citizens Divided: Democracy and Economy in a Corporate Key'. *American Ethnologist* 45(4): 546–560.

Hinton, Alexander Laban. 2010. 'Introduction: Toward an Anthropology of Transitional Justice'. In Hinton (ed.), *Transitional Justice: Global Mechanisms and Local Realities after Genocide and Mass Violence*. New Brunswick, NJ: Rutgers University Press, 1–24.

Kesselring, Rita. 2016. 'An Injury to One Is an Injury to All? Class Actions in South African Courts and Their Social Effects on Plaintiffs'. *Political and Legal Anthropology Review (PoLAR)* 39(S1): 74–88.

Kesselring, Rita, Elif Babul, Mark Goodale, Tobias Kelly, Ronald Niezen, Maria Sapignoli, and Richard Ashby Wilson. 2017. 'The Future of the Anthropology of Law. Emergent Conversation'. *PoLAR: Political and Legal Anthropology Review Online*, 10 February. Electronic document: https://polarjournal.org/2017/01/10/emergent-conversations-part-6/.

McCormack, Fiona. 2016. 'Indigenous Claims: Hearing, Settlements, and Neoliberial Silencing'. *Political and Legal Anthropology Review (PoLAR)* 39(2): 226–243.

Merry, Sally Engle. 2006. *Human Rights and Gender Violence: Translating International Law into Local Justice*. Chicago: University of Chicago Press.

Moore, Sally Falk. 1969. 'Law and Anthropology'. *Biennial Review of Anthropology* 6: 252–300.

Nader, Laura. 1965. 'The Anthropological Study of Law'. *American Anthropologist* 67(6): 3–32.

Nader, Laura (ed.). 1980. *No Access to Law: Alternatives to the American Judicial System*. New York: Academic Press.

Pirie, Fernanda. 2013. *Anthropology of Law*. Oxford: Oxford University Press.

Pirie, Fernanda, and Judith Scheele (eds.). 2014. *Legalism: Community and Justice*. Oxford: Oxford University Press.

Rosen, Lawrence. 2000. *The Justice of Islam: Comparative Perspectives on Islamic Law and Society*. Oxford: Oxford University Press.

Shaw, Rosalind, and Lars Waldorf. 2010. 'Introduction: Localizing Transitional Justice'. In Rosalind Shaw, Lars Waldorf, and Pierre Hazan (eds.), *Localizing Transitional Justice: Interventions and Priorities after Mass Violence*. Stanford, CA: Stanford University Press, 2–26.

Theidon, Kimberly. 2012. *Intimate Enemies: Violence and Reconciliation in Peru*. Philadelphia: University of Pennsylvania Press.

Valverde, Mariana. 2009. 'Jurisdiction and Scale: Legal "Technicalities" as Resources for Theory'. *Social and Legal Studies* 18(2): 139–157.

Vera-Lugo, Juan Pablo. 2017. 'The Humanitarian State'. PhD diss., Rutgers University.

Weiss, Erica. 2016. 'Best Practices for Besting the Bureaucracy: Avoiding Military Service in Israel'. *Political and Legal Anthropology Review (PoLAR)* 39(S1): 19–33.

Wilson, Richard Ashby. 2001. *The Politics of Truth and Reconciliation in South Africa*. Cambridge: Cambridge University Press.

INDEX

veridiction, 14
vernacularisation, 97–98, 101–102,
    213
victims, 116
Vienna, 40
    graffiti in, 45
viewshed boundaries, 139–140
vigilantism, 38
Village Courts Act, 185–186
visibility, justice and, 27–28

waiting room, 9–11
war crimes, prosecution of, 111
Wastell, Sari, 9–11, 21, 84–85
Waters, Alice, 143–144, 148

watershed boundaries, 139–140
West New Britain Province (WNB), 182,
    195–196
    flag of, 194–195
Western legal tradition, 18
Wienerwand, 40, 45
wilderness, 24–25
WNB. *See* West New Britain Province
women's rights, 42–43
Worker's University, 128–129
working cultures, 91–95
working landscape notion, 146–147
worlding, 63–64

Young, Iris Marion, 75–76

CAMBRIDGE STUDIES IN LAW AND SOCIETY

Books in the Series

Diseases of the Will: Alcohol and the Dilemmas of Freedom
Mariana Valverde

The Politics of Truth and Reconciliation in South Africa: Legitimizing the Post-Apartheid State
Richard A. Wilson

Modernism and the Grounds of Law
Peter Fitzpatrick

Unemployment and Government: Genealogies of the Social
William Walters

Autonomy and Ethnicity: Negotiating Competing Claims in Multi-Ethnic States
Yash Ghai

Constituting Democracy: Law, Globalism and South Africa's Political Reconstruction
Heinz Klug

The Ritual of Rights in Japan: Law, Society, and Health Policy
Eric A. Feldman

Governing Morals: A Social History of Moral Regulation
Alan Hunt

The Colonies of Law: Colonialism, Zionism and Law in Early Mandate Palestine
Ronen Shamir

Law and Nature
David Delaney

Social Citizenship and Workfare in the United States and Western Europe: The Paradox of Inclusion
Joel F. Handler

Law, Anthropology, and the Constitution of the Social: Making Persons and Things
Edited by Alain Pottage and Martha Mundy

Judicial Review and Bureaucratic Impact: International and Interdisciplinary Perspectives
Edited by Marc Hertogh and Simon Halliday

Edited by Richard Rottenburg, Sally Engle Merry, Sung-Joon Park, and Johanna Mugler

Contesting Immigration Policy in Court: Legal Activism and Its Radiating Effects in the United States and France
Leila Kawar

The Quiet Power of Indicators: Measuring Governance, Corruption, and Rule of Law
Edited by Sally Engle Merry, Kevin Davis, and Benedict Kingsbury

Investing in Authoritarian Rule: Punishment and Patronage in Rwanda's Gacaca Courts for Genocide Crimes
Anuradha Chakravarty

Contractual Knowledge: One Hundred Years of Legal Experimentation in Global Markets
Edited by Grégoire Mallard, and, Jérôme Sgard

Iraq and the Crimes of Aggressive War: The Legal Cynicism of Criminal Militarism
John Hagan, Joshua Kaiser, and Anna Hanson

Culture in the Domains of Law
Edited by René Provost

China and Islam: The Prophet, the Party, and Law
Matthew S. Erie

Diversity in Practice: Race, Gender, and Class in Legal and Professional Careers
Edited by Spencer Headworth and Robert Nelson

A Sociology of Constitutions: Constitutions and State Legitimacy in Historical-Sociological Perspective
Chris Thornhill

A Sociology of Transnational Constitutions: Social Foundations of the Post-National Legal Structure
Chris Thornhill

Shifting Legal Visions: Judicial Change and Human Rights Trials in Latin America
Ezequiel A. González Ocantos

The Demographic Transformations of Citizenship
Heli Askola

Criminal Defense in China: The Politics of Lawyers at Work
Sida Liu, and Terence C. Halliday

Constituting Religion: Islam, Liberal Rights, and the Malaysian State
Tamir Moustafa

The Invention of the Passport: Surveillance, Citizenship and the State,
Second Edition
John C. Torpey

Law's Trials: The Performance of Legal Institutions in the US "War
on Terror"
Richard L. Abel

Law's Wars: The Fate of the Rule of Law in the US "War on Terror"
Richard L. Abel

Transforming Gender Citizenship: The Irresistible Rise of Gender
Quotas in Europe
Edited by Eléonore Lépinard and Ruth Rubio-Marín

Muslim Women's Quest for Justice: Gender, Law and Activism in India
Mengia Hong Tschalaer

Children as "Risk": Sexual Exploitation and Abuse by Children and
Young People
Anne-Marie McAlinden

The Legal Process and the Promise of Justice: Studies Inspired by the
Work of Malcolm Feeley
Jonathan Simon, Rosann Greenspan, Hadar Aviram

Sovereign Exchanges: Gifts, Trusts, Reparations, and Other Fetishes of
International Solidarity
Grégoire Mallard

Measuring Justice: Quantitative Accountability and the National
Prosecuting Authority in South Africa
Johanna Mugler

Negotiating the Power of NGOs: Women's Legal Rights in South Africa
Reem Wael

Indigenous Water Rights in Law and Regulation: Lessons from
Comparative Experience
Elizabeth Jane Macpherson

The Edge of Law: Legal Geographies of a War Crimes Court
Alex Jeffrey